Metaphysics and the God of Israel

Metaphysics and the God of Israel

Systematic Theology of the Old and New Testaments

Neil B. MacDonald

Baker Academic
Grand Rapids, Michigan

12 11 10 09 08 07 06   7 6 5 4 3 2 1

First published jointly in 2006 by Paternoster in the UK
and Baker Academic in the USA

Paternoster is an imprint of Authentic Media
9 Holdom Avenue, Bletchley, Milton Keynes, Bucks, MK1 1QR, UK
and
285 Lynnwood Avenue, Tyrone, GA 30290, USA
OM Authentic Media, Medchal Road, Jeedimetla Village,
Secunderabad 500 055, A.P.
www.authenticmedia.co.uk/paternoster
Authentic Media is a division of Send the Light Ltd., a company
limited by guarantee (registered charity no. 270162)

Baker Academic is an imprint of Baker Publishing Group,
PO Box 6287, Grand Rapids, MI 49516-6287
www.bakeracademic.com

British Library Cataloguing in Publication Data
A catalogue record for this book is available from the British Library

ISBN-13: 978-1-84227-178-0
ISBN-10: 1-84227-178-4

Library of Congress Cataloging-in-Publication Data
Library of Congress Cataloging-in-Publication Data is on file at the
Library of Congress, Washington, DC

ISBN-13: 978-0-8010-3243-1
ISBN-10: 0-8010-3243-1

Cover design by fourninezero design.
Print Management by Adare Carwin
Printed in Great Britain by J.H. Haynes & Co., Sparkford

Contents

Preface   xi

Prologue   xxi
Some Reflections on the Concept of Rationality for a
Systematic Theology of the Old and New Testaments

Part One

1. "The First Two Days of Creation": Time and Space   3

2. YHWH the God of Israel, Divine Self-
    Determination, and the Mechanics of Divine
    Action   24

3. God the Self-Determining Self and Some Classical
    Problems of the Doctrine of Creation   44

4. "The Sixth Day of Creation": The Creation of
    Humankind and the *Imago Dei*   53

5. "The Seventh Day of Creation": "Our God Who
    Art in Heaven" in the World   67

6. The Self-Determining Self and Israel's Historical
    Experience of YHWH   100

Part Two

7. YHWH in the Exodus Narrative: The Self-Determining Self Who is also a Desisting, Forbearing Self   117

8. God and the Primeval History   139

9. God and the Deuteronomistic History   161

Part Three

10. The Gospel Narrative, Substitutionary Atonement, and the "Directorial Eye" of the Evangelist   183

11. Substitutionary Atonement and the Origins of Divine Triunity   225

     Name Index   246

For my wife, Sheralyn

Acknowledgements

The publication of this systematic theology of the Old and New Testaments owes not a few debts. There are people like Dr Robin Parry of Paternoster Press who, as a biblical theologian himself, had every sympathy with the kind of work I was striving to produce. There is Trisha Dale, who worked under pressure – and with great patience and skill – to render the text more accessible to a wider audience. Both I thank. I would like to mention St Anne's Lutheran Church, in Gresham Street, London EC2, served most ably by Pastor Jana Jeruma-Grinberga; it has sustained the necessary emotional impetus involved in thinking that the endeavours of the mind may still have a role to play in the church having the greatest of confidence in its intellectual foundations. Finally, I thank Roehampton University, London SW15. It has warmly encouraged and facilitated the research necessary to bring this book to completion.

Preface

The greatest of our medieval theologians were no strangers to the subtle and esoteric language of philosophy. Above all they knew that the creative application of the traditional philosophical skills could make sense of Scripture and doctrine in unexpected and frankly thrilling ways – ways that made one's soul soar at the providential necessity of things that had previously borne the ring of contingency about them. Perhaps Anselm's *Cur Deus Homo* is the single greatest example of this kind of genius in action. Whether one accepts the mechanics behind Anselm's conclusions, his philosophical reflection on the doctrine of atonement seemed to indicate that Anselm had gone where "mere mortals feared to tread" in bringing back home to us ordinary mortals the simple sheer rationality and indeed necessity of the truth of this doctrine.

With the age of the Enlightenment the age of Christian philosophy seemed to have come and gone forever. True, the spirit of philosophical theology lived on. But it lived on at the behest of the Enlightenment rather unworthily – given its past – justifying its existence with the merely generic question of God's existence. This is all epistemological skepticism would permit. The rest – the particularities of the Christian belief – were (more or less) declared off-limits as the language of myth.

Let me say at once that I do not believe the great classical era can ever come back in the form it took in the past. *Modernity's legacy in bequeathing among other things a thoroughly historical understanding of the literary formation of the Bible cannot be undone: to put it baldly, we "know" too much about the Bible, both about its form and about its meaning for us to affirm the classical tradition of Augustine, Anselm, Aquinas, Luther, and Calvin just as it stands.*

This does not mean, however, that the characteristic classical ('medieval') modes of philosophical thinking have no role to play in a modern appraisal of the Bible. On the contrary: quite paradoxically, it is this very understanding of the Bible – the great modern tradition of biblical scholarship reaching its apogee as it did in the twentieth century – that provides the opportunity once more to articulate a "biblical metaphysic" that passes the canon of rationality. In one sense then this book is a reaffirmation of the intellectual ambitions of the medieval theological tradition to understand God in all his truth. But it retrieves their modes of thought under the presumption that these modes of thought can actually take advantage of a histori-cal understanding of the formation of the Bible in quite striking and even counterintuitive ways that nevertheless gain our intellectual assent.

It is one thing to insist that the breach between biblical and theological studies that opened up during the Enlightenment be healed. It is quite another to demonstrate that biblical and theo-logical studies can be part of the same theatre of rational perfor-mance. Accordingly: in the following pages you will find the names of Gerhard von Rad, Claus Westermann, Karl Barth, Martin Noth, Aristotle, Thomas Aquinas, Anselm of Bec, William Alston, Hans Frei, Augustine of Hippo, Albert Schweitzer, Gregory of Nyssa, Brevard Childs, James Barr, Nicholas Wolterstorff, Robert Jenson, N. T. Wright, Richard Bauckham, Christopher Seitz, and others. In this sense the book endorses Francois Lyotard's definition of the postmodern condi-tion as the juxtaposition of present and past – of the juxtaposition of nuclear power station and cathedral as it were (John Milbank's example in *Theology and Social Theory*). Milbank has spoken out against theology's false humility when encountering or more pertinently when encountered by the academic disci-plines of modernity. He and radical orthodoxy are right about this. Yet to my mind radical orthodoxy is more successful in diagnosing the present malaise in academic theology than in providing the solution. The right response cannot be to orientate oneself in the direction of affirming the whole classical theological tradition (Duns Scotus apart), as if it were a unified "argumentative" narrative to be advocated wholesale against the mainly negative judgements of modernity (even though, as Wolterstorff points out, something like this was the way the classical tradition was understood by our medieval ancestors). In lieu of Lyotard's definition I would say that the postmoderns must become more postmodern to suit me (Karl Barth!): the figures of modernity are palpably missing from their pantheon of heroes. Nicholas Wolterstorff has said that one must earn the right to disagree with the likes of Augustine, Anselm, and Aquinas. One must also earn this same right *vis-à-vis* the modern tradition, and in the context in which I am writing this means the high tradition of modern biblical scholarship on the Bible: Von Rad, Martin Noth, Weiss, Schweitzer, and others who have made a decisive difference to the landscape of modern thought on the Bible.

To be sure, the Cambridge theologian Catherine Pickstock has spoken honestly of the lacuna in radical orthodoxy respecting the Old Testament, but any correction must also include reference to modern scholarship. *There is a very simple and decisive reason for this.* In 1936 Gerhard von Rad published a famous paper entitled "The Theological Problem of the Old Testament Doctrine of Creation." In this paper Von Rad argued that the doctrine of creation was ancillary to the doctrine of salvation in Israel's Scriptures and history. Israel first knew of YHWH as a saving or soteriological identity and only later inferred that this same God was the creator of all things.

Crucially, Von Rad's insight that Israel's foundational experience of YHWH was of a soteriological identity implied a historical experience of YHWH acting in her life then and there. This was Israel's primal experience. This alone must mean that there is something deeply problematic about the whole precritical theological tradition as regards Old Testament narrative. If one looks at Augustine through Anselm and Aquinas to Calvin, one sees that all of them presuppose a God acting from eternity predestinating all that was to happen in human history from eternity. *If Von Rad is right this cannot be the appropriate hermeneutical category for the locus of divine action in the life of Israel.* The trajectory of systematic theology must be one that "rewinds" backwards in time from Israel's experience of YHWH in the exodus phenomenon to that of YHWH creating the heavens and the earth. It will be a minimal requirement of any theory descriptive of this trajectory that it presupposes a *God acting in the same time frame as the people Israel* ; not a God who as it were acts from eternity. The exodus narrative is quite clear that God speaks to Israel and Moses in particular *then and there*; the narrative-agent that is God is not speaking from eternity.

Is this any more than an academic exercise unrelated to the exigencies of the modern world? *Not if one wants to affirm what I believe to be the most persuasive truth about Jesus of Nazareth, which is that he is to be included within the divine identity of YHWH, he too as a soteriological identity.* The reason is that the sentence you have just read presupposes that there *is* such a soteriological identity as YHWH in which Jesus *is* to be included – a real person or historical identity. But if the plain sense of Scripture is that this God is to be believed in through his actions – as in the exodus narrative – then we must find some way of rationally affirming divine action in the world. I argue that the witness of the Old Testament, and Old Testament narrative in particular, is that YHWH is essentially a judging yet desisting forbearing self. But this God may remain an essentially fictional self, condemned to remain within the literary confines of the narrative unless we can find some way for this God to break into historical reality.

Much of Parts One and Two of this book are devoted to providing a solution to this problem. The solution proposed, in effect reverses Von Rad's extrapolation from YHWH the soteriological identity to YHWH the creational identity. The mechanics of divine action in creating the world are also the mechanics of divine (soteriological) action in the world. Essentially the two modes of action can be explained in terms of the singular concept of *divine self-determination*. There is no essential difference between, on the one hand, YHWH the God of Israel who determines *himself* to be "the one who releases Israel from the bondage of Egypt" and, on the other, YHWH the God of Israel who determines himself to be "the one who is the creator of all things."

Notwithstanding this, we must be clear that the epistemic priority lies with this God acting in the world rather than with his acting to create the world. This is because it was as the former historical identity that the people "Israel" first experienced their God. Though philosophers of the Enlightenment (for reason of their respect for the newly discovered laws of nature) thought it much easier to conceive of God creating the world than his acting in the world, such a presumption ran contrary both to Von Rad's insight and to the history of canonical shaping. Not to put too fine a point on it: if it is irrational to affirm God acting in the world, then the question of this same God acting to create the world doesn't arise – for the simple reason that the God so identified (as the creator of all things) cannot be the God of the Scriptures.

Parts One and Two provide the essential theological and historical framework for the culminating claim of this book: on their backs do we move the conclusion by the end of the book (Part Three) that the God of Israel who reveals himself to be a judging yet desisting, forbearing self in the Old Testament is the one who in the gospel narrative ultimately takes his own judgement on himself – in the form of his Son, Jesus of Nazareth.

The two greatest influences in this book are undoubtedly Karl Barth and Gerhard von Rad. I credit Barth with three path-breaking insights. The first is regarding the unique nature of God's action in both creating the world and acting in the world. The metaphysic that enables me to unify God's action in both realms under one kind of action surely has its origins in the *Church Dogmatics*. The second is what Barth had to say regarding divine spatiality. When I thought this through I realized that Barth had provided a means of taking both the concept of "heaven" and of "the man Jesus being in heaven" within our conceptual reach even within the confines of modernity: a remarkable feat! Third, I credit him with showing how a doctrine of substitutionary atonement could be understood to be objectively present in the Synoptic Gospels. Much of the work in this book sought simply to develop the implications of Barth's seminal insights on these matters.

Von Rad's insights were perhaps no less important though they were much more exegetical in nature (though no less theological). I owe to Von Rad's exegesis of the primeval history in Genesis 2 – 11 the insight that YHWH the God of Israel in the Old Testament can be understood to be a judging yet desisting forbearing divine identity. His influence is clear throughout much of the book.[1]

Brevard Childs has also made a decisive difference to my thinking as regards the philosophical consequences of canonical shaping. Especially significant in this respect is his idea of the impact on canonical shaping of the literary priority of the priestly creation narrative. I have sought to show what this impact is for the rationality of affirming the rationality of historical experience of God (Israel's and ours). More fundamentally: if there is a "Protestant" impulse in this work in any sense, it is due to Child's insight (very much implicit in his *Introduction to the Old Testament as Scripture*) that systematic theology cannot ignore the gains and insights of two or three hundred years of critical biblical scholarship (precisely because a lot of what it has to say is rational to believe). Instead, it must work with these insights to produce a truly satisfying and credible theological position. Only in this way can we join together what has been put asunder in "the parting of the ways" of theology and biblical studies. The current trend to promote Thomas Aquinas from either a classical or postmodern perspective – with very little else – can only "preach to the converted." It has very little to say to the outside world.

And then there is Nicholas Wolterstorff whose influence has been two-fold. First there is his work on divine speech and how it would be possible for God to speak without having physical speech organs: "Thus saith the Lord." Second, there is the simple yet brilliant argument that he presents in favour of the "a-series" over the "b-series" of time: the priority of the concept of present event over either the past or the future as regards God's knowledge of tensed facts. While I cannot be sure that I have appropriated either idea exactly in the way he would have wanted, I remain in his debt for my vision of how it would be possible for God to act in history. I should also mention Richard Bauckham's

---

[1] Since I wrote these comments, another, final, chapter was added to the book, namely Chapter 1. It will be evident there that the influence of Claus Westermann's brilliant analysis of Genesis 1:3–10 from his commentary on Genesis is central to it. Perhaps Westermann's influence is greater than I originally envisaged.

God Crucified: New Testament Christology and Jewish Monotheism.
This brilliant little book provided much of the initial impetus to
thinking about God in terms of the concept of divine identity
instead of the patristic concept of divine *ousia*.

But perhaps more than anyone else it is Professor of Old
Testament and Theological Studies at St. Andrews University,
Christopher Seitz, who in a number of conversations over recent
years made the arguments and perspective in this book at all
possible. It was only after many discussions with Christopher
Seitz over the question of the unity of the Old and New Testament that it became possible to transcend some of the classic
christocentric weaknesses in Barth's theology. As Seitz would
say: we do know something about God other than through Jesus
of Nazareth, Jesus Christ. We know something about the God of
Israel even as this knowledge is elevated by the man Jesus. The
Kantian conception of God contradicts what we read in the Old
Testament, Israel's Scriptures. This book is in a sense an attempt
to show how valid this seminal insight is.

Finally, a word of enduring thanks. In 2002–3 I was invited to
become a member of the Center of Theological Inquiry in Princeton where I did a great deal of the groundwork for this book. I
hope the end result justifies their invitation and, in particular,
Wallace Alston's, to come to Princeton. It is a work that I hope fits
in with the notion of advanced theological inquiry. During my
time at the Center, I had the great honour to discuss issues such
as those raised in this book with Robert Jenson. Jenson is to many
discerning theologians the greatest living English-speaking
theologian. Like Bauckham, Jenson holds that the man Jesus is
divine insofar as he is included within the divine identity of
YHWH – not added but included. This is what it means to say
that Jesus is divine – not that he is, in a crude realist sense, to be
acknowledged "in two natures": one human and one divine as
Chalcedon may have it. But Jenson (perhaps again under the
influence of Barth) has also made an audacious attempt to put
"heaven" back on the modern theological map in the context of
his doctrine of the divine identity of God. To say that "Jesus is in
heaven" is to say that the man Jesus is in God's own space – the
space that is a property of God himself. These are lofty thoughts
that would not be out of place in the great classical discussions of

the past. The challenge is to make these – for us – "extraordinary" thoughts, "ordinary" once again.

I once heard a famous film director say that what he was after was not realism but life, that what he wanted to see through the lens of the camera was something that was alive rather than real. I took him to mean that the distinction between, on the one hand, a "real" or perhaps more accurately "realistic" presence on the screen and, on the other, a presence that, as it were, "became alive," was the difference between ordinary and great cinema. Ordinary cinema merely reinforces the obvious truth that film is film and reality reality; great cinema suspends awareness of the demarcation between celluloid and reality. This difference can be put in terms of Erich Auerbach's words made known to theologians by Hans Frei's *The Eclipse of Biblical Narrative*. The Greek poet Homer in the *Iliad* and the *Odyssey* seeks, as Erich Auerbach famously put it, "merely to make us forget our own reality for a few hours"; in contrast, the Bible, he said, "seeks to overcome our reality: we are to fit our own life into its world, feel ourselves to be elements in its structure of universal history" (Auerbach, *Mimesis*, [Princeton: Princeton University Press, 1953], 15).

The task of the theologian is not quite the same as the filmmaker but he or she must strive to be an artist to the extent that the overall objective of any theologian must be to delineate a world which the reader comes to recognize as real, as the ordinary real world we all live in. The postmodernist in Lyotard would endorse this project. But it cannot be achieved by eschewing the simple canons of good argument, which unfortunately for us are not ideological constructs no matter what the Frankfurt school of sociology said. A rose is a rose is a rose, said Gertrude Stein. A good argument is a good argument is a good argument . . . for it enables us to look at the world and see that it might be just as the Bible says it is. It brings alive what we thought was dead. It is to transpose to the Bible what T. S. Eliot called in poetry "the presentness of the past", to affirm with Luther the importance of "the meaning of 'meaning it'," and to repudiate Nietzsche's tragic sense that "the desert is growing."

Thomas Mann once observed that human beings were at their most natural, perhaps more themselves sitting at rest in a church where what really did not matter in the end could be seen for what it was. This kind of sentiment was not lost on Peter Fuller in his *The Face of God: The Consolation of Lost Illusions* when he lamented that the loss of the religious dimension in the visual arts had brought in its wake a meaner more mediocre art. Yet, much in the spirit of Arnold's *Dover Beach*, Christianity was for him no more than that which his subtitle intimates: the consolation of an illusion. The aim of this book is to say: carry on sitting in the church pew, carry on praying, carry on saying "thank Christ." The pew in which you are sitting is part of the world which God created, in which God acted in history (with his people, Israel); in which Jesus died (for our sins). Amen.

Neil B. MacDonald
Roehampton University
February 2006

Prologue: Some Reflections on the Concept of Rationality for a Systematic Theology of the Old and New Testaments

Let me say a word about the concept of "rationality" employed in this book. It is a concept that I invoke frequently and its meaning is not transparently obvious. In the *Cambridge Dictionary of Philosophy* the entry under "rationality" runs as follows: "In its primary sense, rationality is a normative concept that philosophers have generally tried to characterize in such a way that, for any action, belief, or desire, if it is rational we ought to choose it."

It then goes on to say: "No such positive characterization has achieved anything close to universal assent because, often, several competing actions, beliefs, or desires, count as rational. Equating what is rational with what is rationally required eliminates the category of what is rationally allowed."

It then says: "Irrationality seems to be the more fundamental normative category: for although there are conflicting substantive accounts of irrationality, all agree that to say of an action, belief, or desire that it is irrational is to claim that it should always be avoided." (Gert, "Rationality," 772).

These are sentiments that I would wish the reader to hold when putting this book under rational scrutiny. It is harder to judge what is rational than what is irrational. In particular, there may be more than one belief on a specific matter that is rational to hold. This means three things in particular.

First, I am not saying that if what I say in the following pages is rational then it follows that if you are rational you ought to adopt this position as your own! There may be an alternative contrary position to the one I hold that is also rational to hold. Therefore, you may find the position I take on the redactional-canonical shaping of the Bible to be a position you do not accept. You may think that the Priestly writing is older than the Yahwist and so on. Fine.

Second, what I do insist upon is that the position presented in this book is "rationally allowable" in the sense of the words of the dictionary entry. One of the virtues of postmodernity is that it allows for a proliferation of truth-claims that in the strict logical sense are to be defined as *contraries*. Contrary truth-claims are defined in the following way: if one is true the other must be false, even though both might turn out to be false. This position is quite consistent with the view that the contraries are both "rationally allowable." Therefore, there may be more than one belief on a matter each of which is rational to hold though one is contrary to the other. I will make claims to which some readers will offer counter-claims, contrary claims. I would wish them to remember that all I ask for is the rationality of the claim. Is it rational to view the priestly narrator as a redactor or are we dealing with a priestly document? Is it rational to hold that God was judging Jesus in the passion narrative?

Third, if the belief is rationally allowable then it does not have to meet the criterion of what is "rationally required." Many classical positions on rationality take just this view. I mention two famous classical criteria of rationality. Descartes' criterion of certainty and Karl Popper's criterion of falsifiability:

1. One ought not to believe something unless the belief is certain. This criterion says that it is irrational to believe something if the belief in question is not certain. We therefore require unassailable foundations. (Descartes)

2. One ought not to believe something unless the belief is falsifiable. This criterion says that the belief is irrational if the belief is not falsifiable. It is irrational to believe something if the belief in question is not falsifiable. (Popper)

Let me say briefly that I do not accept either as a criterion of rationality. Many of the truth-claims I make in the course of this book are neither certain nor falsifiable but I would say rational.

In response to Descartes' equation of rationality, with either logic or incorrigible belief, I would say the truth-claims are rational precisely because though they may well lack certainty, it doesn't follow they ought not to be held. I can think of many beliefs that I hold that I know are not certain. Bur I think I should hold them and indeed would deem it irrational not to hold them. I reject foundationalism as a criterion of rationality. Similarly I can think of beliefs that are not falsifiable that I nevertheless think I ought to hold. One of them it seems to me might be belief in the existence of God. As a postscript to these eminently classical approaches to rationality, one might mention in the context of Popper's principle of falsifiablity another principle which, though weaker than proof (and therefore proved certainty), has also been citied as the hallmark of rationality. This is the criterion of (deductive) provability. In this sense, mathematics has often been hailed as the very paradigm of rationality. Mathematical rationality entails provability if not actual proof. But Gödel's famous incompleteness theorem put an end to this dream. If the mathematical system is consistent – and therefore generates no inconsistencies – then there will be true statements that are not provable by the system. The system is therefore incomplete: there are some true – certain – statements in the system it will not be able to prove (certainty doesn't entail provability!). One can't have both consistency and completeness is the moral of the story.

Finally, and more recently, probabilistic decision-theory, in the context of rational choice theory, has been employed as a means of assessing relative rationalities of contrary beliefs and with a view to making a rational choice which to believe. But it is evident that the task of applying these sciences to the present field is one of great complexity, and by no means uncontroversial. I am not sure how it would be done, but if it can be, it should be left to another day, once the contents of this book have been fully assimilated. At present, I seek only to satisfy the criterion of rationality in the broader old-fashioned "Enlightenment" sense.

Bibliography

Audi, Robert and William J. Wainwright (eds.), *Rationality, Religious Belief, and Moral Commitment* (Ithaca: Cornell University Press, 1986).

Descartes, René, *Meditations on First Philosophy*, translated by John Cottingham (Cambridge: Cambridge University Press, 1996).

Elster, Jon (ed.) *Rational Choice* (Oxford: Basil Blackwell, 1986).

Gert, Bernard, "Rationality." In *Cambridge Dictionary of Philosophy*, 2nd ed., edited by Robert Audi, 772–73 (Cambridge: Cambridge University Press, 1999).

Hollis, Martin and Stephen Lukes, *Rationality and Relativism*. (Oxford: Basil Blackwell, 1982).

Kline, Morris, *Mathematics: The Loss of Certainty* (Oxford: Oxford University Press, 1980).

Pelikan, Jaroslav, *Christianity and Classical Culture: The Metamorphosis of Natural Theology in the Christian Encounter with Hellenism* (New Haven: Yale University Press, 1993).

Popper, Karl, *The Logic of Scientific Discovery*, rev. ed. (London: Hutchison, 1968).

Swinburne, Richard, *The Existence of God* (Oxford: Clarendon Press, 1979); *Is There a God?* (Oxford: Oxford University Press, 1996).

Toulmin, Stephen, *Cosmopolis: The Hidden Agenda of Modernity* (Chicago: University of Chicago Press, 1990).

PART ONE

As steals the morn upon the night,
And melts the shades away
So truth does fancy's charm dissolve,
And rising reason puts to flight
The fumes that did the mind involve,
Restoring intellectual day.

G F Handel, *L'Allegro, il Pensero ed il Moderato*

Logic is doubtless unshakeable,
but it cannot withstand a man who
wants to go on living.

Franz Kafka, *The Trial*

1

"The First Two Days of Creation": Time and Space

It is entirely reasonable to understand the Priestly creation narrative as a redaction of an already extant narrative whose subject-matter is the personal and historical relationship – beginning at the exodus from Egypt – between the God of Israel and his people "Israel." The people "Israel" have the historical experience of being in a presently occurring personal relationship with this God. When "Israel" claims that the God who is responsible for this historical experience is the creator of all things, they are compelled to say that what this God creates is among other things the space and time in which they experience this relationship. Hence God is posited as creating the time and space Israel – and the rest of humankind – experience. This means that God creates whatever is necessary for the existence of *events* other than himself. Since events necessarily have duration this implies the creation of *time*.[1] And since events other than those predicated of God himself are for the most part embodied in *objects* this implies the creation of space. Moreover, insofar as the experience of being in a presently occurring personal relationship with God is not an illusion, this must mean that there can be such

---

[1] See Swinburne's *The Christian God*, pp. 72–74 for a convincing argument for this:

> To say that an object is green at 2pm is to say that it is green for some period which includes 2pm. It is difficult to see what is meant by an object being green at 2pm although it was not green either before or after 2pm. It was green for a period of zero duration, and how could that differ from its not being green at all (p. 72).

an event in which God is in such a relationship with Israel. Such events occur when they *presently* take place – it is true of the very "being" of an event that, to be an event, it has to take place in the present tense, it has to be presently occurring to be an event at all. God therefore has to create what is necessary for such a historical relationship with humankind to take place. To say that God creates time and space is to say that he creates the possibility of presently occurring events[2] – events other than himself. This concurs with what the Priestly creation narrative has to say. In order to see how this is so, we take recourse to the distinction between the distinction speech-act theory makes between locutionary and illocutionary acts: God does not speak literally about "time," "space," or "the possibility of (presently occurring) events" (in his locutionary actions) but this is what he means and does (in his illocutionary actions). I begin this chapter with some pertinent words about this distinction.

The Priestly creation narrative: locutionary acts and illocutionary acts

As Nicholas Wolterstorff points out in his book *Divine Discourse*, fundamental to the theory of speech-acts is the distinction between *locutionary acts* and *illocutionary acts* (Wolterstorff, *Divine Discourse*, 13). *Locutionary* acts are, as he says, acts of uttering or inscribing words: the basic act of speaking or writing and what is produced in the process of such an act. So, to take an example to which I will frequently return: when God is described as saying "Let there be light" in Genesis 1:3, this is a locutionary act, the simple act of uttering words. *Illocutionary* acts are acts performed *by way of* locutionary acts. The most common examples of these cited are: asking, asserting, commanding, and promising. In the context of a marriage ceremony for example, when the bride or groom says "I do," this is the bride or groom promising to be a loving wife or husband. The

---

[2] The phrase "presently occurring events" is therefore something of a "tautology": there is no such thing called an event which could be other than presently occurring. I discuss this point in more detail in Chapter 5.

latter is the illocutionary act performed of course by way of uttering the words, "I do."

The illocutionary actions commonly cited by speech-act theorists can be summarized in the following way. They are what the speaker *means or does* by way of the performance of the locutionary action. (When the bride or groom says "I do" they mean that they are doing something – promising to be a loving wife or husband.) It is because of this implication of speaker meaning or intention that speech-act theory has been applied to our understanding of language writ large. What we mean or do by way of what we say is the illocutionary action; what we say directly and literally so is the locutionary action. *Crucially, sometimes the illocutionary action is the same as the locutionary action; sometimes the illocutionary action is other than the locutionary action.* As we will see, this latter insight is central to the understanding of God as creator.

Let me take the former case first. Often when we speak we mean what we say: we mean the literal sense or what Wolterstorff calls the *noematic content* of the utterance (*Divine Discourse*, 138). The illocutionary action is identified with the locutionary action. We mean the literal sense of our utterance. We utter the sentence "The cat is on the mat" and we mean that the cat is on the mat.

But speakers can often mean other than what they say (to the philosopher Stanley Cavell's famous question, "Must we mean what we say?", the answer must be, no). A speaker's illocutionary action does not have to be the same as his locutionary action. *The illocutionary action can be – and often is – other than the locutionary action. In such a case, the speaker means other than his locutionary action.* The most obvious example of this that comes to mind is when the speaker's illocutionary stance is a metaphorical one. A simple example of this would be someone uttering "Jones is a pig." This sentence might be used to mean that Jones treats people dreadfully or that he has abominable eating- or table-manners. If such is the case the speaker's illocutionary action is clearly not the same as his locutionary action. His illocutionary action is not to be identified with his locutionary action. He does not mean what he says literally – unless for example there is a pig he knows who is called "Jones."

As Wolterstorff points out, the assumption that the illocutionary action is the same as the locutionary action is normally the
first strategy we try in interpreting someone's utterances: "the
base-line from which we operate is that we reckon people having
said what their sentences mean – in other words reckoning them
as having spoken literally, strictly and directly so. We reckon
people as speaking in strict and direct literal fashion unless we
have good reason for not doing so" (*Divine Discourse*, 191).
Therefore if someone utters the sentence "The cat is on the mat"
then, since his sentence means that the cat is on the mat, "we conclude that that's what he said, that that's the noematic content of
his illocutionary act – unless we have good reason for not doing
so" (Wolterstorff, *Divine Discourse*, 191).

But it is precisely because of the simple fact that speakers can
often mean other than what they say that we employ other strat-
egies of interpretation. In the case of the utterance "Jones is a
pig" it is not assumed that a speaker's illocutionary action is the
same as the locutionary action. This is because there is good
reason to believe that the speaker's illocutionary action here is
not the same as the locutionary action embodied in what was
said or uttered. The illocutionary action is taken to be other than
the locutionary action. The illocutionary action performed by
way of the locutionary action is not the same as the locutionary
action. The speaker did not mean that the man Jones was literally
a pig.

As readers of Augustine will recognize, this is the strategy
Augustine advocated we employ in the interpretation of Scripture in his *On Christian Doctrine*. Start with the literal sense, he
said, but if this conflicts with the divine identity and in particular
his moral character then we make the assumption that the
meaning of Scripture at this point is other than the literal sense.
He applied this insight in his own exegesis of the literal sense of
Genesis.

"Let there be light!": the creation of the possibility of temporal order

Historically, exegesis of Genesis 1:3 has followed the lines of
God creating light by divine fiat. In saying, "Let there be light,"

God is commanding light to come into existence. If we fit the traditional exegesis of 1:3 into the language of speech-act theory, we see that God saying, "Let there be light" can be understood as the locutionary action and his meaning the creation of light can be understood as the illocutionary action. If this is right then we have a paradigm-case in which locutionary and illocutionary are the same: God said, "Let there be light" – the locutionary action; and he meant light – the illocutionary action. However, as we have seen, speech-act theory opens up an alternative strategy of interpretation precisely because it allows for the fact that the illocutionary action performed by way of the locutionary action can be other than the locutionary action itself. And it may be that there are alternative traditions of exegesis of Genesis 1:3 which require precisely an approach sanctioned by speech-act theory in which illocutionary action is other than locutionary action.

In this respect, let us look at Claus Westermann's exegesis of Genesis 1:3 in his monumental commentary on the book of Genesis: "And God said 'Let there be light'." It is fundamental to note that Westermann does not deny that 1:3 says literally that God said, "Let there be light." Furthermore, he does not deny that the literal sense of the utterance "Let there be light" is as it reads: the locutionary action that God performs is "Let there be light." Nevertheless, what Westermann's exegesis of 1:3 implies is that, in effect, the illocutionary action performed by way of this utterance, this locutionary action, is other than the locutionary action itself. Here is what Westermann says: "The first thing that God created was light . . . [But] light is not meant to be 'the most subtle of all elementary forces' or 'a material full of mystery' (A. Dillman), 'the most sublime element, a subsistent thing, a subtle material'(H. Gunkel)" (Westermann, *Genesis 1 – 11*, 112).

We pause at this juncture in an important passage in Westermann's exegesis of Genesis 1:3. He is quite clear that God says, "Let there be light." This is what he means when he says, "The first thing that God created was light." There is no question but that this is the locutionary action the narrator narrates God as performing. Whether we can make sense of God performing such a locutionary action – God actually speaking – is a question to which we will return below. But for the moment I want to take the event or action in question for granted and presume that God did say, "Let there be light," and literally so.

But though the literal sense of the narrative is that God created light, Westermann goes on to divest us of any notion we might have that light is to be understood here as referring to the evanescent or diaphanous force or substance with which we all think we are familiar. For the Priestly writer, light is not to be categorized under the various descriptions that more traditional biblical expositors have suggested, namely "the most subtle of all elementary forces" or "a material full of mystery," "the most sublime element, a subsistent thing, a subtle material." It is neither "force," nor "material," nor "element," nor even – "thing." It is not to be imagined as something that travels through space precisely because space has yet to be created. It is not meant to be any of these things because it is meant to be *the condition of the possibility of time*. Westermann explains why as follows:

> Such descriptions are impossible because for P the first three acts of creation are not as it were the manufacture of substances, but the basic divisions of the universe. The separation of light from darkness is temporal, not spatial. The creation of light is put before these divisions because it renders possible the temporal succession into which, according to P, the world is set. God creates brightness and thereby makes possible the basic cycle of time and order (*Genesis 1 – 11*, 112).

If we are tempted to think that Westermann's exegesis is counterintuitive, we must understand what he says within the context of what is the fundamental presupposition behind his exegesis of Genesis 1 (and indeed his exegesis of the primeval history running through Genesis 1 – 11). This is that the object of the Priestly creation narrative is "not to communicate a description of the course of the events of creation. It is much more; it is to establish the reality that conditions present existence; what is narrated in the cosmogony is not directed to the description of creation but to what exists as a result of creation" (Westermann, *Genesis 1 – 11*, 120).

This means that the motivation behind the narrative is to explain that which the Priestly writer believes presently exists in his own time (and, in the case of time itself, has existed since "the beginning"). It is what presently exists that has to be explained. So if you asked the Priestly writer what presently exists, he would answer: created time exists, created space exists, and (as we will see in Chapter 4) distinct and unalterably fixed – immutable – species, including most importantly humankind, exist. In particular, "the category of time and the categories of space . . . are the basic categories in which creatures, and above all living beings, live out their existence" (Westermann, *Genesis 1 – 11*, 119). This means that the light and the separation of the light from the darkness referred to in 1:3–5 are not ontological particulars in the sense in which the category of time, the categories of space, and living beings are. It is not that light does not exist as part of created being – as an ontological particular itself – but in fact, as we shall see below, it comes into existence on the fourth day of creation, particularly as an emanation of the "greater heavenly body," the sun, and plays a central role in the metric of time, the measurement of time.

In fact, it gets even more strange: what Westermann wants to say is that in saying "Let there be light" God isn't really creating *anything*; he is creating the possibility of *something. God is creating the condition of the possibility of time* which in turn can be understood as the condition of the possibility of order (Westermann, *Genesis 1 – 11*, 112). If one thinks about it, a condition of possibility is an abstraction, it isn't really an "anything." It is really in the narration of God separating the light from the darkness in Genesis 1:4 that *God is creating something – time.* As Westermann puts it: "It is not the creation of light but the separation of light and darkness that sets in motion the march and rhythm of time. What is reported in v.4 then belongs to the first act of creation" (Westermann, *Genesis 1 – 11*, 112).

The first act of creation is the creation of time, temporal successiveness. Without the narration of the act of God's separating the light from the darkness, there is no actual temporal successiveness – and therefore no unfolding temporal structure as presumed by the description of seven days of creation. In the story then, the narration of the separation of light from the darkness is itself the condition of the possibility of the ensuing six days of creation. In this sense it belongs to the first creative act which should be understood as making possible the unfolding of the temporal structure of the ensuing six days of creation (days two to seven and beyond). In particular, the creation of time is the presupposition of the creation of space: the creation of space takes place in created time.

What Westermann is in effect saying is that in the locutionary act of saying, "Let there be light," God is performing the illocutionary action of creating the condition of the possibility of time, creating the possibility of temporal successiveness. God's illocutionary action is other than his locutionary action. But further, in the locutionary act of separating the light from the darkness, God is creating time itself, temporal successiveness itself. But this separation is temporal, not spatial. To reiterate: whatever "light" is here, it is not to be imagined as something that travels through space precisely because space has yet to be created.

It is the distinctive contribution of the Priestly writer that the creation of time "takes precedence" over the creation of space (Westermann, *Genesis 1 – 11*, 120): "creation does not begin with the division of space, but with the division of night and day as the basis of time" (p. 114). Following the creation of time, there are in fact two divisions of space in the Priestly narrative. Together, the three acts of division – of separation – "are the source of the three basic categories of existence . . . The alteration of night and day is the basis of time, the creation of the firmament – the separation of the heavens from the earth – the basis of the vertical dimension of space, the division – separation – of the water and the land, the basis of the horizontal dimension" (Westermann, *Genesis 1 – 11*, 119).

God speaks and God creates time; God speaks and God creates space. But what do the latter two respective claims mean? The categories of space and time – and especially their relation to God or God's relation to them – have perplexed the greatest minds throughout history. What is time? What is space? What is it that God creates?

What is time? What is space?

In the eleventh book of his *Confessions* Augustine famously asked, "What is time?" One of the responses he made to this question implied that we could not ask another question, namely, "What was God doing before the creation of the world?" Since time only came into existence with creation it followed that the presupposition behind the question, namely that there was a "before" prior to creation, was without foundation. With this undoubtedly brilliant insight Augustine set the theological agenda for how the classical Christian tradition – Anselm and Aquinas to take the two greatest examples – was to think about God and time thereafter. God was eternal or, apophatically speaking, timeless (he did not endure through, and had no location in time). In contrast, the time that God had created for humankind "waited for no man" and brought in its wake change and inevitable decay.

Even in the twentieth century Augustine's insight that time came into existence with creation appeared to receive scientific corroboration when the twentieth-century physicist Albert Einstein and his theories of relativity concluded that time (and space) came into existence with the world and its laws of nature, and could not be defined or measured apart from it and them. (Aristotle's definition of time as the measure of bodies in motion was of course the precedent of the theory that time was in essence measurable; see Jenson, *Systematic Theology*, vol. 2, 332). The view that all events in time were present simultaneously to God's eternity or timelessness became something like the classical view of the relation between God eternity and created time (see Pannenberg, *Systematic Theology*, vol.1, 256–57). With the advent of Einstein's theories of relativity, it is arguable that the received theological wisdom (informed by science) became that God's obviously nonmeasurable timelessness was to be juxtaposed to (created) measurable time. This juxtaposition was posited on the implicit assumption that these temporal categories were exhaustive categories: either nonmeasurable timelessness (obviously!) or measurable time – but nothing else.

Yet intriguingly, Richard Swinburne is one philosophical theologian who challenges this assumption. For him God can be understood according to a concept of nonmeasurable time – as opposed to nonmeasurable timelessness; and the time he creates for us could be understood in terms of just this concept of time too.

As has been said, Einstein's theories of relativity apply to measurable time (and space): time and space are defined operationally by him in the sense time and space *cannot be other than measurable time and space*. But Swinburne has argued that we can make perfect sense of nonmeasurable time (and presumably nonmeasurable space too). This is because we can distinguish between, on the one hand, time understood *topologically* and, on the other, time understood *metrically*. Topology is concerned with the *ordinal* scaling of events, the mere ranking or ordering of events; it allows for the question whether one event is before or after another event. But it makes no sense to ask of time of this kind how much earlier or later one event is relative to another, or how long did a particular event take. In this sense is such time nonmeasurable. Such questions do apply to metrical time since it presupposes *interval* scaling, which does involve the size of the interval between any two events, or the duration of any particular event (Swinburne, *Christian God*, 75).

Since, according to Swinburne, metrical time is dependent on the existence of laws of nature, and in particular periodic mechanisms that function as natural clocks, time *without* laws of nature – topological time – is nonmeasurable time. Hence it is possible that God existing by himself (existing with the property of topological time only) – and therefore not having yet created a universe in which there are laws of nature – could have created time *understood only as temporal successiveness or temporal order*.

In such a scenario there "would be no 'cosmic clock' ticking unstoppingly away – that is, there would be no temporal intervals of any definite length" (Swinburne, *Christian God*, 140). There would "not be a truth that any event had lasted a particular length of time rather than any other" (Swinburne, *Christian God*, 140). This has the entirely counterintuitive consequence that there "would be no difference between an event which lasted a millisecond and one that lasted a million years" (Swinburne, *Christian God*, 140).

Swinburne suggests that the view that "God created time" can be understood in either of the two above ways: "either in the sense that he created a temporal order of qualititatively distinct events, or in the sense that he created a temporal metric" (Swinburne, *Christian God*, 144). If we apply this insight to Genesis 1:3–5 and take up the former alternative, we can say that God initially creates the possibility of time, then time itself, understood only as temporal successiveness. The content of the first day then does not necessarily say anything about metrical time. This dovetails nicely with Westermann's own observation that the creation of the heavenly bodies on "the fourth day of creation" is "to be for the signs and for seasons and for days and years" (Westermann, *Genesis 1 – 11*, 129). He continues: "One of humanity's earliest and most significant achievements was to derive chronological order from the course of the stars" (Westermann, *Genesis 1 – 11*, 129–130). In other words, one could argue that the first day of creation is about the creation of time understood as temporal order, and the fourth day of creation concerns itself with metrical time..

If Swinburne is right in his assumption that we can distinguish between "ordinal" temporal successiveness and "interval" metrical time, it is possible to say that the time God is narrated as creating in Genesis 1:3–5 is precisely the former. Since the "relativity of simultaneity" presupposes operational – therefore metrical – time (relativity presupposes metrical time), it may be that even were the universe and its laws of nature to evaporate as it were, there would still exist temporal successiveness. God created the latter and the universe disappearing as it were does not imply that it would cease to be. William Lane Craig argues that there exists an ontological time experienced only by God called "true temporality" (Craig, "God and Real Time"). It is conceivable that it is this that God gives to us in his creation of time. With the laws of nature he gives us measurable time.

God possesses the property of nonmeasurable and therefore ordinal time.[3] *It is this time which he creates. It is the laws of nature that give us measurable time. Hence there is no a priori reason why God should be considered as eternal and timeless or created time assumed to be only measurable time. Both can be considered as ordinal temporal successiveness though one is noncreated and the other created.*

---

[3] Interestingly, Swinburne points out that though the Greeks in general saw a close connection between time and change, they seemed less committed to a connection between time and measurable change. For Swinburne this implies that the thought of time existing in the absence of measurable change was not entirely alien or inconceivable to them (Swinburne, *Christian God*, 80). See also Sorabji, *Time, Creation,*

A similar argument could be made about space. It is possible to conceive of space in nonmetrical, non-interval, ordinal terms. Though modern science under the influence of Einstein appears to be committed to the conception of space as a "plenum" – as something that is, quite literally, "full" – "full of matter – or its modern equivalent, energy" ($e=mc^2$); and though we have "good empirical reason to suppose that there is no part of space which is not suffused of energy," it remains the case that the "field equations of Einstein's general theory of relativity – which forms the basis of modern scientific cosmology – admit of solutions in which space is entirely devoid of matter and energy" (Lowe, *Survey of Metaphysics*, 256). This means that "mathematically at least . . . the notion of perfectly empty space is perfectly consistent" (Lowe, *Survey of Metaphysics*, 256). It is logically possible to speak of perfectly empty space even given General Relativity. Einstein's equations allow for zero content of space.

---

[3] (*continued*) *and the Continuum*, ch. 6. Similarly, "the scholastics too sometimes seemed to allow for the possibility of there being time with a topology yet lacking a metric. For when they discuss the life of the angels, they sometimes allowed for the possibility that they might have come into existence before the physical universe with its regular motions (of the heavens about the earth, or something else)" (Swinburne, *Christian God*, 80). See Aquinas, *Summa Theologiae*, 1a, 63. 6 ad 4 for an example. Though God was timelessly eternal, this did not mean that the angels trod the realm of ordinary worldly temporality as humans do. Rather, they existed in "sempiternity," a kind of intermediate duration between eternity and measurable time (and therefore change). If it can be argued that such a view insinuates such "intermediate" time possessing ordinal but not interval (metrical) properties, this would imply that the account of nonmeasurable (non-interval) time offered in this chapter has at the very least a medieval precedent. The crucial difference between this account and the medieval account is that nonmeasurable time (let us call it "eternal time" since it, among other things, continues to exist if nothing but God does) has been attributed to God as a perfection in place of "apophatic" "timeless eternity," thereby being elevated from the realm of angels to that of God. Boethius' famous definition of eternity as "unending life all at once" – which Barth enthusiastically endorsed in *Church Dogmatics* II/1 (Barth, *CD* II/1, 610f.) – as "sheer duration" – is not sufficiently temporal though it is sufficiently non-apophatic.

As Lowe puts it: "Just because Einstein's theory advertises itself as the general theory of *relativity*, we shouldn't assume that it is committed to a *relationist* theory of *space*" (Lowe, *Survey of Metaphysics*, 267).

This means, among other things, that space – just like time – can exist without the laws of nature that make space – like time – measurable. Intriguingly, it can also be said of God – and I will say it in Chapter 5 – that he possesses the property of space which, being nonmeasurable, is another way of giving us what the concept of infinity gives us, namely nonmeasurability (it was thought by the medievals under the influence of the ancients, notably Aristotle, that only infinity was nonmeasurable). It is this particular property of space that God possesses for us in terms of it constituting a place for us, which historically goes under the name of "heaven" (Chapters 5 and 10 say more about this difficult concept). Moreover, it is this space that God creates for us to live and die in (created space as opposed to noncreated heavenly space). It is the laws of nature that enable created space to be measurable space.

The conclusion must be that it is possible to endorse the Priestly writer's conception of God creating time before he created space. At the very least we want to say that what is going on in Genesis 1:3–10 is, among other things, the claim that God created the possibility of events other than himself.[4]

---

[4] To the extent that the category of time precedes the category of space in the Priestly creation narrative, it follows that the Priestly writer thinks of time and space coming into existence independently or separately of each other. This is what existed in the realm of being; hence, this is what God created – separately and independently. That created being is actually like this was of course challenged in the twentieth century with Einstein's celebrated theory of special relativity published in 1905. Einstein rejected Sir Isaac Newton's assumption that space and time are independent aspects of reality. As the mathematician Herman Minkowski famously put it in 1908, the consequences of Einstein's theory for the absoluteness and independence of space and time appeared to be fatal: "Henceforth, space by itself, and time by itself, are doomed to fade away into mere shadows, and only a kind of union of the two will preserve an independent reality" (Minkowski, "Space and Time," 75). Here Minkowski referred to a quintessential

⁴ (*continued*) Einsteinian concept: space–time. E. J. Lowe supplies a penetrating description of the fundamental implications of this concept:

> For Einstein, physical reality as a whole is a unitary, four-dimensional space-time manifold and events which have a purely space-like separation with respect to one frame of reference may have a time-like separation with respect to another: the only kind of "separation" between events whose measure is not frame-relative is neither purely space-like or purely time-like – it is their *space-time* separation (Lowe, *Survey of Metaphysics*, 268).

This means among other things that the temporal simultaneity of any two events separated in space may be true with respect to one frame of reference, but false with respect to another. This is Einstein's famous principle of *the relativity of simultaneity*. It is only with respect to a unitary space–time continuum that *all* judgements of simultaneity (and nonsimultaneity) are absolute. Crucially: it is not that there are *no* absolute truths about the temporal simultaneity and nonsimultaneity of any two events in space; it is that, according to Einstein, any theory which posits a space–time continuum, rather than space and time independently, will be a more comprehensive theory encompassing *all* judgements of simultaneity and nonsimultaneity – rather than the vast majority *but not all* (as is the case with Newton's conception of the absoluteness of time).

But this theory presupposes that space, and time, in particular be defined operationally. Only that which is measurable could be time; only that which is measurable could be space. Hence, if only measurable time can go by the name of "time" and only measurable space could go by the name of "space" then such a time and such a space existed only as one indivisible continuous reality called "space–time." So Einstein. The theory of special relativity and its postulation of space–time as an indivisible reality depend upon the time-dilation effect and the Fitzgerald–Lorentz contraction of space (the spatial counterpart of the time-dilation effect). Both effects are measurement effects and, as such, presuppose laws of nature not only as the means of measurement but as the operational meaning of the term "measurement" itself. Hence if we can speak of ordinal time and space such that operational definitions of time and space do not exhaust what we can mean by the terms "time" and "space," then clearly the special theory of relativity has no theoretical, far less empirical, application to these concepts.

Moreover, not only does Einstein's theory presuppose a metric of time and therefore the existence of laws of nature, it also purports to be

[4] *(continued)* a description of certain fundamental laws of nature. It is noteworthy that as regards operationally defined time and space, we must also recognize the priority of time over space: the ability to measure time is a requisite for the theory of space. Hans Reichenbach states that space and time are different concepts which remain distinct in the theory of relativity. The *real* space is three-dimensional and the *real* time is one-dimensional; the four-dimensional space–time used in the theory of relativity is a mathematical artifact (Reichenbach, *Philosophy of Space and Time*, 34).

But even as regards its application to metrical time, the theory is not without its critics. Lowe points out that Einstein's theory is dependent on the claim that the speed of light is constant. But since the constancy of the speed of light is not capable of empirical confirmation but only the constancy of the *average* speed of light, it is possible, he says, to reject the Einsteinian view on the grounds that it is still rational to affirm that time and space "are wholly separate and independent aspects of reality" (Lowe, *Metaphysics*, 269). (The philosopher of science Hans Reichenbach took the view that there is no way of measuring the velocity of light and proving it is constant, because the measurement of the velocity of light requires the definition of simultaneity which depends on the speed of light. Einstein – Reichenbach claimed – does not prove that the speed of light is constant. Rather, the special theory of relativity assumes it is constant [Reichenbach, *Philosophy of Space and Time*, 33]). This would imply that Einstein's "time-dilation" effect does not reveal anything about the nature of time (and so is ill-named), but only something about certain distorting influences on our *measurement* of temporal duration, "arising from variations in the speed of light as it travels in different directions" (Reichenbach, *Philosophy of Space and Time*, 269). Lowe draws on some brilliant arguments made by Michael Tooley in his recent book *Time, Tense, and Causation*, Chapter 11. The "time-dilation" effect refers to the experimental demonstration that "a clock with a high velocity (an appreciable fraction of the velocity of light) with respect to a given frame of reference appears to 'run slow'" (Lowe, *Metaphysics*, 268). This "has been confirmed by the observation that the half-lives of radioactive particles with high velocities are measurably longer by an amount predicted by the theory, than those of similar particles moving at lower velocities" (Lowe, *Metaphysics*, 268). The Fitzgerald–Lorentz contraction is the spatial counterpart of the time-dilation effect where bodies travelling at high speeds cause a contraction of the space complementary to the dilation of time.

Question: How did God create time and space? Answer: He determined himself to be the creator of time and of space

Let us now bring together the two main lessons from the previous two sections. From speech-act theory we have learned that the illocutionary action performed by way of the locutionary action can be other than the locutionary action itself. The simple example I offered was our saying, "Jones is a pig," and meaning other than the literal sense of this utterance. Not only do we have two actions which take place simultaneously, we have two different actions (as opposed to two identical actions if we were to mean what we say). From Claus Westermann's exegesis we learned that in saying, "Let there be light," God was creating temporal successiveness. Putting speech-act theory and Westermann together, we can see that there are two different actions at work here. One is the locutionary action corresponding to the God saying, "Let there be light." The other is the illocutionary action – which is other than the locutionary action – corresponding to God creating the possibility of time. Similarly, God performs the locutionary action of saying "Let there be an expanse between the waters to separate water from water" (Gen. 1:6), and performs the illocutionary action of creating space. Nevertheless, in both cases God literally speaks. Can we make sense of this notion? We can if we endorse the view that God can speak in virtue of determining himself to be the one who speaks. And, in particular, we can say that God performs the act of creating time and space in virtue of the same type of act: the act of divine self-determination.

What does it mean to say that God spoke (and speaks)?

Can God speak? Does he physically have to speak to speak (so to speak)? Clearly if the answer to the latter question is, yes, then there is problem unless of course we commit ourselves to some kind of materialist doctrine of God. Wolterstorff has famously provided an ingenious solution to this problem in his book *Divine Discourse*. He has shown how speech-act theory provides for the coherence of saying that God speaks without attributing him any kind of physical organ such as a larynx. The core of the argument goes something like this. Human beings can speak (speech-act theorists would say, perform this illocutionary act) without physically saying anything.

Here are two persuasive examples from Wolterstorff (see Wolterstorff, *Divine Discourse*, 38–45). You send someone a birthday card which someone else, say, at a factory, actually created, physically made. Nevertheless it is true to say that you spoke to the person to whom you sent the card – even if you are mute. Or again: you send your ambassador to speak on your behalf. Again, even if it is the case that you never physically actually said a word, it is true to say that you spoke in this case – performed this illocutionary act. Therefore it is not a logically necessary condition of human beings speaking that they have physically to speak, physically inscribe their words.

Wolterstorff applies this analysis to the case of God speaking through the prophets (*Divine Discourse*, 45–50). The prophet Isaiah or Jeremiah speaks – performs the locutionary action – but in fact what he is doing is inscribing the word of the Lord: "Thus saith the Lord." In performing the illocutionary action, God can be said to speak without physically saying anything. God too – like human beings – does not need a larynx (or any physical embodiment of a voice organ) in order to speak! Think of Jeremiah or Isaiah as God's ambassador and you get the idea.

However, the case of Genesis 1:3 poses a trickier problem. It may be objected that in both of Wolterstorff's examples, something else had to happen. In the first case a person physically made the card in a factory; in the second, there was an ambassador who physically did the speaking. The difficulty posed by God saying, "Let there be light" in Genesis 1:3 is that God has to say it. Though there is no real difficulty posed in the context in which God speaks through the prophets to Israel as it were, there appears to be with God speaking when nothing has yet been created. How do we solve this problem?

My answer comes in the form of a theory of divine action that I wish to apply to both God acting in the world and God acting in creating the world. Much of this book is taken up with this theory. As regards God speaking in Genesis 1:3 I wish to say that it is true that God says, "Let there be light" because he determines himself to be the one who says, "Let there be light'; therefore he says, "Let there be light." Similarly, I want to say that in saying, "Let there be light" God is the creator of temporal successiveness. How does he come to be the creator of temporal successiveness? The answer is that he determines himself to be the creator of temporal successiveness; therefore he *is* the creator of temporal successiveness; therefore (created) temporal successiveness exists. God cannot determine himself to be the creator of temporal successiveness and (created) temporal successiveness not exist. There are in fact (at least) two acts of divine self-determination, one corresponding to the locutionary action of speaking and another corresponding to the illocutionary action of creating time. It does not take a great deal of thought to see that speech-act theory would also dictate the occurrence of two actions were we to say that the locutionary and illocutionary action were the same – a state of affairs in which God says, "Let there be light" and means – and does – what he says. What my theory says is simply that the illocutionary action is other than the locutionary action in the context of Genesis 1:3–5.

If this theory of divine self-determination turns out to be coherent, there is no need to take recourse, as Augustine did, to the concept of "spiritual speech," when facing the question of the nature and sound of God's voice. For the theory asserts no more than that God spoke *because he determined himself to be the one who spoke*; which is to say, such divine self-determination does not require a physically embodied voice organ. Indeed, such a claim makes sense of the assertion that God – without a physically embodied voice organ – can speak to individual human beings. Indeed, if God determined himself to be the one who spoke to a profoundly deaf person – say the great Ludwig van Beethoven – then God spoke to Beethoven. Crucially, this would be the case without Beethoven as it were "hearing voices," in this case the "voice of God." No such implication is warranted: God's *self*-determination is basic and sufficient for it to be rational to say that God spoke to the great composer (whether or not this actually happened). Of course, as Wolterstorff points out: as a speaking person, God acquires the obligations and responsibilities attached to such a person (see Wolterstorff, *Divine Discourse*, chapter 6). He therefore satisfies the apparatus philosophers of language attribute as necessary conditions for such a speaking person: God does not merely determine himself to be the one who utters a random string of words, "Let-there-be-light" as a basic automaton might do; he enters into the linguistic realm of the language he speaks following its syntax and semantics!

We can even say, along with the simple literal sense of the text, that God spoke in Hebrew (both Barth and the great Old Testament scholar Herman Gunkel affirm this) since this is what is in the direct-speech quotational marks! (When Luther translates the narrative into German in his publication of the full Bible in 1534, he cannot be taken to be claiming that the translation inside his quotational marks corresponds to actual spoken reality!) If God determines himself to be the one who says, "Let there be light" then he said it! If God determined himself to be the one who spoke in Hebrew then he said it in Hebrew! The theory simply states that if God determines himself to be the one who does this or that action, then he does this or that action because he is the one who does this or that action.

Concluding remarks

In Book 11 of his *Confessions* Augustine distinguishes between, on the one hand, God's speaking at the creation of the world and, on the other, the voice at Jesus' baptism saying, "This is my Son, whom I love" (Matt. 17:5). The reason he makes this distinction is that he clearly thinks that the latter, being in time, is unproblematic: "That voice is past and done with; it began and is ended" (Augustine, *Confessions*, Bk 11, 225). Indeed, according to Augustine, it isn't in fact really God's voice but some mediating created thing who or that is doing the speaking (Augustine, *Confessions*, Bk 11, 225).

For Augustine, God speaking at Genesis 1:3 is quite another matter. Since time and creation do not yet exist, nothing can act as a "mediating thing." But worse, all that exists is God's timeless eternity. This means that the divine speaking cannot be an event in time such that it has a beginning and an end. Augustine's affirmation of timeless eternity means – predictably – that he has great conceptual perplexity with the literal sense of the text, which does seem to speak of God's actions having a

beginning and an end. The assumption of temporal successiveness has no such difficulty. According to the theory of divine
action espoused in this book, God speaks through divine self-
determination: he says, "Let there be light" by determining
himself to be the one who says, "Let there be light." (I thereby
endorse Wolterstorff's insight that God can speak without a
physically embodied speech-organ.) Timeless eternity does not
seem able to cope with the event of divine self-determination.[5]
As explained earlier, the concept of "ordinal" temporal successiveness as prescribed by Swinburne can; we can say that the
event of divine self-determination began and ended without
having to say how long it endured.

Is this theory of divine self-determination rational? In the following chapter I will expound this theory of divine self-determination in its most general form, namely, in reference to: God is
the creator of all things. Clearly the analysis encompasses both
God speaking as a locutionary action and God creating time as
an illocutionary action. I believe, as I say, that it can unify God
acting in the world as well as his acting in creating the world. But
the proof will be in the pudding in Chapter 2.

---

[5] I argue in effect that God speaking in Gen. 1 – and especially at 1:3 –
undermines the very notion of timeless eternity. But God possesses the
property of temporal successiveness because nothing else exists at this
"time." There is therefore nothing problematic about his speaking.
Likewise, I am going to argue that, just as God speaking requires a
concept of temporal successiveness, then so the affirmation of God
raising the man Jesus from the dead requires that God also possesses
the property of spatiality. This symmetrical proposal will be made in
Chapter 5.

Bibliography

Aquinas, *Summa Theologiae*. In *Basic Writings of Saint Thomas Aquinas*, edited by Anton Pegis (New York: Random House, 1945).

Augustine, *Confessions*, translated by H. Chadwick (Oxford: Oxford University Press, 1991).

Barth, Karl, *Church Dogmatics* II/1, translated by T. F. Torrance and G. Bromiley (Edinburgh: T. &T. Clark, 1957).

Craig, William Lane, "God and Real Time." *Religious Studies* 26 (1990): 335–47.

Einstein, Albert, *Relativity: The Special and the General Theory*, translated by R. W. Lawson (London: Routledge, 2001).

Jenson, Robert W., *Systematic Theology*, vol. 2 (Oxford: Oxford University Press, 1999).

Lowe, E. J., *A Survey of Metaphysics* (Oxford: Oxford University Press, 2002).

Minkowski, Herman, "Space and Time." In *The Principle of Relativity*, edited by H. A. Lorentz, A. Einstein, H. Minkowski and H. Weyl, translated by W. Perrett and G. B. Jeffery, (New York: Dover, 1952) 104–11.

Pannenberg, Wolfhart, *Systematic Theology*, vol. 1 (Grand Rapids: Eerdmans, 1991).

Reichenbach, Hans, *The Philosophy of Space and Time*, translated by M. Reichenbach and J. Freund (New York: Dover, 1958).

Sorabji, Richard, *Time, Creation and the Continuum* (London: Duckworth, 1983).

Swinburne, Richard, *The Christian God* (Oxford: Oxford University Press, 1994).

Tooley, Michael, *Time, Tense, and Causation* (Oxford: Oxford University Press, 2003).

Westermann, Claus, *Genesis 1–11* (Minneapolis: Fortress Press, 1994).

Wolterstorff, Nicholas, *Divine Discourse* (Cambridge: Cambridge University Press, 1995).

2

YHWH the God of Israel, Divine Self-Determination, and the Mechanics of Divine Action

The brilliant physicist Richard Feynman once said of the celebrated double-slit experiment of quantum mechanics that, if you understood this experiment, then you understood the essence of quantum reality; any difficulties in understanding and accepting the implications of quantum theory could, Feynman claimed, be tempered by reminding oneself of the paradoxical results of the experiment. I mention this famous story from the world of physics because the theory of creation that I am going to propound in this chapter – which I also take to be the basis for a theory of divine action in the world – is also a decidedly paradoxical one. The late and great philosopher and logician Willard van Orman Quine wrote a famous essay called "The Ways of Paradox" in which he argued that one must be distinguish between apparent paradoxes and real paradoxes. He gave as examples of the former the so-called barber paradox. Of the latter category, he cited Kurt Gödel's famous incompleteness theorem. I am inclined to think that what I have to say about the doctrine of creation does not belong to the exalted class of real paradox but is only apparently paradoxical. My claim will be that God creates the world precisely by determining himself to be the creator of the world. The paradoxical aspect of this is that it seems to put things the wrong way round. Our natural inclination is to say that God determines himself to be the creator precisely by creating the world. My thesis is that God does not create the world in order for it to be the case that he determines himself as creator. God determines himself as the creator of the world; therefore, he is the creator of the world.

Question for a catechism: How did God create the world? He determined himself to be the creator of it

Hans Frei once made the observation that the *material* mode of Christian theology was that of the Bible. By this he meant simply that the matter on which Christian theologians reflected was the Old and the New Testaments. This material mode was to be distinguished from the *formal* mode of theology. The latter mode was to be identified with the form theological reflection was to take on this material. He professed the view that the specific formal mode most likely to solve the outstanding problems of theology in relation to the Bible was that of analytic philosophy. I agree with Frei on this. I think that Nicholas Wolterstorff's work on divine speaking (see Chapter 1), and God and time (see Chapter 5, "The Seventh Day of Creation"), demonstrates just how powerful and illuminating a tool analytic philosophy can be when allied to biblical interpretation. But my objective here is not as it were to bang the drum for analytic philosophy as a Christian conceptual enterprise; it is to show how adopting this mode of thought might solve some outstanding problems in the area of the doctrine of creation – and do so in such a way that provides a means of affirming the rationality of Israel's experience of YHWH acting in their history as narrated in the Old Testament.

Let me begin with what I take to be the analytic philosopher's core strength. It is that he or she will tend to view a proposition or a declarative sentence as alive with certain implications. In his or her eyes – or ears for that matter – a proposition is not an inert thing which just says what it says; it is dynamic in the sense that if it is true then it generates other truths, entails other truths. Another way of saying the same thing is that: *if the proposition under scrutiny is true, its truth is a logically sufficient condition for another proposition being true.*

My contention will be that if you can grasp the simple formal idea that propositions are alive in the sense that they beget other propositions then you can go far toward understanding how we can reach our objective of affirming the historical experience of Israel as told in Old Testament narrative.

Let me begin with some simple distinctions. Theologians commonly distinguish between on the one hand God in himself (God *ad intra*) and God in his works (God *ad extra*). In the present context this distinction becomes God in himself and God the creator of the world. More obviously perhaps, theologians also draw a distinction between, on the one hand, these two concepts of God and, on the other, the concept of the work itself – the world. Theologians commonly explain the existence and reality of the world in terms of the fact that it is the work of God the creator (God *ad extra*).

I want us to ask the question, How far might we go toward reaching the conclusion that the world was created by God if we were to focus entirely on – restrict ourselves exclusively to – a concept of God the creator (*ad extra*) in which God acts on himself – inwardly as it were – rather than acting outwardly and directly toward the creation of the world? A concept in which God's work of creation is directed at himself and only indirectly outwards? How far might such a conception take us? The answer I want to suggest to you is that we might be able to go quite far towards our desired conclusion. This is how we might do it.

There are many analogies and models used to describe God as creator of the world. If we look at the standard textbooks of Christian theology – Daniel Migliore (*Faith Seeking Understanding*); Alister McGrath (*Christian Theology: An Introduction*) – we find the following selection of analogies:

(1) A *procreational* analogy in which God begets or gives birth to the world as in a mother's generation of her offspring.
(2) The world as an *emanation* from God as in the light and heat radiating from the sun or a fire, water flowing from a spring as its source, and so on.
(3) A *constructional* analogy in which God is understood as the fabricator or builder of the formation of world.
(4) The world as the product of God's *artistic expression*. The world understood as the "handiwork of God" as a work of art.

Common to all these analogies is that the divine act of creation is understood as a basic action directed outward from God toward the creation of the world. This is most clearly evident in the anthropomorphic analogies of human construction and human artistic creation. In the creation of a work of art for example the artist commonly does something to the canvas (external to him or her) – with his or her paintbrush and paint, and thereby creates the work of art. My basic observation of all these analogies is that they are inadequate, not least because they bear absolutely no relation to the historical formation of the Old Testament.

In contrast the analogy I want to examine is one in which the fundamental idea is that God's basic action in creation is not first directed outward in this sense but is in fact something that God first does to himself in his divine sovereign freedom. The proposition I want to examine is the one that says quite simply that the basic act of divine creation is: *God determines himself to be the creator of all things.*

The important thing for our present purpose is that when God determines himself this is something that God does to himself. He does not determine anything or anyone else. Our proposition says something solely about God and not about anything or anyone else. It is a statement solely about God determining his being or identity – not about God determining the existence of any other being or identity – or at least not directly. *God is both the subject and – crucially – the object of his action.*

To determine oneself to *be* this or that identity is not merely to do something to one or other of one's properties; it is to orientate one's whole identity. God determines himself *to be* the creator of all things; God determines himself to *be* (one who is) present within the constitution of the world. My first reaction when I first reflected on the nature of God's self-determining self was that it was a kind of self-reflexive action, similar in kind to the actions indicated in self-reflexive verbs such as "I wash myself" or "I shave myself." But the similarity is only superficial. My washing myself is merely to do something to one or other of my properties, in this case my body. Self-determination carries a connotation that mere self-reflexive action does not. So, while determining himself to be the creator of all things may be something that God does to himself, it is something God does to his *whole* identity. He acts on himself to become an identity he was not before, though without becoming someone else. God remains God even as he becomes the creator of the world in the sense that he determines himself to be the creator of the world. When God determines himself to be the creator of all things he is acting on himself; more precisely, he is acting on his identity, orientating his identity.[1]

Yet though the work of creation is an action restricted to God's identity in this sense, it is, I submit, able to derive the conclusion that the world was created by God.

If we put this thesis in the form of a question asked in a Catechism we get:

---

[1] It is conceivable that there is a historical precedent in Aristotle's *Metaphysics* for some aspects of the conception of divine action outlined in this chapter. It is conceivable that there is a formal similarity with ideas promulgated by Aristotle in his *Metaphysics* (and perhaps also in his *Physics*). In a fine contribution to the Blackwell *A Companion to Philosophy of Religion* correcting some popular misconceptions of Plato and Aristotle, Kevin L Flannery writes: "Aristotle . . . speaks of the unmoved mover as 'thought thinking itself'" (*Metaphysics* xii, 9, 1074b33–5) and has been criticized for thereby positing a self-absorbed, distant God. But this is quite irreconcilable with his overall theory and should be resisted as a possible interpretation. Aristotle rejects the notion that God might think of something other than himself precisely because it would diminish his power (*Metaphysics* xii, 6, 1071b12–32). The power that Aristotle is concerned about is the power whereby God has an effect in the world (*Metaphysics* xii, 6,1071b12–32). (In *Physics* viii, 5, Aristotle also says of Anaxagoras' Mind that "it could only cause motion the way it does being unmoved, and it can only *rule* unmixed" – 256b26–7; emphasis added.) So we must conceive of God's thoughts about himself as bound up with his immanency (*Metaphysics* I,2,983a8–10; iii,4,1000b3–6; (Flannery, "Ancient Philosophical Theology," 77). The difference I perceive between Aristotle's conception and the proposal on offer in this book is that I want to apply such a notion in the context of God determining himself to be a specific historical identity picked out by identifying descriptions such as "the one who is the creator of all things" and "the one who released Israel from the bondage of Egypt."

Question: How did God create the world?
Answer: God determined himself to be the creator of it. He determined himself to be the creator of all things.

It is a highly counterintuitive theory. As was said, the paradoxical aspect of it is that it seems to put things the wrong way round. Our natural inclination is to say that God determines himself to be the creator precisely by creating the world. In contrast, the present thesis is that God does not create the world *in order* for it to be the case that he determines himself as creator. God determines himself as the creator of the world; therefore, he is the creator of the world.[2]

God's self-determining self is a sufficient truth

Let me try to view the statement "God determines himself to be the creator of all things" as I think an analytic philosopher would. What propositions does it beget? All analytic philosophers would agree that if this statement is true then it follows that God is the creator of all things. Philosophers would say that God determining himself to be the creator is a logically sufficient condition of it being true that God is the creator. There is the premise that God acts in a certain way – determines himself to be the creator – and there is the logically deduced conclusion that God is the creator. To put it another way: it is a simple logical truth that if God determines himself to be the creator or the one who creates all things then he *is* the creator. They would also agree that a further proposition would follow, namely that all things were created by God. If God is the creator in virtue of determining himself to be the creator then it follows that God determining himself as the creator of the world is *sufficient* for it to be the case that the world was created by God. This much is uncontroversial.

---

[2] Counterintuitive this doctrine might be – but in my judgement it is able to resolve some hitherto intractable doctrinal problems. I mention just two: the first is creation out of nothing which Augustine perceived was still a problem late in the fourth century; the second is the problem of how a nonmaterial creator can create a material world – a problem which worried the patristic fathers and especially the Cappadocian father, Gregory of Nyssa. I discuss these matters in Chapter 3.

God's self-determining action is a basic action

What is more controversial is the following claim. The statement is a *basic action*. This is in fact the key claim. The mechanics of logical implication as outlined above are only significant for divine action in the context of the claim that behind the whole logical edifice we are speaking of an action of God and, in particular, a basic action of God. To say that "God determines himself to be the creator of all things" is a basic action is to make an actual claim about God's relation to the world and *how* God creates the world.

What is a basic action in this context? A basic action is such that there are no actions other than the one of God determining himself to be the creator of all things for it to be true that God *is* the creator of all things.

What is of course controversial about this claim is that it is likely to prompt the response: but doesn't God *have* to do something other than determine himself, to be the creator of the world? Doesn't God *have* to do something to determine himself to be the creator of the world? If God *has* to do something other than determine himself in the appropriate way then of course God' self-determining self cannot be a basic action. That much is clear. But it will not do as an argument to say that God *has* to do something else because this is simply to beg the question – unless it is something like a necessary truth that God has to do something else (and most analytic philosophers would agree that it is no such truth).

Undoubtedly the Christian tradition thought in terms of God "creating" or "making" – or even "speaking" – being the basic action involved in divine creation. In this way did God determine himself to be the creator (he "creates," he "makes"; ergo he determines himself as the creator). There is no act of self-determination that could take place independently of these implicitly more basic acts.

In actual fact, the assertion that *God has to do something in order to be the creator* (other than simply determines himself appropriately) is almost certainly based on the example – the analogy – of human self-determination. It seems quite clear that when human beings determine themselves to be some person or some identity, self-determination is not the basic action involved in being the person or identity. By this I mean that human beings do things in order to determine themselves. For example, in order to become – determine oneself as – the person who picks up the coin in front of me, I will have to pick up the coin in front of me. I will have do something in order to become this person, this identity. Similarly, suppose I determine myself to be the winner of the Olympic hundred metres then it is clear I also do something. I win the Olympic hundred metres. I don't just determine myself as this as in a thought or as in a dream. Self-determination is not the basic action involved in my being the hundred metres Olympic gold medal winner. Winning the race is. This is what I do directly. I determine myself as the winner *through* winning the race. Self-determination is indirect.

In contrast, *God's self-determination of himself is basic in the sense of being irreducible.* God's self-determining self is basic in this sense. There is a fundamental disanalogy between divine self-determination and mere human self-determination. In divine self-determination God does not *do* anything as a condition of self-determination (what he *does* is determine himself). In other words, God does not create the world *in order* for it to be the case that he determines himself as creator. God determines himself as the creator of the world; therefore, he is the creator of the world. This is the sense in which his action is an *efficient cause* – although as we shall see in dealing with the question of *creatio ex nihilo* this is to be sharply distinguished from a *material cause*. In a slightly different though theologically relevant context, Robert Jenson says that God *is* his own decision (*Systematic Theology*, vol. 1, 140) – which is to say his own self-determining decision. *God possesses unrestricted, sovereign freedom. Indeed, only a doctrine which says this does justice to the majesty and Godness of God!*

Putting this doctrine of creation in its most general terms we should say: if God is the creator of the world then it follows that the world was created by God. And because God being the creator of the world is true in virtue of God *determining himself* as the creator of the world, then it follows that God determining himself as the creator of the world is *sufficient* for it being the case that the world was created by God. God's determining himself as creator is both *basic* and *sufficient* for it being the case that the world was created by God. When Childs speaks of the Priestly narrative as indicative of God the creator of all things "whose intention and execution are identical," he is exactly right (*Biblical Theology*, 352. See also MacDonald, *Karl Barth*, 58).

Divine self-determination with and without natural theology

The theory of divine self-determination espoused here is compatible with natural theology. This is the first thing that must be said. The statement that God determines *himself* to be the creator of all things is not *in itself* incompatible with natural theology. To say that God determines *himself* to be the creator of the world does not *exclude* the possibility that he imbues his creation with "signs" that he created it, that he leaves his "fingerprints" on it, as it were. But equally, *divine self-determination does not entail natural theology*. In other words, to take an example: in the context of God creating time, we can say one of two things. We can say that God determined himself to be the creator of time in such a way that a natural theology of time is possible (theologians and philosophers could then propose a proof of God's existence based on some observed or deduced property of time just as Aquinas did in the case of motion); or we can say that God determined himself to be the creator of time in such a way that natural theology is impossible – or at the very least, impotent (there is nothing distinctively theological about time *per se* which would lead us to infer that it was created by God).

I am of the opinion that divine self-determination without natural theology is on the whole the preferred option (though I am not averse in principle to a theology of nature). This is because the former does not commit itself to any particular way science construes or discovers the world to be – excepting perhaps that it had a beginning and "there was when it was not." This means that, no matter what science discovers about the world, the claim that God created it by determining himself to be the creator – no less and no more – remains entirely feasible even in the face of competing explanations of the existence of the world. This is the fundamental reason Barth claimed that there is "free scope for natural science beyond what theology describes as the work of the Creator" (Barth, *CD* III/1, x). Though positive natural theology – natural theology purporting to reason from the world to God – is impossible, so too is negative natural theology, which is to say, natural science purporting to claim that this world could not have been created by any personal creator. To say that God determined himself to be the creator of all things, including (created) time, does not imply that God's act of self-determination leaves "fingerprints" on the natural properties of creation; but it is to say that such an act is sufficient for it being the case that the predicate "created by God" designates the world.

Further explanation: "only incidentally about the creation"!

If God created the world then the world was created by God. If God created the world merely by determining *himself* to be the creator then the world was created by God (if God determined himself to be the creator of time, then time was created by God). We can agree to these innocuous logical truths! But because the world, including time, was created by God determining *himself* – nothing more – then all that must be true of the world created by God is that it is designated by the predicate "created by God." If we were to represent the world in terms of a package, we could imagine it to be stamped with the words "created by God." But note well: the stamp itself tells us nothing about the package itself other than the fact it was created by God. It tells us nothing about the package itself, regarding its contents, for example. In other words, the stamp tells us nothing about the *natural properties* of the package. The stamp acts simply a designator, not a description.

Crucially then, we cannot infer from the natural properties of the package to the claim that it was created by God. The natural properties of the package are not the reason that the package is stamped with the words "created by God." What explains the stamp is that God determined *himself* to be the creator of the package. Nothing more and nothing less.

This means – and this is a very big claim – that were the God of Israel *not* to have created this world then all that would be necessarily true is that the *very same (identical) world* which we inhabit was not created by God and therefore is not designated by the predicate "created by God." What makes it true it was *in fact* created by God is that God determined himself to be the creator of it. Conversely, were we to suppose that the divine action of creating did not take place we would simply say: God did not determine himself to be the creator of this world, because he didn't create it! We are not saying this world – this very same world – would be a different world in terms of its natural properties – were it not created by God. We are simply saying that God did not determine himself to be its creator because he didn't create it! Back to the package: it doesn't have the stamp "created by God" on it simply because, according to my story, God did not determine himself to be the creator.[3]

Barth saw the importance of this implication for his doctrine of creation. In *Church Dogmatics* III/1, he is quite adamant that the world in which we live might well not have been created by God (Barth, *CD* III/1, 7). It is possible, for example, that it had always existed in some such form or another – a view held by the classical Greek philosophical tradition including of course Plato and Aristotle. Barth did not demur from such a conclusion: all this was possible! Though Barth believes that the actual world we live in was in fact created by God, he is also of the view that counterfactually it might not have been created by God. There could well have been then a world identical to the one we inhabit that was not created by God.

Is this possible? Could there really have been a world identical to the one we inhabit – *identical in all respects as regards its natural properties* – that was not created by God? Barth made

---

[3] Of course, if one argues that necessarily, anything that exists is created, then it cannot be the case that there is something that exists that was not created by God. Clearly, if we say that there could be a world that existed which was not created then the assumption of two identical worlds one of which was not created by God implies that both the argument from design (or to design) and the cosmological argument are invalid. Perhaps Kant was right but for reasons or premises with which he would not have been comfortable!

good on showing how this could be so. *He says that the world created by God is designated by the predicate "created by God" and the other is not.* The reason it is designated by this predicate is because of God's act in determining *himself* to be the creator of all things. The reason the other (identical) world is not designated so is because there is no corresponding act of divine *self*-determination. *Otherwise there does not have to be any difference between the two worlds.* The natural or material properties of each world are the same because the predicate "created by God" does not say anything about the natural or material properties of the world it designates. But what it does do is tell us something about the properties of God instead – i.e. that he is the creator – and this is the crucial point. Basic and sufficient.

How can the predicate "created by God" be true of the world without it being the case that anything is said or implied about the natural or material properties of the world? The simple answer is that God determining *himself* to be the creator of all things does not imply anything at all about the natural and material properties of the world – yet is sufficient for it being the case that this world was created by God. What makes this predicate designate our actual world is the fact that God determined *himself* to be the creator of all things, and this means the actual world we live in. The other identical world is not designated by the predicate "created by God" simply in virtue of the fact that God did not determine himself to be its creator.

Did Barth really say something like this?[4] Speaking of God the creator in the context of the apostles' creed, Barth wrote: ". . . the confession does not speak of the world, or at all events it does so incidentally, when it speaks of [God the creator] of heaven and earth. It does not say, I believe in the created world, nor I believe in the work of creation. But it says, I believe in God the Creator"

---

[4] For anyone who is of the opinion that this is too philosophically sophisticated a view to attribute to Barth, I ask them to consider his interpretation of Anselm's *Proslogion* where he insists that Anselm's famous formula "that than which a greater cannot be conceived" must be understood as a *noetic conception and not an ontic conception.* That is: it does not *describe* God's *nature* but rather acts to *designate* God without telling us anything at all about his nature. See MacDonald, *Karl Barth,* chapters 6 and 9.

(Barth, *Dogmatics in Outline*, 50). The ultimate consequences of this claim are not entirely clear until Barth concludes his point with the following sentences:

> . . . everything that is said about creation depends absolutely [*hängt ganz und gar*] upon this Subject [*Subjekt*]. The same rule holds always, that all the predicates [*Prädikate*] are determined by Him [*sind bestimmt von ihm*]. This holds also for creation. Fundamentally, what is involved here is the knowledge of the Creator; and after that and from that viewpoint, His Work must be understood (Barth, *Dogmatics in Outline*, 50).

This is in my opinion revolutionary stuff and the basis for a new biblical metaphysics. What Barth *ultimately* means here is that the claim, the world was created by God, depends absolutely upon this subject, God. It depends on whether the predicate "created by God" predicates the world. This in turn depends on whether the predicate "creator of all things" predicates God. And *this* in turn depends on whether God determined himself to be the creator of all things. If we know that God determined himself to be the creator, then we know that the world was created by God. We do not have to look at any of the properties of the world, either individually or collectively, to deduce God's creation of it; we do not have to look at any of the properties of human beings, either individually or collectively, to deduce God's creation of human beings or the world in general. Indeed, for the reasons given above, we *cannot* look at any of the properties of the world, either individually or collectively, to deduce God's creation.

The creation narrative, Barth said, was "only incidentally about the creation" (Barth, *Dogmatics in Outline*, 51); it was about God revealing himself, determining himself to be the creator – the creator of all things. It was really *all* about God – what God "does" to himself.[5]

---

[5] As a number of biblical scholars have noted, the Priestly narrator's emphasis in his creation narrative is not so much on the *created beings* as it is on *God the creator*. As Von Rad points out, "the form and content of the former are shadowy and vague" (Von Rad, *Genesis*, 65). The Priestly creation narrative has been also described as nothing other than a form

Rationalism, voluntarism, Aquinas, and Ockham

Clearly, the above analysis – divine self-determination without natural theology – implies that the celebrated "five ways" of Thomas Aquinas cannot prove what they are meant to prove. This follows from the observation that there could be a world identical to this one in all respects which God did not create. There could be a world identical to this one in precisely the sense that it contains all the phenomena described by each of the "five ways", yet that world not have been created by God.[6]

But this does not mean that divine self-determination without natural theology closes off the possibility of the kind of *rationalism* espoused by Aquinas. According to Aquinas, the creation of the world is preceded by ideas in the infinite intellect of God, and these ideas are realized by way of God's infinite will because they are seen to be good by God's infinite intellect. This is one legacy Plato bequeathed to Aquinas. God created according to something akin to the Platonic Forms and these ideas are to be understood as existing in God in some sense in God's mind. The supreme principle of rationalism was that God created according to an idea, a Form. (In theological terms the Logos was accorded pride of place as the supreme Form, the Form of Forms, as it were.) None of this is ruled out and, indeed, if we talk of God as being a person (though not merely a person) we can see that this kind of description of God's action may be entirely appropriate. The truth is that divine self-determination neither entails or excludes it. Rationalism of the kind Aquinas endorses is one thing, and natural theology another.

---

[5] (*continued*) of praise for God the creator. Westermann argues that Gen. 1:1 could be rewritten as a hymn of worship: "God, creator of heaven and earth" (Westermann, *Genesis 1 – 11*, 94).

[6] Denys Turner has recently argued that it is possible to prove the existence of God on the basis of natural theology (see Turner, *Faith, Reason, and the Existence of God*, chapter 1). If we take 'possible' to mean what it means within the context of analytic philosophy then I agree. Nevertheless if divine self-determination without natural theology is true – which means that there could have been an identical world which was not created by God – then it is simply a false assertion. "One can prove the existence of God by natural theology" is false.

What is the relation between, on the one hand, divine self-determination without natural theology and, on the other, the voluntaristic doctrines of a theologian like William of Ockham? In his book *Act and Being*, Dietrich Bonhoeffer compared Barth's later theology (the early part thereof) to the voluntarism of Duns Scotus and his most famous pupil William of Ockham in the context of an exposition of Luther (Bonhoeffer, *Act and Being*, 78). Since Barth's ideas on creation are a major influence on the theory of divine action being endorsed in this chapter – and in the book as a whole – one might think that if Bonhoeffer is right in his analysis then the relation must be a positive one. But things are less straightforward than might appear.

In contradistinction to Thomas Aquinas, one of the fundamental inferences to be made from the thought of a theologian like William of Ockham appeared to be an emphasis on the distance between God and humankind. Creation is an act of divine will. But though God had willed this world into existence, it is out and out *contingent*, and if it had pleased him, God could have created a world entirely different from the one we have now. The history of ideas at this point in time seemed to be saying that we could no longer infer from the world to God with any degree of confidence. In fact: we could not infer from the world to God at all. God, being all-powerful and absolutely *free*, could have created *an entirely different world* and, given this, there is no necessary chain linking the world with God. The nature of the world tells us nothing about the nature of God because God could have created a world that had absolutely no continuity with his nature. Humankind from its position in the world could not reach God epistemologically, which is to say, it could not prove the Deity's existence. One could only affirm God's existence *through faith*.

The implication of this kind of reasoning – if valid – was to undermine the kind of natural theology held by Aquinas. In the wake of this, humankind was thrown back on the Bible – on revelation – as the only source of knowledge and belief in God. Historically, this insight was of great importance to Luther's theology since it implied that humankind was thrown back into the arms of God's saving identity in Jesus Christ in the absence of any provable knowledge of God the creator. In such a context the only refuge – the only epistemological sanctuary – was *trust* in God (Luther's most famous twentieth-century successor Rudolf Bultmann carried on this Lutheran orientation in that he demythologized and reinterpreted the doctrine of creation in terms of an existential soteriology: to affirm God as creator is to affirm *in faith* my dependence on God for my existence.)

Nevertheless, there is a crucial distinction to be made between divine self-determination without natural theology and this understanding of Ockham's view of creation. The thesis that God determines *himself* to be the creator of all things without leaving a "fingerprint" on nature does not of itself exclude the possibility that God would *only* have created the actual world we inhabit (God has reasons: herein lies residual rationalism at the very least!). This is a very un-Ockhamish assumption (unsurprisingly, divine self-determination does not start from the premise of an arbitrary God working within the parameters of logical possibility since it is fully compatible with Aquinas's rationalism). Notwithstanding this, however, divine self-determination without natural theology – and here is the affinity with Ockham – refutes the possibility of the project of natural theology. Natural theology becomes impossible – *but for a completely opposite reason to the one voluntarism gives.* Voluntarism typically argues that natural theology is to be rejected because God could have created many different worlds, none of which bear any natural continuity with their creator. The theory of divine self-determination proposed here says that natural theology is rendered impossible because our very same world might not have been created by God. It is therefore impossible to infer from any of the natural properties of the actual world to God as the creator of it.

Divine self-determination without natural theology – if it is true – refutes *naturalism*. Naturalism is the doctrine which says that the natural properties of the world provide sufficient resources to derive the truth about the world itself. David Hume's "stratonician atheism" is an example of this kind of naturalism which, in the modern age, goes under the name of the philosophy of immanence. For example, to anticipate some conclusions of Chapter 4: if humankind created in the image of God is true solely and sufficiently in virtue of God's self-determining history then naturalism must be false. That is: understanding the image of God in terms of God's self-determining creation history provides the basis on which to reject naturalism. Clearly, if humankind created in the image of God is true solely and sufficiently in virtue of God's self-determining history then this doctrine must be false. The natural properties of a part of the world – in this case, our natural properties as human beings – are not sufficient to derive the truth about this same world. The same goes for the world writ large.[7] To repeat: God determining *himself* to be the creator of all things does not imply anything at all about the natural and material properties of the world – yet is sufficient for it being the case that this world was created by God.[8]

Concluding remarks

When I first mooted the idea that God created and acted in the world by respectively determining himself to be the creator of

---

[7] It is my belief that such a doctrine minimizes the importance of any kind of fruitful interaction between theology and science. One could have *two identical worlds* one of which it would be true to say that God determined himself to be the creator of it and the other not. What would make one world created by God and the other not would be whether God had determined himself to be the creator of it or not. But God's having determined himself as creator is solely and sufficiently confined to the creation history. Hence this self-determination cannot be established by looking at the natural properties of each world. See MacDonald, *Karl Barth*, 148–150. Explaining the existence of the universe in terms of, for example, quantum fluctuations trading on the quantum uncertainty of time and energy and providing a basis for cosmological inflation leading to the "big bang" may be fascinating in its own right; but it has no direct bearing on the issue of God as creator understood as a self-determining self.

[8] To be sure: divine self-determination *with* natural theology also refutes naturalism. It also opposes the claim that the natural properties of the world provide sufficient resources to derive the truth about the world itself. This is because it itself makes the claim that the natural properties of the world themselves – at least some of them – bear witness to the "fingerprints" of God. This allows it to make an inference to God the creator. The natural properties of the world do not provide sufficient resources in the above sense because something outside of it – God – created it.

and actor in it, I had the sensation or so it seems to me, of what the seventeenth-century poet Henry Vaughan called "seeing eternity the other night." Is this really how God created the world? Is this really how he acts in it? I also thought though not entirely seriously, Is there an aspect of profaning the sacred in all this? Of trespassing into the "holy of holies"? I concluded not. First, the mystery is still intact. When I assert that God determining himself is a basic action – that God can and does act in this way – the question how he is able to do this remains unanswerable. I submit that we have gone as far we can toward grasping God's being in this respect. Beyond this point is the retention of mystery.

Second, the act of discerning the "mind of God" is not without precedent in the history of theology. To the modern mentality, the idea of medieval school philosophers constructing comprehensive systems proactively and pedantically anticipating answers to potential objections is the stuff of eccentricity, of faintly absurd comedy. "How many angels can one get on the head of a pin?" is perhaps the most famous example of a scholastic curiosity taken to extremes. Yet it should be remembered it was also a world in which the great thinkers of the time debated the actual mind of God and in doing so made it utterly real, present, and alive to their audiences or their addressees. An example would be the intellectualist–voluntarist debate. Intellectualists such as Aquinas and Eckhart thought choices of the will result from that which the intellect recognizes as good. In the case of God this meant that God's will itself is determined by his reason, his intellect as it were. Voluntarists such as Duns Scotus and William of Ockham held that the will determines which objects are good. In the case of God, this meant that the divine will is the ultimate origin of the good. Did God reason before willing or was will the ultimate origin of his action? These were all attempts to peer into "the mind of God."

There is also a modern precedent to this aspect of the medieval mind. It has found itself at home in no less a subject than fundamental theoretical physics. Physicists in effect are the minds who attempt to peer into the mind of God. Perhaps Steven Hawking's *A Brief History of Time* is not a particularly good example; a better one might of course be Paul Davies' *The Mind of*

God. But even then both examples are too secular in nature. It is time for a reappropriation of "the mind of God" – as it were – on the part of the Bible and theological studies.

Bibliography

Barth, Karl, *Church Dogmatics* II/1, translated by T. F. Torrance and G. Bromiley (Edinburgh: T. & T. Clark, 1957).

Barth, Karl, *Church Dogmatics* III/1, translated by T. F. Torrance and G. Bromiley (Edinburgh: T. & T. Clark, 1958); *Dogmatics in Outline,* translated by G. T. Thomson (London: SCM Press, 1949).

Bonhoeffer, Dietrich, *Act and Being*, translated by Bernard Noble (New York: Harper & Row, 1962).

Childs, Brevard, *Biblical Theology of the Old and New Testaments: Theological Reflection on the Christian Bible* (London: SCM, 1992).

Davies, Paul, *The Mind of God: The Scientific Basis for a Rational World* (New York: Simon & Schuster, 1992).

Feynman, Richard P., Robert B. Leighton and Matthew Sands, *The Feynman Lectures on Physics: Vol III, Quantum Mechanics* (Reading, Massachussets: Addison-Wesley, 1965).

Flannery, Kevin L., "Ancient Philosophical Theology." In *A Companion to Philosophy of Religion*, edited by Philip L. Quinn and Charles Taliaferro (Oxford: Blackwell, 1999) 73–79.

Hawking, Stephen, *A Brief History of Time: From the Big Bang to Black Holes* (New York: Bantam Books, 1988).

Jenson, Robert W., *Systematic Theology*, vol. 1 (Oxford: Oxford University Press, 1997).

MacDonald, Neil B., *Karl Barth and the Strange New World within the Bible: Barth, Wittgenstein, and the Metadilemmas of the Enlightenment*, rev. ed. (Carlisle: Paternoster, 2001).

McGrath, Alister, *Christian Theology: An Introduction*, 3rd ed. (Oxford: Blackwell, 2003).

Migliore, Daniel, *Faith Seeking Understanding* (Grand Rapids: Eerdmans, 1995).

Ockham, William of, *Quodlibetal Questions, Volumes 1 and 2.* translated by Alfred J. Freddoso and Francis E. Kelley (New Haven: Yale University Press, 1991).

Quine, Willard van Orman, "The Ways of Paradox." In *The Ways of Paradox and Other Essays*, rev. ed. (Cambridge, MA: Harvard University Press, 1976) 1–21.

Rad, Gerhard von, *Genesis,* translated by J. Bowden, 3rd ed. (London: SCM, 1972).

Taylor, Charles, *The Sources of the Self: The Making of the Modern Identity* (Cambridge MA: Harvard University Press, 1989).

Turner, Denys, *Faith, Reason, and the Existence of God* (Cambridge: Cambridge University Press, 2004).

Westermann, Claus, *Genesis 1 – 11* (Minneapolis: Fortress Press, 1994).

3

God the Self-Determining Self and Some Classical Problems of the Doctrine of Creation

One central claim for the biblical metaphysic expounded in this book will be that it unifies God's action in creating the world with God's acting in the world. Both are "token" actions of the same "type." Such unification as any physical scientist might tell you (pointing to James Clerk Maxwell's success in the field of electromagnetic radiation) is one criterion by which one judges the success of a theory. Moreover, the biblical metaphysic is also able to encompass the view held by such as Gerhard von Rad that Israel's experience of YHWH was (primitively) of its God – the God of Israel – acting "then and there" in its life, in the same "spatial" and "temporal" frame. Nevertheless, for this theory of biblical metaphysics to pass muster it must at the very least be capable of doing justice to the classical problems of divine creation to the same extent as the kind of tradition to which Thomas Aquinas belongs. Here I speak of the main ingredients of the standard "credal" fare of the doctrine of creation. These are that:

(1) God created out of nothing;
(2) as a nonmaterial identity, God created the material world; and
(3) as a personal self, he created a being with whom he could be in personal relationship.

The third issue will be a matter for Chapter 4. Here I focus on the first two issues, what might be called "the fundamental metaphysical problems of creation." How does the concept of God the self-determining self compare with the more traditional approach in which divine creation is thought of as more analogous to human creation and action?

My implicit argument is that the traditional approach is too invested in commonsense "empirical" human analogy. With his "five ways" of proving the existence of the Deity it might be said that Aquinas is too much the Aristotelian scientist (he thought his proof from motion – the first proof – his most interesting proof). Perhaps Aquinas is too much the advocate of the "science of his day" as regards the doctrine of creation – an unashamedly Aristotelian framework which is superseded by Newton's revolutionary concept of gravitational "action at a distance" interfering with "inertial motion." Whatever the reason, Aquinas understands "creating," "making," and so forth as the basic actions of creation entirely analogous to human action and creation, and in terms of Aristotelian causality and continuity (Einstein similarly maintained the "commonsense" concepts of causality and continuity in the context of the "quantum-mechanical" interpretation of Bohr and Heisenberg). Had he been asked to translate the action of divine self-determination into his own terms, Aquinas would have said that God determines himself to be the creator precisely by the basic actions of "creating," "making," and "separating," and all understood in exemplary commonsense Aristotelian fashion.

It is because of this that certain fundamental ideas in the history of Christian doctrine such as *creatio ex nihilo* have remained more or less intractable. Under the traditional interpretation of Genesis 1, creation out nothing is simply affirmed as an article of faith. The interpretation remains stubbornly neutral about the doctrine, neither implying or excluding it. We are simply informed that God "creates," "makes," and so on the world – all that is – and that he does this out of nothing. Thomas's solution was to say that God created both form and matter (though he saw a problem, as did Augustine, in the idea of created matter without form). In contrast, under the interpretation being offered here, the doctrine follows quite naturally from the text. God's speaking is a determining himself to be the creator of all things. Therefore he is the creator of all things. This really is *creatio ex nihilo* – and God's self-determining self provides a simple yet powerful explanation of it which is neither emanationist or dualistic. The power of understanding divine self-determination as both sufficient and basic is readily seen.

"How can a nonmaterial creator create a material world?" The question may presuppose the notion that the cause of the material world must be present in its effect, precisely the same material world. But, how can the latter be the case if the cause is nonmaterial and the effect material? The Cappadocian Father, Gregory of Nyssa, sought to provide a satisfactory answer to this question. He presumed that cause and effect must share some kind of "ontic" similarity. Divine self-determination wonders whether this assumption is necessary.

Creatio ex nihilo, pre-existent matter, and emanationism

Creation out of nothing first played a prominent part in the exegesis of the Priestly narrative at the end of the second century in defence against the distinctively gnostic doctrine of creation out of pre-existent matter. But in the history of the doctrine there were those who thought that a satisfactory exposition of *creatio ex nihilo* must entail some kind of emanationism in which God created out of himself. In essence, it seemed that one was faced with the choice between, on the one hand, the Charybdis of creation out of pre-existent matter (dualism) and, on the other, the Scylla of emanationism (monism). Augustine is instructive in his understanding of this dilemma. In *Concerning the Nature of Good* Augustine argues against those who assert that God is the material cause, so to speak, as well as the efficient cause of the world. Augustine distinguishes between *de ipso* and *ex ipso*. The world may be said to be from God (*ex ipso*) because he created it; but it is not of God (*de ipso*) because it is not of his substance. As Augustine puts it: to say something is *from* God does not entail it is *of* God (though the converse holds: to say that it is *of* God implies that it is *from* God).

Augustine finds it necessary to invoke this distinction since he faces opponents who argue as follows: "To state that God created the world from nothing (i.e., not from an eternally pre-existent matter) is to render the doctrine of creation unintelligible unless 'creation out of nothing' is simply a way of saying 'creation from *nothing other than out of God*' – so that God is both the efficient cause of the world and the substance out of which the world emanated." Augustine rejects this reasoning arguing that what is of God can only be God. Thus the Son is God begotten of God (*de deo*) and the Holy Spirit is of God proceeding from God (*de deo*). If the world were from God then it would be equal to the Son and the Holy Spirit, i.e. it would itself be God. The best orthodox response remained along the lines of Augustine. Anselm too in the *Monologion* affirms God as an efficient cause but not as an material one.

I think Augustine's argument for rejecting emanationism is a valid one. But what remains behind after his refutation is precisely the same dissatisfaction with the concept of "creation out of nothing" which had led to emanationism in the first place! Augustine undermined emanationism without providing any other explanation of "creation out of nothing." It seems to me that we now have a way of resolving this impasse in doctrine in the form of the concept of God determining himself to be the creator.

Wolfhart Pannenberg provides the most immediate context to the introduction of this concept in modern systematic theology. In *Systematic Theology*, vol. 2, Pannenberg argues that God's creation of the world through speech was not unique to Genesis 1.1–2.4a, given that a similar claim had been made by Egyptian Memphis theology in the third millennium (as in creation through the magical word) (Pannenberg, *Systematic Theology*, vol. 2, 131). What was unique was what it came to *signify*: God's unrestricted freedom. This concept later found expression in the formula "creation out of nothing." The logic of the case was that if God has unrestricted freedom then he must be able to create out of nothing (otherwise there would be a restriction on his freedom); ergo, he created the world out of nothing.

Though Pannenberg was right in what he said, I would argue that the concept of God's unrestricted freedom signified something else more ultimate: it signified – pointed to – the concept *of God's determining himself as the creator of all things*. This takes the doctrine of creation to a deeper explanatory level. God's speaking is in fact a revealing of himself, a revealing of himself as a personal self. It is the event of God determining *himself* as creator. Von Rad describes it as a doctrine of God the creator – "it contains doctrine throughout" – in which "the whole interest is focused exclusively on what comes from God, his words, judgements, commands, and regulations" (Von Rad, *Genesis*, 27–28). Therefore as a logical consequence of this exclusive orientation toward God the creator, "P resists the temptation of an actual description of the acts of creation" (Von Rad, *Genesis*, 65). (One can see this more clearly if one compares P with the J creation narrative in which the acts are described.) Similarly, as another consequence of this, the presence of the created humankind in the narrative consists of no more than "shadowy figures" (Von Rad, *Genesis*, 65). We are mentioned out of logical necessity: God cannot be the creator and what he creates not come into being. But the focus is all him.

God's self-determination of himself as creator explains "creation out of nothing"

What then of the dilemma brought on by rejecting creation out of pre-existent matter and affirming creation out of nothing? It is resolved in this way. If the rationale behind God's unrestricted freedom as regards creation is God determining himself as creator then it must follow that God determining himself as creator is able to move the conclusion of creation out of nothing. This it is able to do. If God determining himself as creator is both basic and sufficient then it follows that God creates the world out of nothing. He does not create it out of himself (monism) nor does he create it out of pre-existent matter (dualism). He determines himself as the creator of the world; therefore he is the creator of the world; therefore the world was created by God. This is creation out of nothing. The creation of the world irreducibly and sufficiently pertains to God's own "being," i.e., in his self-determination as creator. It is indeed the sufficiency of the action that is the key. An ancient and recurring dilemma is resolved: there is no temptation to affirm emanationism (or any kind of process theology) given the rejection of pre-existent matter if we understand God determining *himself* as creator in the above sense.

An interpretation of the Priestly creation narrative that resolves an ancient dilemma and simultaneously provides a way of affirming in canonical fashion that the historical experience of the people of Israel is rational has much to commend it in terms of explanatory comprehensiveness. (Interpreting "creation out of nothing" in terms of divine self-determination coheres with the ultimate objective of interpreting Old Testament narrative – exodus, the history culminating in Babylonian exile, etc. –in the same way.)

Gregory of Nyssa's theory of creation

In a brilliant book, *Time, Creation and the Continuum*, Richard Sorabji argues that in Gregory of Nyssa's theory of creation we have the origins of the kind of idealism with which Bishop Berkeley's name is eponymous. As Sorabji succinctly puts it, "Berkeley moves from idealism to a conclusion about cause and creation; Gregory moves from a view about cause to a conclusion about creation which involves idealism" (Sorabji, *Time, Creation and the Continuum*, 179). Gregory's context is creation (as opposed to Berkeley's which is the quintessentially modern one of skepticism). Gregory ponders the question, How could a purely immaterial creator have produced matter? The idea which causes his worry is a thesis about causation, namely that a cause needs to be somehow like its effect. So for example, Gregory writes in his *Hexaemeron*:

> You can hear people saying things like this: if God is matterless, where does matter come from? How can quantity come from non-quantity, the visible from the invisible, some thing with limited bulk from what lacks magnitude and limit? And so also for the other characteristics seen in matter: how or whence were they produced by one who had nothing of this kind in his own nature?

Drawing on the Platonic legacy, Gregory's solution is that material objects consist of nothing but qualities like colour, and extension, and that these qualities are not themselves material things, but mere thoughts and concepts. As Sorabji points out, Gregory's solution is strikingly reminiscent of Berkeley's celebrated doctrine of *esse est percipi*: to be is to exist as an idea in a mind and, in particular, to be an existing object is to exist as perceptions or ideas. Both doctrines say that objects are not in essence physical, material things. In Gregory's case, this means that God does not create physical material things but rather collections of qualities which are themselves incorporeal.

It is not difficult to see that the root of Gregory's perplexity lay in his assumption that cause must be like effect, and his problem would have vanished had he dispensed with this assumption. But it seems to me that we would still be left with something like his original question, How *did* a nonmaterial creator produce matter?

The traditional interpretation of the Genesis creation story is no less susceptible to this kind of critique. When it says that God "created," "made," and so forth, not only is it an unexaminable article of faith that the world was "created," "made" *out of nothing*, it is also a similar such article of faith that this *nonmaterial creator produced this material world* out of nothing.

The thesis of God's self-determining self solves the problem easily and effortlessly and, most importantly, without artifice. God simply determines himself to be the creator of the (material) world. Therefore – again, the sufficiency principle – he *is* the creator of the (material world); therefore there *is* a material world. There is no likeness between "cause" and "effect" and yet it explains how God who is not world creates the world, and how world which is not God was created by God. Thus we have an explanation *of creatio ex nihilo* that simultaneously resolves the problem faced by Gregory of Nyssa.

Concluding remarks

Divine action understood as divine self-determination can unify the concepts of, on one the hand, God acting to create the world and, on the other, God acting in the world. But if the theory can simultaneously resolve some outstanding classical issues in the former domain, such success further advances its claim to be the best available explanation of how God could have created the world. This way of speaking – "theoretical unification," "best available explanation," etc. – unashamedly employs the language of the philosophy of science. Questions about the relative merits of instrumentalist and realist explanations of the realm of event – even if one is talking divine event and divine self-determination in particular – are not irrelevant at this point. But they are deep metatheoretical issues. There are those learned in the philosophy of language and the philosophy of science respectively who might insist, for example, that speaking of God really determining himself to be this or that identity may at best only be analogically true (as Aquinas might say); at worse, not really true at all. This is so, they would say, because we can quite uncontroversially say that God does what ever it takes to make the assertion "God determines himself to do action a" true. But if this is so, it allows for the possibility God may make the assertion "God determines himself to do action a" true in some way *other* than actually determine himself to do action a (remember, God is omnipotent). And if we can say this we cannot justifiably claim that God actually, *actually* executes an act of self-determination. Instrumentalism would then seem to have won the day. There is an argument to be had on this but, as one might expect, I remain resolutely realist on the matter. I believe it rational to do so; God actually does execute the action of self-determination. Either way, I still say that divine self-determination has two important advantages over rival accounts: it solves some outstanding classical problems of the doctrine of creation; it brings God's action in creating the world and God's action in the world under a single category of explanation. The latter if true not only has explanatory value, it also has aesthetic value pertaining to the beauty and effortless economy of God.

Bibliography

Anselm, *Monologion*. In *Anselm of Canterbury: The Major Works*, edited by Brian Davies and Gillian Evans, (Oxford: Oxford University Press, 1998) 5–81.

Aquinas, *Summa Theologiae*. In *Basic Writings of Saint Thomas Aquinas*, edited by Anton Pegis (New York: Random House, 1945).

Augustine, *Concerning the Nature of Good, Against the Manicheans*. In *Nicene and Post-Nicene Fathers*, vol. 4, edited by P. Schaff, translated by A. Newman (New York: The Christian Literature Publishing Co., 1890).

Barth, Karl, *Church Dogmatics* III/1, translated by T. F. Torrance and G. Bromiley (Edinburgh: T. & T. Clark, 1958).

Gregory of Nyssa, *Hexaemeron*, translated by D. Salomon http://www.bhsu.edu/artssciences/asfaculty/dsalomon/nyssa/hex.html

May, Gerhard, *Creatio Ex Nihilo: The Doctrine of Creation Out of Nothing in Early Christian Thought* (Edinburgh: T. & T. Clark, 1995).

Pannenberg, W., *Systematic Theology*, vol. 2, translated by G. Bromiley (Grand Rapids: Eerdmans, 1994).

Rad, Gerhard von, *Genesis*, translated by J. Bowden, 3rd ed. (London: SCM, 1972).

Sorabji, Richard, *Time, Creation and the Continuum* (London: Duckworth, 1983).

Westermann, Claus, *Genesis 1–11* (Minneapolis: Fortress Press, 1994).

4

"The Sixth Day of Creation": The Creation of Humankind and the *Imago Dei*

One central claim for this biblical metaphysic will be that it unifies God's action in creating the world with God's acting in the world. Moreover, the biblical metaphysic is also able to encompass the view held by such as Gerhard von Rad that Israel's experience of YHWH was (primitively) of its God – the God of Israel – acting "then and there" in its life, in the same "spatial" and "temporal" frame. I will argue that the "eternalist" tradition from Augustine, through Aquinas, to Calvin does not have adequate conceptuality to capture Von Rad's insight that the initial historical experience of YHWH was that of the exodus from Egypt; which is to say, a historical experience of YHWH acting then and there in Israel's own time frame. The "eternalist" tradition has a God whose personal self is "fixed" in eternity from whence he acts or has acted.

Nevertheless, both the "eternalist" tradition and the theory of biblical metaphysic being espoused here have to face the following challenge. Both have to give an account of the acts of creation by which God creates and, in particular, an account of the acts of creation by which God creates humankind. Let us assume that Genesis 1:26–28 means that God created a being with whom he can be in personal relationship.[1] This presupposes that God

---

[1] In a wide-ranging survey of biblical and theological interpretation of "God creating humankind in his own image," Jónnson argues that there are two serious contenders for what it means (*Image of God*). One is the view that Genesis 1:26–28 means that humankind is put on earth

created this same being (the latter is indeed presupposed in the claim that God is the creator of all things). The claim that God created humankind faces the challenge not only of internal validity (is it internally coherent in itself?) but also of external validity (is it reconcilable with other truth-claims, notably those of evolutionary genetics, if these claims were true?).

A quintessential Victorian tragedy

The account that the tradition – from Augustine through to Calvin, for example – gave of living being is that, according to Genesis 1, God created living creatures as *distinct and unalterably fixed species-specific natures*: humankind, the other animals, the birds of the sky, the fish of the sea, the creeping things on the earth, the plants of the field – all have fixed species-specific natures which by implication excluded the possibility of evolutionary change and adaptation. God so ordained this in the beginning. This view on creation and species-specific natures was held right down to the eighteenth century, not just by the church but also by some of the greatest scientists who ever existed: Newton, Kepler, Pascal, Boyle, and Galileo.

When Darwin's theory of the natural origins of humankind – and of species-specific nature in general – broke upon the world in the second half of the nineteenth century, Victorian scientists who professed belief in the biblical story of creation, of Adam and Eve, and the fall and so forth, did not have the academic luxury of taking recourse to one or other versions of cultural relativism in which the implications of evolution by natural

---

[1] *(continued)* as a representative of its creator. The other is the view that it means that God created a being with whom he can be in personal relationship (Jónnson, *Image of God*, 78). The two are of course not mutually exclusive (or indeed exhaustive). More importantly, both are rational interpretative claims. I emphasize the latter on the grounds that it makes more sense in the context of the canonical shaping of the Old Testament, grounded as it is in Israel's historical experience of being in personal relationship with YHWH. Within its creation tradition, Israel's historical experience of being in personal relationship with YHWH was to be traced back to a God who *created* a being with whom he could be in personal relationship.

selection could be dismissed as just one other story no more valid or invalid than the traditional Genesis story itself.

When one reads for example of the English zoologist and writer Philip Gosse's attempt to draw the sting of evolutionary theory – which was (so it seemed) then threatening to undermine the whole of biblical history by striking at its very origins – one encounters a tragic spirit brought near to breaking-point by a quintessentially Victorian sense of intellectual integrity born of conscience and concern for the truth. (In his classic account *Father and Son*, which tells of growing up in a household of fundamentalist Christians who rejected Darwin's theory of evolution, Philip Gosse's son Edmund wrote that "The comedy was superficial and the tragedy essential"; Gosse, *Father and Son*, "Preface").

In 1857 (two years before Darwin's publication of *The Origin of Species*) Gosse published a book he entitled *Omphalos* (Greek for "navel"; Gosse had spoken with Darwin in the same year about the theory of natural selection which Darwin was soon to make public). In this book he expressed the ingenious thought that even though Adam and Eve were the first human beings they would have been misled by the existence of their navels into thinking that they had ancestors (which they hadn't had since they were the first human beings!). But not only would Adam and Eve have been misled by the presence of their navels, so would any scientist who might have examined their bodies. In other words, the anatomical facts of the matter – when employed as the premises of an argument – would have derived a false conclusion even though the facts so unambiguously seemed to imply that Adam and Eve did in fact have ancestors (a navel implies an umbilical cord which, by definition, is attached to the mother of the child, which implies ancestry). But given that Adam and Eve were in fact the first human beings and therefore did not have ancestors, the fact of their having navels cannot be taken to imply that they had ancestors. (It is not only Gosse who thought that Adam and Eve had navels. The most famous artist who ever painted the creation of humankind, and of Adam in particular – Michelangelo – also believed so. His celebrated painting on the ceiling of the Sistine Chapel in Rome depicting God creating Adam has Adam clearly possessing a navel where his umbilical cord would have been – had he not been the first human being.)

Even in his own time Gosse's argument was perceived to be a desperate intellectual maneuver born of the psychological need to reconcile a deep conflict between religious belief and scientific theory. But though Gosse's solution was ridiculed in some quarters in Victorian England, it signified the plight of many Christian intellectuals in the mid-nineteenth century. For what Gosse nostalgically hoped to keep alive in "the academy" was, among other things, the notion of fixed distinct species in a manner not unlike the Aristotelian–Thomistic synthesis of a great "chain of being" (the system of classification the Swedish biologist Carl Linnaeus had invented the previous century still assumed a "chain of being" of fixed non-evolving distinct species). The concept of the "chain of being" describes the medieval belief in a hierarchical universe from the lowest to the highest in which each individual species of being, creature, or object was allocated a distinct place and status dependent on the degree of perfection natural for its kind. God of course was at the top of the chain; angels were below him; and below the angels, mortal humankind, who were in fact the highest and most perfect of living mortal beings (plants and minerals were near the bottom of the chain). Implicit in this world-picture was the view that species were fixed and immutable and ordained into existence by God in the beginning, at creation. The idea that evolution or adaptation might take place, from one species into another, was simply not part of the medieval mindset.

In so far as the medieval chain of being represents an alternative picture of the natural world, most if not all mainstream biologists deem it to have been decisively refuted by Darwin's theory of evolution (as opposed to the now discredited Lamarkian version of evolution in which what were inherited were acquired characteristics). Darwin's theory became incorporated into the "Darwinian synthesis" which duly combined Darwin's principle of natural selection with the genetics of evolution giving us what goes under the name of "the genetical theory of evolution via natural selection."

Today, in the wake of Crick and Watson's historic discovery that the double-helix structure of DNA is the basis of genetic inheritance, it is all but accepted by the scientific community that the subdisciplines that constitute the biological sciences – genetics, molecular biology, immunology, medicine in general, and so so on – cannot function either theoretically or experimentally without one or another version of the theory of genetical evolution via natural selection. Whatever revisions have been made to Darwin's original theory over the last century and a half, his essential insight about evolution via natural selection has remained at the core of – as the presupposition of – any biological theory purporting to be the truth. Species are no longer understood to be unalterably distinct and fixed in a "chain of being." Instead, species have evolved through natural selection acting on genetic mutation, and this means that the evolution of species can be traced back to a common source of ancestry (which is subtly different from saying that apes evolved into *Homo sapiens*).

The precocious sixth-century (BC) Darwinian

The account that the tradition from Augustine through to Calvin gave of living being, namely that God created living creatures as *distinct and unalterably fixed species-specific natures,* is almost certainly an accurate picture of Genesis 1. This is what the Priestly writer did in fact believe (whether or not it was a tradition he himself inherited). But it is undeniable that the Priestly writer conceived of his creation narrative the way he did because he believed that historically immediate, temporally adjacent products of creation are *what had been created.* Putting it even more boldly: his view of what had been created *preceded* his view of *how* God had created what had been created. He first fixed his view about what had been created and worked backwards from his view to how God had created what had been created. So for example: it is almost certainly true to say that the Priestly writer thought that *what had been created – and therefore what existed –* was unalterably distinct and fixed species. Therefore, according to him, *this* is what God had created (this is what was identical with the *diversity of life*). Accordingly, he relates a narrative in which separate days of creation are allocated to distinct species without reference to any kind of evolutionary process (when the Priestly writer looked at his fellow people during the exile, this is what he saw: a being who had been there from the beginning of natural history as a fixed and unalterable species-being). Similarly, it is clear that the Priestly writer thought that what existed – and therefore what had been created – was a Ptolemaic universe (something akin to Bultmann's famous "three-decker" universe in which the sun went round the earth); therefore again, *this* is what God had created. Accordingly, he relates a narrative in which the earth is stationary and the stars and the sun move round it.

Moreover – and this is crucial – *these beliefs about what had been created were not exclusive to Israel.* If you had asked any other Near Eastern religion of the same period you would have been met with the same answer: fixed species and "Ptolemaic" universe.[2] These beliefs for want of a better description can be classified as the "scientific" beliefs of the day. In this sense it can be said that there is nothing sacred about them. What is in fact unique about Genesis 1 is the theological proposition that not just any God but the God of Israel created all things and therefore is the creator of all things. Israel in exile makes the astonishingly bold claim that its God is the creator of the whole world.

Hence, had the writer of the Priestly creation narrative encountered the genetical theory of evolution via natural selection in the sixth century, there is no need to think that he would have necessarily have sided with the kind of view Gosse had of "Adam" as against Darwin's. He may well have rejected fixed species in favour of evolution.[3] The question is not what we would do with

---

[2] See for example, S. G. F. Brandon, *Creation Legends of the Ancient Near East*. Westermann claims that common to these creation legends is the fact that "the question, what was created, precedes the question, how did creation take place" (Westermann, *Genesis 1 – 11*, 22–23).

[3] Therefore, a narrator who implicitly believes in fixed distinct species has a doctrine of creation which can designate Darwin's human being with the predicate "created by God" without fear of contradiction. It is as if the Priestly narrator who extrapolates back from Israel's foundational experience of YHWH in the exodus tradition subsequently discovers that between that point in time and the beginning, the human species came into existence as the result of a process of genetical evolution via natural selection. Counterfactually, would this necessarily

the contents of Genesis 1 were we writing it now in the light of what we know from Darwin. Rather, it is what the Priestly redactor would have said in Genesis 1 had he encountered a staggeringly precocious Darwinian then – in the sixth century BC.

But does any of this matter as much as we are wont to think? No! It is often said that the creation story is theology and as such to be demarcated from the terrain of science (in a post-Kantian world this is often stated in terms of a value–fact distinction: creation as value, science as fact). Schleiermacher seems to advocate something like this in *The Christian Faith* with his advocacy of "inward facts" (see Schleiermacher, *Christian Faith*, 152). But if this was a retreat in the face of what appeared to be the unpalatable facts, it was an unnecessary one.

If we reflect on the argument propounded in Chapter 2 regarding identical worlds, one created by God and the other not, we see that the theory of divine self-determination without natural theology moves the conclusion that the natural properties of the world tell us nothing about whether the world was or was not created by God. This depends solely on God determining himself to be the creator of all things, inclusive of course of God determining himself to be the creator of humankind. Therefore, counterfactually, had the claim of fixed, nonmutable species been an accurate picture of the world, this would have told us nothing about whether human beings had been created by God, since there could have been a world inhabited by fixed, nonmutable species which had not been created by God. Similarly, if it turns out that evolving species is an accurate picture of the origins of species then, again, this would have told us nothing about whether human beings had not been created by God since there could have been a world inhabited by evolving species which had been created by God (and an identical one in which evolving species had not been).

If divine self-determination without natural theology is true then what is traditionally thought to go under the titles of

---

[3] *(continued)* bother him? No, because his doctrine is first and foremost about the fact that God determined himself in his speaking to be this personal self, namely the creator of humankind. Therefore it follows that God is the creator of humankind, no matter how human beings came into existence.

"positive natural theology" (fixed, nonmutable species) and "negative natural theology" (evolving species) respectively, are complete misnomers. Neither positive nor negative natural theology exists in a world in which divine self-determination without natural theology holds sway. This is the fundamental reason that assertions regarding the realm of natural being are not theological propositions: they do not impinge one whit on the legitimate designation of human beings by the predicate "created by God," which latter is completely and utterly and exclusively a matter of God the self-determining self.[4]

"In the image of God": God created a being with whom he could be in personal relationship

According to the traditional interpretation from Augustine, through Anselm and Aquinas, to Luther and Calvin, God "created" or "made" humankind in his own image in such a way that the image of God was a property of the species-specific nature of humankind. A typical trajectory of events would be something like the following. God first created formless matter and subsequently out of this formless matter, He created humankind "in his own image" – however this happened in detail. He "made" humankind in his own image.[5] Whether this

---

[4] Therefore, if the evolutionary biologist Richard Dawkins is correct to say in his books (*The Blind Watchmaker* is an outstanding example) that the principle of natural selection is sufficient to explain the diversity of life we perceive, I do not disagree. But it must be noted that, to say this principle is sufficient does not exclude the possibility that this world is designated by the predicate "created by God" in virtue of divine self-determination without natural theology. The principle of natural selection is – if true – sufficient to explain the origins of humankind in particular. But even if true, it is not incompatible with God determining himself to be the one who created a being with whom he could be in personal relationship. Indeed Dawkins' subtitle is intriguing. It is: *Why the Evidence of Evolution Reveals a Universe without Design*. Everything I have said in this book is quite compatible with such a claim!

[5] Two features define this tradition philosophically as it were. One is that the natural properties of humankind and of the world writ large are indicative of divine creation. Humankind made in the image of God

inclined one to think in terms of a physical similarity or a spiritual similarity, the customary presumption was that the quality of humankind which made humankind "made in the image of God, after his likeness," was a property or characteristic possessed by humankind, a property possessed by his species-specific nature analogous to the way in which the eye or ear was. When God made humankind he imbued our person with this quality. Perhaps it did indeed reside in humankind's physical form; perhaps it resided in our rationality, in humankind's capacity for thought and conscience; perhaps it was to be found in our spirituality. Augustine – as remorselessly logical as ever – concluded that just as God was threefold in Father, Son, and Holy Spirit, then so humankind was body, mind, and soul. Later, the Reformation with its emphasis on salvation thought in terms of original uprightness or righteousness.

Furthermore, to say that God created made humankind "in his own image, after God's own likeness," was to say in effect that humankind possessed whatever it was that made it "created in the image of God." It possessed it as one of its natural properties, a property it did not share with the other animals. Hence it became quite natural to say that humankind could have lost what it had previously possessed. This property could be destroyed. And indeed it was argued by a number of theologians that human beings had lost the image of God in Adam's

---

[5] (*continued*) meant that we possessed as a natural property the image of God; Augustine and Aquinas tended to think of this property in terms of rationality, the reformers thought of it in terms of an original "moral uprightness" or righteousness. The point in general is that God creates in a manner analogous to human creation and leaves his mark on creation. An artistic analogy is often used to explain this truth. On seeing a painting by Leonardo or in the modern age, Picasso, one says, "That's Leonardo!" or "That's a Picasso!" on the grounds that each painter has left his characteristic signature or style of painting on the canvas. Similarly, God left his "signature" on the world, and in particular on humankind who accordingly bear the property of the divine image. The other feature is that, as the classical tradition understood it, created being – human being – was a historically immediate, temporally adjacent, product. God did it then and there: he said, "Let us make humankind in our own image" . . . "and it was so."

fall. The theologians who argued this – Calvin and Luther for instance – understood the reference to "likeness" in the text as mere repetition (albeit for rhetorical reasons) of the concept of image. But even those theologians like Irenaeus who distinguished between *ṣelem* (image) and *dᵉmut* (likeness) – he was followed by Augustine and Aquinas in this – and who argued that humanity didn't lose human nature (the likeness to God) but rather lost its original relation to God (lost the image) – even these theologians still thought of the property of relation in a decidedly naturalistic sense, as something that was possessed in itself and could be lost in itself, by every human being. In the modern period Emil Brunner has persevered with this kind of view (see Brunner, *The Christian Doctrine of Creation and Redemption: Dogmatics*, vol. 2, 55–58). He argued that the biblical concept of the image of God possessed both a "structural" (or "formal") and a "material" dimension. The formal dimension corresponded to the freedom that God had bequeathed to humankind in its personal relationship with him; the material aspect of the concept corresponded to the use to which humankind had put this freedom, precisely an abuse of this freedom. The latter corresponded in some sense to the loss of the image of God in a material sense but not in a structural or formal sense. Both the formal and material aspects of the image of God are properties either of the self or of human nature. In this sense they are *immanent* properties.

Brunner is not entirely wrong here in his view that God creating humankind in his own image involves the concept of personal relationship. As the Priestly writer saw it from the historical perspective of exile in the sixth century, just as YHWH was in personal relationship with his people Israel from the exodus onwards – inclusive even of exile – then YHWH created a being with whom he could be in personal relationship. In other words, the wider canonical context is that of the Priestly narrator extrapolating back from YHWH acting in the life of his people "Israel" then and there – and doing this precisely in his speaking – to that of YHWH creating a being with whom he can be in personal relationship – and doing this precisely also in his speaking.

But – and this is the big "but" – none of this implies anything about the natural properties of humankind. Humankind is in no wise different from the other living species. What gives human-kind its special existence is the fact that God determined *himself* to be in personal relationship with humankind (and pre-emi-nently the people "Israel"). He determined himself to be the one who said, "Let us make man in our image, in our likeness" (Gen. 1:26) – the locutionary action; and in so doing he determined himself to be the creator of humankind, a being with whom he could be in personal relationship – the illocutionary action. Therefore subsequently, he is in personal relationship with humankind. Therefore, humankind is in personal relationship with God, with the God of Israel.

This means that humankind is truly designated by the predi-cate "created by God in his own image" no matter what the natural properties of humankind turn out to be. God's divine self-determination is basic and sufficient for this to be the case. God does not create in order to determine himself thus, he deter-mines himself to be the creator of humankind "in our image" – in the image of God (Gen. 1:27) – therefore humankind is created in the image of God. The event of divine self-determination is a basic action sufficient for it being the case that humankind was created in the image of God.

Just as the identifying description, "the one who is the creator of all things" tells us nothing about the natural properties of the world writ large, then so the identifying description, "the one who is the creator of humankind is his own image" tells us nothing about the natural properties of humankind. The same logic applies. The latter description simply says that God deter-mined *himself* to be the creator of humankind in his own image.

God creates a being with whom he can be in personal relation-ship. This event is restricted to God's own creation history (that which is depicted in the seven days of creation).[6] Therefore, though it is true of humankind that it was created in the image of God it is not a natural property of humankind. Humankind can

[6] As a corollary of this, what Von Rad has to say of the P narrative in this regard is pertinent: "No effort is given to depicting man as the recipient of revelation or to the circumstances, the conflicts, the spiritual or social uncertainties attending that experience. The figures of the Priestly account are in this respect completely colourless and shadowy" (Von Rad, *Genesis*, 28).

in no wise look at any of its natural properties and derive the conclusion that it was created "in the image of God." Humankind cannot even look at any of its natural properties and conclude that it was created by God. This is solely and sufficiently a matter of God's creation history and his determining himself to be the creator of a being with whom he could be in personal relationship. And as long as this is the case, our talking to God – characteristically in prayer – is a simple rational action. God's self-determining self – in relation to us – makes it so. It is basic and it is sufficient, and it is – a miracle. But that is the fact of it.

In so far as this kind of doctrine can be attributed to Barth, it would explain why, as against the Reformation, and Calvin in particular, he rejected the doctrine that the image of God was something that was *destroyed* – either partially or completely – in the fall. It could not have been destroyed because it was not something that humankind ever possessed (see Barth, *CD* III/1, 200–202). The locus of its truth resides in God's self-determining self in the creation history; therefore it did not at any time reside in the created world as the natural property of *homo sapiens*. As Barth put it in his own inimitable way:

> it is not surprising that neither in the rest of the Old Testament nor the New is there any trace of . . . the partial or complete destruction of the *imago Dei*. What man does not possess he can neither bequeath or forfeit. And on the other hand the divine intention at the creation of man, and the consequent promise and pledge given with it, cannot be lost or subjected to partial or complete destruction (Barth, *CD* III/1, 200).

Concluding remarks

Claus Westermann claims of all Near Eastern religions and *Weltanschaungen* that the question, what had been created, preceded the question, how did creation take place. Paradoxically, for a doctrine of creation that advocates a theory of divine self-determination without natural theology as an explanation of divine action, this must imply a downgrading of the significance of what we discover to be the nature of (created) being and, in particular, the nature of the creature. To recapitulate: had the claim of fixed, nonmutable species in fact corresponded to the biological data (which it likely does not), this would have told us nothing about whether human beings had been created by God. There could have been a world inhabited by fixed, nonmutable species which had not been created by God. Similarly, if it turned out that evolving species did in fact correspond to the facts regarding the origin of species then, again, this would have told us nothing about whether human beings had *not* been created by God. This is because there could have been a world inhabited by evolving species which had been created by God (and, of course, an identical one in which evolving species had not been). Darwin's famous worry about negative natural theology in *The Origin of Species* was unwarranted.

Less hypothetically, on the claim of humankind created in the image of God in Genesis 1:26–28, I concur with the modern tradition of scholarship of Von Rad and Westermann – and Barth – as against the classical tradition that runs from Augustine through to Calvin. According to the classical tradition the image of God was some "static" property like rationality or righteousness. Modern scholarship can be said to take a more "dynamic" view, appreciative of the redactional role of the Priestly creation narrative in the historical formation of Israel's Scriptures. The Priestly writer did not envisage that human beings ever lost the image of God. This was because creation "in the image of God" meant being created as one with whom God could be in personal relationship. Moreover the Priestly writer did not envisage that God ceased to be in personal relationship with human beings – and this in spite of their misrelation or downright disobedience. This was his view even from the sixth century in exile. God had not abandoned the people "Israel" even in exile. He remained in personal relationship with them.

Bibliography

Aquinas, *Summa Theologiae*, edited by Anton Pegis, *Basic Writings of Saint Thomas Aquinas* (New York: Random House, 1945).

Augustine, *On the Trinity: Books 8–15*, edited and translated by G. B. Matthews and S. McKenna (Cambridge: Cambridge University Press, 2002).

Barth, Karl, *Church Dogmatics* III/1, translated by T. F. Torrance and G. Bromiley (Edinburgh: T. & T. Clark, 1958).

Brandon, S. G. F., *Creation Legends of the Ancient Near East* (London: Hodder & Stoughton, 1963).

Brunner, Emil, *The Christian Doctrine of Creation and Redemption: Dogmatics*, vol. 2 (London: Lutterworth Press, 1952).

Calvin, John, *Commentary on Genesis* (Edinburgh: Banner of Truth, 1984); *Institutes of the Christian Religion* (1559 ed.) edited by J. T. McNeill, translated by L. Battles (Philadelphia: Westminster Press, 1960).

Dawkins, Richard, *The Blind Watchmaker: Why the Evidence of Evolution Reveals a Universe without Design* (London: Penguin, 1990).

Gosse, Edmund, *Father and Son*, edited by M. Lawson (Oxford: Oxford University Press, 1994).

Jónnson, G. A., *The Image of God: Genesis 1:26–28 in a Century of Old Testament Research*, Coniectanea Biblica, Lund, 26, 1988.

Rad, Gerhard von, *Genesis*, translated by J. Bowden, 3rd ed. (London: SCM, 1972).

Schleiermacher, David F. S., *The Christian Faith* (Edinburgh: T. & T. Clark, 1928).

Westermann, Claus, *Genesis 1–11* (Minneapolis: Fortress Press, 1994).

"The Seventh Day of Creation": "Our God Who Art in Heaven" in the World

God determines himself to be the creator of a being with whom he can be in personal relationship. Such a being is a historical being. To be in personal relationship with this being is to be in the same "time and space" frame as this being. This is what it means to say that God rested on the seventh and not the sixth day – that a whole day is allocated to this event. Accordingly, God "gets himself into" the very world he has previously created, in both a temporal and a spatial sense. Instead of the apophatic property of timeless eternity, God possesses the property of nonmeasurable "ordinal" time. Instead of the apophatic property of infinity God possesses the property of (non-measurable) spatiality. By the characteristic act of divine self-determination the eternally temporal God gets himself into the presently occurring time or "time frame" as his human creatures. He is also present to all presently occurring created spaces. But the one who, by an act of divine self-determination, determines himself to be present to all presently occurring created spaces possesses a space which is peculiar to him, identical with him, and which therefore he is in (God is in himself since this space is identical with him, given the thesis of divine simplicity). This implies that God has a place in the world – the space peculiar and exclusive to him. This is what it means to say that God "dwells within the 'highest heaven'," the "heaven of heavens" – in the created reality – in such a way that he is omnipresent: the heavens "cannot contain him."

God also blesses this rest, which is to say he determines himself to be the one who does not withdraw from being in personal relationship with this being. The action of blessing on the seventh day is the primal enactment of YHWH's identity as the identity he is – a soteriological identity. As such the action serves to explain why YHWH's personal relationship with Israel is one in which he reveals himself as a judging yet forbearing, desisting divine identity in Old Testament narrative. (At most, as the medieval mystic Meister Eckhart put it, a judging YHWH "only gets as far as the door of the 'House of Israel'".)

The incomplete creation narrative: "the six days of creation"

The Greek translation of the Old Testament – the Septuagint – understood the Priestly creation narrative fundamentally in terms of six days of creation: God completed the world in six days as it were. Subsequently, the dominant influence on the history of the doctrine of creation has been those theologians – Basil of Alexandria and Ambrose of Milan in the patristic period, Aquinas (in both the *Summa* and his commentary on Genesis) in the medieval period, to name but three examples – who restricted their understanding of creation to six days rather than seven: the *hexamaeron* rather than the *heptamaeron*. Jaroslav Pelikan argues that Christian theology was only storing up trouble for itself in the future when it used the *hexamaeron* as the standard framework for reflection on creation. For, retrospectively, it meant that the seeds of confrontation with Enlightenment thought on creation had long been sown within Christian theology itself by shifting the *theological* focus of creation to issues of *origins* and *causality* (see Pelikan, "Creation and Causality", 10–24). Stated in these terms, the biblical doctrine of creation became easily assimilated to – and criticized by – philosophical concepts whose natural context was to become the classical arguments for and against the existence of God during the Enlightenment: the teleological (design), cosmological, and ontological arguments, dealt with negatively by Kant in *The Critique of Pure Reason* (who offered a moral alternative that was in reality born of the same philosophical vocabulary).

But there was yet a more damaging consequence of using the *hexamaeron* rather than the *heptamaeron* as a framework for creation than simply the one of leaving oneself open to this kind of Enlightenment criticism. It was natural for theologians who restricted creation to the *hexamaeron* rather than to the *heptamaeron* to conceive of God remaining "where he is" "time-wise" even when in the act of creation. God is in eternity before he commenced creation; therefore he remained in eternity as he created. When Augustine speaks of God creating from eternity in a way that is compatible with the simultaneous creation of everything, it is clear that God remains in eternity as he creates. *Moreover, God remains there after creation.* Consequently God's action in this same world cannot but be brought about except by God providentially predestining from his vantage point in eternity what is to happen in the realm of human history. He remains outside his creation.

Crucially, any interpretation of Old Testament must conform to this theological construction. Calvin's exegesis of Old Testament narrative exemplifies the pattern nicely (though one also finds it in Aquinas and any other theologian of the precritical tradition you care to name).[1] As T. H. L. Parker put it, Calvin believes that "all the actions, words, and thoughts of men are determined by God in order to bring his will to pass" (Parker, *Calvin's Old Testament Commentaries*, 90–91). This is the real reason that Calvin treats historical narrative "as if it were purely an account of man's self-moving activities." Indeed as Parker puts it: "We find Calvin in his element here. There seems to be nothing he enjoyed more that reconstructing from the course of events, filling in the missing connections in a narrative, working out motives of behaviour, relating Biblical history to what he knew of ancient history in general, understanding the past by his experience of the present and from his reading." (Parker, *Calvin's Old Testament Commentaries*, 91).

---

[1] "The classical Christian view of God's relation to time" is that "God does not exist in time, he exists 'outside' time . . . this view (let us call it 'eternalism') has an impressive pedigree in the history of western theism – it is the 'mainstream' view represented by Augustine, Anselm, Aquinas, Calvin, and hosts of others" (Helm, 'Divine Timeless Eternity', 28). See also Helm, *Eternal God*, for a more comprehensive exposition of the classical view.

When one juxtaposes this framework to Von Rad's 1936 thesis one encounters an insurmountable conflict. If one is to affirm Von Rad's thesis that Israel's initial experience of the God of Israel in the exodus phenomenon was of a saving identity then and there, of a historical identity in their historical midst as it were, it cannot do to interpret the Priestly creation narrative in an "eternalist" sense as the precritical tradition – Augustine, Aquinas, Calvin, and so on – did and then impose hermeneutical constraints on the historical narratives such that they are to be interpreted as if God is acting providentially from eternity. Rather the development of the canonical shape of the Old Testament implies the reverse process such that Israel's historical experience of a God acting then and there in her life imposes a constraint on how we interpret Genesis 1:1 – 2.4a.

This means that the theologian whose star seems most in the ascendancy at the present time suffers from the same theological and biblical inadequacy as Calvin as regards the canonical shaping of the Old Testament. Perhaps the most comprehensive theological system ever produced was that which is sometimes known as the great medieval synthesis of Thomas Aquinas in the thirteenth century, especially in the *Summa Theologiae*. Aquinas' system was a bold compromise of various facets of the most influential and leading science of the day embodied in the achievement of Aristotle – the Islamic guardianship of his metaphysics and epistemology, the Latin perseverance with and preservation of his logic, and so forth – combined with Augustinian theology and aspects of neoplatonic ideas (especially ethics) introduced into Christian thought by the early church fathers. Since it was the ultimate synthesis – one that Hegel saw could be taken no further than Aquinas had with its constituent parts – it has continued to exercise (though not without at times waxing and waning) a fascination characteristic of a theological system which promises to be "the theory of everything."

Yet as a means of embracing the canonical shape of the Bible – and here I speak specifically about the Old Testament – is the Thomistic synthesis comprehensive enough? A product of the thirteenth century, can it satisfactorily elucidate the canonical shape of the Old Testament as delineated by the last two hundred years of biblical scholarship? Let us suppose that Von

Rad is right to say that Israel's initial historical experience of YHWH was that of the exodus from Egypt; which is to say, a historical experience of YHWH acting then and there in Israel's own time frame. Aquinas – and this judgement must include Augustine, Anselm, and Calvin – does not have adequate conceptuality to account for Israel's historical experience as it is expressed in the plain sense of Old Testament narrative.[2] Aquinas's God acts in history by decreeing in eternity what is to be in history, inclusive of the history of the people of Israel. His is an "eternalist" God in this sense, whose every real act is done from eternity, in eternity. The Thomistic synthesis – and here Aquinas relies heavily on Augustine (as did Anselm and Calvin) – cannot do justice to the canonical shape of the Old Testament. One indication of this is the tendency among all of them – particularly recognizable in Aquinas but also it has to be said in Calvin too – to interpret the divine name "YHWH" as the name of divine being rather than as a reference to what YHWH will do in history ("I will be whom I will be" is the most accurate translation we have of this in English). "I will be who I will be" is therefore a name closely aligned with the identifying description "the one who released Israel from the bondage of Egypt." The soteriological emphasis of the name is unmistakable and remains so throughout Israel's history.

Repairing the damage

What must be done if one is to make sense of Von Rad within the context of creation is the following. *We must be able to plot a trajectory backwards and forwards in time – from creation to history and vice versa – that is compatible with the fact that YHWH is at the time of the phenomenon of the exodus (for example) in a presently occurring personal relationship with Israel.* YHWH "gets himself into" (if this is not too blasphemous a way of putting it!) his own creation – the

---

[2] It is of course of great irony that the much maligned tradition of modern biblical scholarship (within certain theological circles), should return us to the plain literal sense of the text after the kind of interpretation imposed on it by those who wanted to affirm a relentlessly, timelessly eternal God!

world he has previously created. This means that YHWH "gets himself into" his own creation at the very least *temporally* so that God can be understood as in personal relationship with the life of Israel *as it was presently occurring then*. Furthermore, YHWH may also be understood as doing this *spatially* or *locatively* – perhaps the most obvious sense in which God would be *present within* his own creation. God gets himself into the world spatially in such a way that it makes sense to speak of the "God of the heavens" or "God in the heavens."

How is this to be done? *The utterly happy coincidence is that it is done by reinstating the very aspect of the Priestly creation narrative underplayed by both the patristic and medieval tradition.* It is done by reinstating the importance of the very thing that distinguishes the *heptamaeron* from the *hexaemeron*: the seventh day of creation. Only then can we provide for a continuous trajectory that runs from creation to history and vice versa. Only then can we reconcile systematic theology with Von Rad's insight.

What I want to say is that the seventh day of creation intimates the sense in which God gets himself into the very world he has created. It is the point in the continuous biblical narrative of the Old Testament where this event is described as happening. Genesis 2.1–3 is more forthcoming on the matter of God "getting himself into" the *time* of our world ("your time is my time"). But it is also possible to argue that God's action of resting on the seventh day can be understood as the point in time when God "gets himself into" the *space* of our world ("your space is my space"). If we understand the canonical shaping of the Old Testament as one in which the Deuteronomist redacts the Priestly redactor or source rather than vice versa (see Childs, *Introduction to the Old Testament as Scripture*, 131ff.) then the former's references to God dwelling in the "heaven of heavens" or the "highest heaven" (e.g. 1 Kgs. 8:27–30) may provides a means of interpreting Genesis 2:1–3 in a manner not excluded by the Priestly narrator himself.[3]

---

[3] I should add that when the Priestly narrator speaks of God creating "the heavens and the earth" (and in particular of creating the heavens at Gen. 1:6–8), he is not speaking of God's location – where God resides or where God's place is – but rather the created visible heavens (the

God "gets himself into" our world in a temporal sense

The seventh day of creation is narrated in Genesis 2:2–3. This is what the verses say: "By the seventh day God had finished the work he had been doing; so on the seventh day he rested from all his work. And God blessed the seventh day and made it holy, because on it he rested from all the work of creating that he had done."

Let us try to understand God's relation to time within the context of this passage. Is a God who remains in eternity after his creative acts compatible with it? I do not think he is. Let me take Aquinas on the seventh day. He is as ever instructive. It is not that he gets it right (in my view) on this issue but that the half-truth undoubtedly present in his thought insinuates what I hold to be the more nearly right understanding of this matter. This is what Aquinas says. He says that prior to the creation history God can be said to be in eternal divine rest; ergo, when God is said to have rested after the six days of creation, it makes sense to understand him as returning to this eternal rest. Now, let us suppose that Aquinas is right about God prior to creation – that he is in some sense in eternity (or his person is "eternal" in some sense) at that point "in time." The question is whether he is right about God subsequent to creation when measured by the meaning of Genesis 2.1–3. I think he cannot be.

Crucial to the validity of this claim is the fact that God's completing and resting is not something that occurs within the context of the sixth day (as a concluding appendage, say) but is given a full day of creation to itself. Von Rad's comment is to be

---

[3] (*continued*) visible as opposed to the invisible part of created reality). As Westermann puts it, the Priestly narrator did not conceive of the heavens created in Gen. 1:6–8 as a place in which YHWH *dwelt* (Westermann, *Genesis 1 – 11*, 131). God is as beyond or as distant from these heavens as he is beyond the earth. In the context of the canonical narrative, this of course is consistent with understanding Gen. 2:1–3 to be referring among other things to God with his uncreated (non-measurable) place or space (identical with God himself since "God is simple") getting himself into created space – such that the Bible speaks of the God of the "highest heaven" or of the "heaven of heavens" (1 Kgs. 8:27–30).

noted: "It is significant that God 'completed' his work on the seventh day (and not, as seems more logical, on the sixth – so the LXX!). This 'completion' and this rest must be considered as a matter in itself" (Von Rad, *Genesis*, 62).

The Septuagint clearly had a problem with God finishing his creative activity on the seventh day since it naturally seemed to follow from the text that God had in fact finished on the sixth day. But the fact that Scripture wants to say that God "finished the work that he had done" on the seventh day precisely by resting seems to indicate that there was a profound asymmetry between God resting prior to the creation and God resting after creation. And the asymmetry seems to be that God's resting after creation is done in our created time. God does not as it were retire back into his own eternal rest indicative of his own eternal time.

To be sure, one might well imagine that once God had created the world he went back to being what he was before he became the creator, retired as it were back to his eternity *ad intra* (returned to what he is in himself), returned to what Aquinas (in agreement with Augustine) called in the *Summa*, the eternal rest God had had before he started creating. This would not of itself preclude God from being in personal relationship with, and therefore acting in the history of, humankind; a God who creates the world and then returns to being what he was before creation is quite consistent with a God who every now and then as it were turns his personal attention to – and even acts in – the human world. But this is not how the concept of divine resting is employed in the creation narrative. It does not signal the *end* of the creation history; rather, the divine resting is *included* in the creation history. God does not create and then retire, as it were, back into his *ad intra* eternity as does the God affirmed by such as eighteenth-century deists. Rather, God going back to being *himself* – as he was before he became creator and as he is when he is not creator – is now defined in the context *of being, and potentially acting, in the time of his own creation*. Only by including this event as an event of the creation history are we able to affirm that God does not turn his back on creation as is the consequence – intended or not – of many traditional philosophical conceptions. In determining *himself* (himself *ad intra* who is not, at that "moment", creator) *as the content of the seventh day of the creation history*, God determines *himself* – posits himself – to be part of, belong to, coexist with, his own creation.

To repeat: as Genesis 2.1–3 understands it, there is a fundamental asymmetry between God before creation and God during and after creation. Or perhaps more precisely, *whatever* turns out to be true of God prior to creation, God remains in time – our time – after creation. God is saying in effect: "Your time is my time" – such is the claim of the Priestly narrator at the end of his creation narrative. Furthermore: if P is a redactor rather than a mere documentary-source – and it seems rational to affirm either! – then one can say that he intends to understand all subsequent history – primeval, patriarchal, and Israelite (pre-eminently the exodus) – in this context. God is not acting from eternity in history as the tradition from Augustine to Calvin thought. He is acting in history from the vantage point of historical time. What the Priestly narrator says at Genesis 2.1–3 is utterly consistent with Von Rad's understanding of Israel's historical experience of YHWH in the exodus narrative.

"Your time is my time"

Von Rad's assertion is that Israel's initial historical experience of YHWH was that of the exodus from Egypt – which is to say, a historical experience of YHWH acting then and there in Israel's own time frame. Integral to this historical experience is the experience – expressed in Scripture – of God's knowing what is presently occurring in the life of the people of Israel (entirely analogous to the fact that if two *people* are of the same time frame then there is no reason in principle why they should not know what is *presently* occurring – going on – in each other's life). What would endorse the rationality of this claim is that God *is* in our time as Genesis 2.1–3 has it. God rested on the seventh day.[4]

---

[4] In understanding the Priestly creation narrative we must always bear in mind that it is the foundation or presupposition of God's historical relationship with Israel. It is, as Jenson points out, the beginning of this historical relationship (Jenson, *Systematic Theology*, vol. 2, 34). Unless we want to say that God conducts his business with Israel from

But what if this historical experience of God in Israel's own time frame does not – in so far as it is a *subjective* experience – correspond to anything *objective*? What if the claim of modern physics, to the effect that the past, present, and future are not objective features of time, is true? Then the experience of historical time would be illusory, and God could not have gotten himself into our time for the simple reason that "our time" has not ever existed as an objective reality.

Against the view that past, present, and future are not objective features of time Nicholas Wolterstorff has argued that the present is in fact *basic* to our understanding of time. He argues that what is wrong with the view of the non-objectivity of past, present and future is that it:

> treats past, present, and future as properties of events and regards the three properties as equal in status. In fact the present is basic, in the following way. What is fundamental in time is the *occurrence* of events – this having for the most part nothing to do with your and my temporal relationship to these events. When an event occurs, that's when it's present; being present at t and occurring at t come to the same thing (Wolterstorff, "Unqualified Divine Temporality," 196)[5].

---

[4] *(continued)* a position outside the universe, I think we would want to say that somewhere between the beginning and this history there occurs an act where God gets himself into our world. The God who "walks in the Garden of Eden in the evening" (in Gen. 2) is not a far-off distant transcendental God in the classical philosophical sense, but a God who is concretely here, temporally present within the constitution of our world. The implication is that from a position outside the world (but not timelessly) God is now seamlessly and effortlessly present within the world. He has "gotten himself into" the world he has created.

[5] Wolterstorff's statement implies that he sides with those who affirm a tense theory of time (otherwise known as "the A-series of time" following the English philosopher J. M. E. McTaggart) in which time is objectively real such that "all events are ordered in terms of some happening now, some having happened . . . and some going to happen"; Wolterstorff, "Unqualified Divine Temporality," 194). This is posited in opposition to a tenseless theory of time (McTaggart designates it the "B-series of time") which argues that the passage of time is not

This means that events can only become past events if they have at some time been presently occurring events. In fact, according to Wolterstorff for something to be an event at all, it has to be a presently occurring event (Wolterstorff, "Unqualified Divine Temporality," 196); a past event too has to have been a presently occurring event!

This argument has fundamental consequences for anyone who wants to claim that God knows of presently occurring events. For if God knows of presently occurring events at all, then God has to be in time, he has to have a history in this sense. For as Wolterstorff says, one can "know that something is presently occurring *only when it is* [my italics]" (Wolterstorff, "Unqualified Divine Temporality," 206). One's knowledge of such events has to take place when the event is taking place. Otherwise it will not be knowledge of the event as a presently occurring event.

Wolterstorff has championed the cause of the precritical tradition running from Augustine through Anselm and Aquinas to Calvin on the rationality of theological belief. But he has stopped short of affirming that same tradition's approach to time and, by implication, the interpretative framework it employs in its understanding of biblical narrative (even if our time is not illusory, God has not gotten himself into it because he is eternal, and this because he is immutable).

Wolterstorff cites the following passage from Aquinas's *Summa Contra Gentiles* which he takes as definitive of Aquinas's understanding of God's action in the world. But he cites it in order to repudiate it, not affirm it. This is the passage:

> Nor, if the action of the first agent is eternal, does it follow that His effect is eternal? . . . God acts voluntarily in the production of things . . . God's act of understanding and willing, is, necessarily, His act of making. Now, an effect follows from the intellect and the will according to the determination of the intellect and the command of the will. *Moreover, just as the intellect determines every other condition of*

---

[5] *(continued)* objectively real. See Wolterstorff, "Unqualified Divine Temporality," 194–95. It may be the case that, if Einstein's theory of special relativity entails the B-series of time, then one would have to reject it if one affirmed the A-series.

the thing made, so does it prescribe the time of its making; for any art deter-
mines not only that this thing is to be such and such, but that it is to be at
this particular time, even as a physician determines that a dose of medicine
is to be drunk at such and such a time, so that, if his act of will were of itself
sufficient to produce the effect, the effect would follow anew from his previ-
ous decision, without any new action on his part. Nothing, therefore,
prevents our saying that God's eternity existed from all eternity,
whereas its effect was not present from eternity, but existed at that
time, when, from all eternity, he ordained it (Aquinas, *Summa*
Contra Gentiles, 2.35; my italics).

Wolterstorff is quite clear what the whole passage means. It
means that, according to Aquinas, God determines in eternity
what is to happen in time without actually acting in time himself.
The physician can determine when the dose of medicine is to be
taken in the future without being around at this particular time
in the life of his patient. Analogously, God does the same as
regards making events happen in the world. In particular, he
acts on and in the world from his vantage point in eternity.
(Wolterstorff describes Aquinas' point in terms of the childhood
toy in which one releases a marble at the top of the toy and then
the marble subsequently emerges at the bottom after having
navigated loops, springs and trapdoors at high speed.)

Wolterstorff's target is Aquinas but it could just as easily have
been any from the tradition from Augustine through to Calvin.
In particular, as regards Calvin, it does not take too great a leap
of the imagination to see that the position Wolterstorff criticizes
is precisely a fundamental presupposition of Calvin's whole
hermeneutical approach to Old Testament narrative as outlined
by T. H. L. Parker above. Granted the stylistic and rhetorical differences between the two theological giants, Aquinas' words
would be wholly endorsed by Calvin. This of course means that
they are entirely inimical to the position implied in the insights
of Von Rad regarding Israel's experience of YHWH as a presently occurring soteriological identity.

How does God get himself into our time?

The answer to this question follows the same rationale as that advanced in Chapter 2: God determines *himself* to be within our time. Therefore he *is* in our time. The action of divine self-determination as in the case of the acts of creation is both basic and sufficient for it being the case that God is in our time. Notwithstanding the sabbatical implication, this is what resting on the seventh day rather than the sixth means – so the Priestly narrator. The days don't "run on" with God "leaving himself behind," as it were, on the sixth – no, God "comes along with us" in personal temporal relationship with us in his resting on the seventh. Therefore, to anticipate: it would be rational to say that Israel's historical experience, of God being in her time, is a valid one. This provides for the rationality of attributing to the people of Israel, and indeed to all of us, experience of God acting in our respective lives, "then and there" and "here and now."

When I say that God determines himself to be the one who gets himself into our time I mean: *our created* time. This is because, following Westermann, I understand Genesis 1:3–5 as narrating God creating time. But our created time – unlike God's *uncreated* time – is also measurable time; or, at least, by the time God gets himself into our created time on the seventh day of creation, it is measurable time – since the world by then is a world inhabited by laws or regularities of nature, including at the very least periodic mechanisms that allow for the measurement of our created time (this among other things is the point of what happens on the fourth day of creation; the creation of the heavenly bodies on "the fourth day of creation" is "to be for the signs and for seasons and for days and years" [Westermann, *Genesis 1–11*, 129]).

Therefore in so far as God gets himself into our created time, he subjects himself to measurable time. It is possible to say that the duration between, on the one hand, God acting as "the one who released Israel from the bondage of Egypt" and, on the other, the same God acting as "the one who raised Jesus of Nazareth from the dead" is a temporal period of some eleven or twelve centuries. In other words, given the periodic mechanisms implicit in the laws or regularities of nature, God's actions subject themselves to metrical time.[6]

Moreover, we can say of such acts that they last longer than zero duration because to say that an act is of zero duration is equivalent to saying that it has not been in existence at all (cf., Swinburne, *Christian God*, 72–74). Whether this means that we can measure the *length* of duration of these events is another question. What we can say from Wolterstorff's analysis of divine knowledge of, or divine acquaintance with, tensed facts is that God's knowledge or acquaintance endures as long as the human action or event in question endures.

But were created time, both nonmeasurable and measurable, to cease to exist it does not follow that time *per se* ceases to exist. This is because, as was said in Chapter 1, God possesses the property of nonmeasurable time. As a property of God, it is uncreated time or what I might call – in opposition to apophatic "timeless eternity" – "eternal time." It is a positive (non-apophatic) property of God indicative of "ordinal" temporal successiveness but not ("interval") chronology; divine actions or events can be temporally ordered but it does not make sense to speak of the elapsed time between such actions or events (i.e., there is no such thing as measurable time).

Uncreated nonmeasurable time is "eternal time" for a second reason, namely that it is the time that remains once the laws and regularities of nature and created nonmeasurable time itself

---

[6] Anselm writes:

> What . . . has no place or time is doubtless by no means compelled to submit to the law of place and time. No law of place or time . . . in any way governs any nature which no time or place limits by some kind of restraint. But what rational consideration can by any course of reasoning fail to reach the conclusion, that the Substance which creates and is supreme among all beings, which must be alien to, and free from, the nature and law of all things which itself created from nothing, is limited by no restraint of space or time . . . The supreme Substance . . . is encompassed by no restraint of space or time, is bound by none of their laws. (Anselm, *Monologion*, chapter 22)

But though God is by no means compelled he does choose freely that his actions be measured by our created time which is subsequently, in the course of creation, metrical time. This is what it means to say that God gets himself into our world in a temporal sense.

ceases to exist – once nothing but God exists.[7] *The same or similar can be said about space.* There is created space and there is uncreated space. Created space may be nonmeasurable space in the absence of regularities of nature (such as those presupposed by the existence of the standard metre in Paris: the definition of *what* it is a metre is) – but like time, it is measurable once such regularities exist.

Divine spatiality

Were created space in all its forms to cease to exist this does not mean that space *per se* ceases to exist. This is because non-measurable space exists as an uncreated property and therefore perfection of God.[8] Attributing to God this perfection has an invaluable benefit: it is a very powerful way of putting the theological concept of "heaven" back in the modern theological vocabulary.

For when Jesus says, at Matthew 24:35, "heaven and earth will pass away" he is speaking of the *created* heavens seen from the earth; he is referring to that which Genesis 1:1 speaks of when

---

[7] Wolterstorff appears not to endorse this notion of created time since he speaks of "time everlasting," an "entity" which has always existed, and in which both he and his creatures coexist once the latter have been created. See Wolterstorff, 'Time Everlasting'. Since I align myself with Westermann on this point I cannot but think that Gen. 1:3–5 narrates God creating time. But this does not imply that God is timelessly eternal. When we say that "he gives us time" he gives in the first instance precisely his own time: nonmeasurable time.

[8] For what follows see Barth, *CD* II/1, 461–90. Barth has decisively shaped the view espoused here, namely that divine spatiality has ontological advantages over divine infinity even though he implicitly acknowledges that both are capable of deriving divine omnipresence (and indeed divine simplicity). One obvious advantage is that divine spatiality allows us to identify this spatiality with "heaven." Divine infinity (unboundedness) is an apophatic assertion that does not designate a positive property of God at all and so cannot qualify in this respect as any kind of (positive) space. And, even were it not an apophatic designation (and I'm not sure what this would mean) it is unlikely that it could do the job that divine spatiality can.

it declares: "In the beginning God created the heavens and the earth." *These* heavens, like the earth below them, are contingent and corruptible (as modern science now knows) and no more eternal than the earth. Medieval theologians tended to think of space as heterogeneous and therefore the upper regions of space and its celestial occupants as noncorruptible and therefore everlasting (see Jenson, *Systematic Theology*, vol. 1, 201–202). We now know that space is everywhere homogeneous – the same everywhere in the universe – and therefore no less susceptible to eventual non-existence.

Hence, unless "heaven" is identified with "God's place" meaning an uncreated place – and therefore property of God – rather than a created place, then heaven or "the heavenly city" is not a "continuing place." And if it is not a "continuing place" it could not constitute a place where humankind could eternally *be*.

Divine spatiality *contra* divine (nonspatial) infinity

The perfection of nonmeasurable space constitutes the spatial counterpart of the nonspatial and indeed apophatic "property" of infinity traditionally attributed to God. Early Greek philosophers such as Democritus assumed an infinite space existing beyond the world. Medieval theologians such as Thomas Bradwardine (ca. 1290–1349) who was briefly Archbishop of Canterbury before succumbing to the Black Death, likewise posited the existence of a similar such infinite void space beyond the world but divinized it in that he identified it with God's infinite omnipresent immensity. God is present everywhere in the world but is also beyond the world in a place, which is to say, in an infinite void (see Duhem, *Mediaeval Cosmology*, 78–83). (Given divine simplicity the property of infinite void space is identical with God himself who is therefore "in" himself, as it were.)

In typical medieval cosmology, the cosmos was understood to be comprised of eleven concentric spheres. The outermost sphere of the cosmos was thought to be the immobile "empyrean heaven" (the motion of the other ten spheres was essentially motion relative to this immobile sphere). Many theologians regarded this realm as the dwelling place of God and the angels, as well as the abode of the blessed. If such an infinite void of space could be affirmed as a property of God, such a property provided an explanation of omnipresence. This was because this infinite void was itself the outermost concentric sphere containing in itself the other (finite) spheres (the innermost comprising the earth). This implied that all the concentric spheres internal to it were contained in it. Therefore if the outermost infinite void space were a property of God it would follow that God would be present to every place internal to this space since every created space was inside his uncreated space.

To be sure, the claim that God possessed the property of infinite void space seemed to imply that God was an extended being, albeit infinitely extended. But such extension appeared to imply divisibility – in which case God violated the doctrine of divine simplicity beloved of medieval theologians. Bradwardine's solution to this problem was to say that God is infinitely extended without dimension. His conception of infinite void space was therefore one of dimensionless space.

Bradwardine thought of this outermost dimensionless sphere as *uncreated* space since it was a property of God. But the other spheres, the spheres contained in it as it were, were *created* spaces. In the seventeenth century Isaac Newton retained the idea that infinite space was a property of God but appeared to reject the notion that this space was dimensionless; accordingly, three-dimensional infinite space was now said to be an attribute of God. But more importantly for our purposes, Newton replaced the Ptolemaic universe with the Copernican one, and in doing so rejected the medieval conception of the universe as comprised of heterogeneous concentric spheres. Instead, infinite three-dimensional space as a property of God was understood to be homogeneous in its entirety. The great scientist therefore rejected the distinction between uncreated and created space. *All* space – since it was homogeneous – was a property of the Deity.

Is there a position that can draw on the valid insights of both the "late" medieval Bradwardine and the "early" modern Newton? With Bradwardine it can be said that God possesses the property of uncreated space. But since space is homogeneous, not heterogeneous, it cannot be said with Bradwardine that uncreated space was to be identified with the outermost sphere of a Ptolemaic universe, while created space was to be identified with those spheres internal to this outermost sphere. Does this mean that we agree with Newton that *all* "empirical" or "visible" space is uncreated space, that *all* "empirical" or "visible" space, homogeneous as it undoubtedly is, was now to be identified as one of the divine properties? No, quite the opposite: all measurable space is created space, not uncreated space. The space that God possesses as a property is precisely nonmeasurable space. (The sense in which the medievals were right in their assumption of heterogeneous space is that there is, on the one hand, uncreated nonmeasurable space and, on the other, created measurable space.)

Divine spatiality and divine simplicity

The property of divine (nonmeasurable) spatiality is compatible with the thesis of divine simplicity. To be sure, the traditional apophatic designation of God as infinite is consistent with the noncompositeness or simplicity of God. But nonmeasurable space is also consistent, in the way that measurable space is not, with the noncompositeness or simplicity of God (were the space of God measurable then *ipso facto* it would be precluded from being a property of God at all). Bradwardine attempted to reconcile his concept of uncreated space with divine simplicity by introducing the assumption that this space – the outermost sphere in the medieval universe – was dimensionless. Though such an assumption achieved its goal, it was difficult to perceive how infinite extension could simultaneously be dimensionless, especially if it was understood to contain created, obviously dimensional, space as Bradwardine thought it did. But dimensional space as a property of God is only incompatible with divine simplicity if it presupposes that such space is *ipso facto* measurable. If it makes sense to speak of dimensional yet nonmeasurable space then such space is not divisible, and this because indivisibility presupposes nonmeasurability (as divisibility presupposes measurability).

We have much to learn from the medieval theologians in our recovery of their characteristic manner of thinking about space even from a pre-Copernican perspective! Does space by definition possess dimensions and, if it does, does this imply that such space is measurable and therefore divisible? But perhaps space – divine space – is dimensional but nonmeasurable? Perhaps space does not have to be dimensional, at least not in our ordinary sense? These are lofty thoughts that we have got out of the habit of thinking in the modern age.

Divine spatiality and divine omnipresence

In the classical tradition represented by Aquinas, God's omnipresence was explained by the attribution of the perfection of infinity. But infinity is not a real (positive) property since it is an apophatic designation (like immutability) conveying the idea that God is not finite, bounded, or limited but is, rather, infinite, unbounded or unlimited. It is a product of the *via negationis*. It is difficult to envisage the sense in which such a designation could constitute a place. Indeed, though Aquinas defines the empyrean heaven – the highest heaven – as outside the region of change, it is the highest of the corporeal places and therefore not a property of God as Bradwardine later has it (see Aquinas, *Summa*, 1, Q102–112). For a later medieval theologian such as Bradwardine, omnipresence was to be explained by God's infinite void space concentrically containing created space.

But in both Aquinas' and Bradwardine's theology, it seems that God cannot be but omnipresent. This I would argue is a limitation on his freedom. *Shouldn't we rather say that God makes himself, freely chooses to be, omnipresent?* Divine spatiality allows for this to be the case: nonmeasurable spatiality does not of itself entail that God is present to all created spaces (though I agree with Barth that without it he cannot be omnipresent; see Barth, *CD* II/1, 468). Just as God is free to choose to be in the same "time frame" as his creatures, to be present to all events (which by definition are *presently occurring events* such that they cannot be present to God *simultaneously* unless they *occur* simultaneously), then so God can choose to be present to all created places or spaces. This means that God determines himself to be one who is present to all created spaces, which is to say: all presently occurring spaces (which by definition do or do not occur simultaneously).[9]

The "spatial" God who "gets himself into" our space: "God is in the highest heaven" which yet "cannot contain him"

The one who determines himself to be present to all presently occurring spaces *is the one who possesses the property of space or place*. "God possesses space, His own space" (Barth, *CD* II/1, 468–69). This means that God's omnipresence (in the world) coexists with God possessing a space particular and exclusive to him in the world. As Barth put it: "It was not too small a thing for Him to reserve a special place in this sphere where he could be all by himself and wholly himself – but in this sphere" (Barth, *CD* III/1, 224). The one who, by an act of divine self-determination, determines himself to be present to all presently occurring created spaces possesses a space which is peculiar to him, identical with him, and which therefore he is in (God is in himself since this space is identical with him, given the thesis of divine simplicity). *This implies that God has a place in the world* – the space peculiar and exclusive to him (which he possesses as one of the divine perfections, in his being *ad intra* as it were).

---

[9] In his sterling contribution to that collection of essays under the title of *God and Time*, Wolterstorff says a very interesting thing in one of his responses to the classical Calvinist philosopher, Paul Helm. Helm says that if Wolterstorff wants to say that God is in time in the sense in which he claims then he, Wolterstorff, must say that God is also in space (Helm, *Eternal God*, 42–46). Wolterstorff rightly rejects the claim that the former entails the latter (Wolterstorff, "Unqualified Divine Temporality," 208–209). However, it seems to me that there is a certain determinate sense in which Scripture also thinks of God as being *spatially* present in the reality he has previously created. God's presence is not only a temporal presence in created reality but also a spatial presence. God is present in the temporal and spatial constitution of the world he had previously created in his identity as the creator of all things. He gets himself into the spatial constitution of the world that he previously created.

This coexistence of particular spatiality and divine self-determining omnipresence is the fundamental rationale behind the biblical claim at 1 Kings 8:27–30 that God is "in heaven" in such a way that not only is it the lunar or sublunar heavens that cannot contain him, the "highest heaven" or the "heaven of heavens" cannot contain him. (Hence, it is not at all clear that the references in Exod. 20:22, 2 Chr. 2:6, Jeremiah, Psalms, and 1 Kgs. 8:27–30 should only be interpreted metaphorically – as a way of referring to God's unassailable transcendence. The uncontainability of God in this respect is not only a way of exalting divine sovereignty; it is a way of saying that God is "larger" than the space of heaven; that God is in fact *omnipresent*; that God is everywhere present, on the earth as well as in heaven [Deut. 4:36; Josh. 2:11]). Nevertheless, one can also say that heaven is to be defined as "the place in the world from which God's action, as an inner worldly action, originates" (Barth, *CD* III/3, 432). Among these actions is God's speaking: "It is from heaven that God speaks and acts" (Barth, *CD* III/3, 433).

What does it mean that to say that God is in our space? Since God *possesses* space (as a divine perfection), he cannot be understood as occupying space in the way that we human beings do; clearly human bodies do not possess their own space in the sense of carrying it around with them as they move through space. Instead, they move or relocate from one place to another, one space to another. God cannot be thought of as moving from one spatial location to another. Hence, when God determines himself to be within the spatial constitution of the world this should not be understood to mean that God is in space as physical objects, inclusive of human bodies, are in space. God is not locally and finitely in space as human creatures and all other material objects are.

Nevertheless, in so far as this God truly and really determines himself to be within the spatial constitution of the world he "gets himself into" our world. Heaven as God's own place or space really is a place in the created world. Therefore it is not beyond the created world. As Barth puts it: "The world is not without the fact that from its beginning in creation the gracious address and lordship and presence of God are concretely true and actual even within its own constitution" (Barth, *CD* III/1, 224). God's presence does in fact *imply* for Barth that God is within the spatial constitution of the world (in the sense of being present to all presently occurring spaces).

"God's presence necessarily means that he possesses a place, or, we may safely say, His own place" in the world (Barth, *CD* II/1, 468). God possesses a place within the spatial constitution of the world but it is his *own* place. The tradition of heaven as the abode of God – as the place where the "Lord [is] seated on a throne, high and exalted" (Isa. 6:1) – must be understood, as the tradition rightly says, in such a way that God is not spatially located in heaven in the same sense in which we are spatially located on earth. The throne of God "is clearly to be found in the same space as the earth. Within this space, however, it is elevated above earthly space. And it is God's space alone" (Barth, *CD* II/1, 474). In this sense can God be said to dwell "in heaven."

To recapitulate: to say that God "dwells in heaven" or the "heaven of heavens" means that God, possessing the prior property of space, determined himself to be within the spatial constitution of the created world ("God dwelling in heaven" must mean more than that God is in our time). But this does not mean that we can spatially locate God within the created world as we can physical objects. As 1 Kings 8:27 puts it, "The heavens . . . cannot contain you." God is in heaven in such a way that the heavens – even the highest heaven – cannot contain him. This is of course a way of exalting the sovereignty and autonomy of God but it is also a way of saying that God, with the space that is particular and exclusive to him, is omnipresent. For the "heavens of heavens" is God's own space, the space that he possesses as a property (hence someone like Barth finds a direct way of affirming one classical belief that heaven is ultimately identical with God!). Hence, no one else has access to it, empirical or otherwise.

Divine spatiality and omnipresence in the Old and New Testaments

The coexistence of divine spatiality and divine omnipresence makes it rational to affirm one very significant dimension of Old

Testament narrative. The biblical witness is *expressive of a histori-cal experience* of YHWH spatially located in the world. In the exodus tradition Moses' first encounter with YHWH is in the form of a burning bush. In the same tradition YHWH is said to dwell in the ark of the covenant. In the Deuteronomistic history, YHWH is said to be spatially located in the temple in Jerusalem in the inner sanctuary, the "holy of holies." Yet as the last refer-ence indicates, this presence or spatiality is not a straightforward presence. It is not for example the simple spatial locatedness common to his human creatures. In Solomon's prayer in 1 Kings 8:27–30 it is asked: "Will God indeed dwell on the earth?" But there is no question but that God actually dwells on earth. This is testified by the later verses. Nevertheless, the passage is quite clear that God dwells on earth *in his own way*, not in the way that *anyone else* dwells on earth. God is present but he is absent. God is immanent but he is inaccessible. We may profitably compare Calvin (and Aquinas) to Luther on this point. Calvin thought of the problem of divine transcendence in terms of "distance." In contrast, Luther understood the problem as a problem of "inac-cessible immanence" (Steinmetz, "Calvin and His Lutheran Critics," 176). Luther's insight here may be said to be closer to Israel's historical experience of YHWH's spatial presence. Regardless of whether this is so, there is no doubt that the concept of "inaccessible immanence" plays a pivotal role in Israel's experience of YHWH acting in her historical life. Not only "Your time is my time" but also "Your space is my space."

Moreover, as regards the New Testament, the motif of the empty tomb in the resurrection stories of the Gospels is closely aligned to the historical truth-claim that the God of Israel raised the man Jesus of Nazareth from the dead. This is the theological purpose of the presence of the angelic figures in the narratives. When the angelic figure exclaims, "He has risen! He is not here" (Mark 16:6), the unmistakable insinuation is that Jesus has been raised to heaven. But to say Jesus has been raised is to say that he is in God's space, the space peculiar and exclusive to God. In fact, to say that Jesus is in God's space is what it *means to say* that God raised the man Jesus from the dead. *God determines himself to be "the one who raises Jesus from the dead" only in the sense that he deter-mines himself to have one who was dead and buried in the space peculiar and exclusive to him. But since there can be no corpses in heaven(!) – in the one who is eternal life – this is what it means to say that Jesus has been raised from the dead. For us also: to be raised from the dead would mean to be "in heaven" in the sense of being in God's space, the space he possesses as a divine perfection.*[10]

---

[10] In the final chapter of this book I attempt to replace talk of the Son being "of one substance with" the Father with talk of the man Jesus being "included in the divine identity of YHWH, the God of Israel." One can see that were this divine identity to be understood as possessing the property of space particular and exclusive to him (as a divine perfection), how natural then it would be to say that the *man* Jesus is included in the divine identity of YHWH. There is no obstacle to understanding a finite man in some sense within this space. But with the important qualification: this man is divine precisely because he exists or has his mode of existence in God's own space. I am of the view that this implies a Lutheran omnipresence of the man Jesus though it also implies "heaven" as a place in created reality for reasons given in this chapter. As in many things it is Robert Jenson who has been ahead of us all on this matter in thinking of the divine identity and the Trinity in terms of the man Jesus of Nazareth included in the same sense in the "space of God." See his *Systematic Theology*, vol. 2, 254–56. To be sure, Calvin too seems to want to affirm heaven as a definite "place" but characteristically, as in his doctrine of the Eucharist, he rejects the inference that the man Jesus' presence there implies *of itself* that he is omnipresent to all created spaces. When speaking of Paul's comment in Eph. 4:10 on Christ ascending "above all the heavens, so that he might fill all things" Calvin writes:

> It is as if he said, "Beyond this created world." When Christ is said to be in heaven we must not take it that he dwells among the spheres and numbers the stars. Heaven denotes a place higher than all the spheres, which was appointed to the Son of God after His resurrection. Not that it is literally a place beyond the world, but we cannot speak of the kingdom of God without using our ordinary language. Others, again, considering that the expressions, above all heavens, and ascension into heaven, are of the same import, conclude that Christ is not separated from us by distance of place. But one point they have overlooked. When Christ is placed above the heavens, or in the heavens, all that surrounds the earth – all that lies beneath the sun and stars, beneath the whole frame of the visible world – is excluded (Calvin, *Galatians, Ephesians, Philippians and Colossians*, 176–77).

The conceptual tension, even anomaly, inherent in talking of God's heaven as a *place* separated from both the atmospheric and the starry

Coda: how does God become present to all presently occurring spaces?

As a definite description, as a uniquely identifying description, "the one who is present to all presently occurring created spaces" is to be understood first and foremost as a property of God. In other words, the predicate "the one who is within the spatial constitution of the world" is to be thought of first and foremost as a predicate – or designation – of God. How does it become true of God? The answer has already been given: God makes it so, he makes it true of himself, he determines himself thus as a basic action. It is true only of this world that God is in its space in so far as the predicate "the one who is present to all presently occurring spaces" is true of God.

This predicate is true of God solely and sufficiently in virtue of the fact that God has determined himself to be such that this predicate is true of him: he determines himself to be within the spatial constitution of the world. We can ask of any created space only whether God being present to it – in it – is a predicate of

---

[10] *(continued)* heavens was not lost on a mind like Calvin's. Nevertheless, as a pre-Copernican, he seems to think of heaven as a created (hence corporeal) though divine place – not an uncreated place that is a divine property. Even though it may be infinite in magnitude, the finite man Jesus who is in it cannot be omnipresent to all presently occurring created spaces. Characteristically, Calvin's explanation of the man Jesus' omnipresence is a matter of his boundless presence through the power of the Holy Spirit (it is a "true" presence, not a "real" presence:

> When we hear of the ascension of Christ, it instantly strikes our minds that he is removed to a great distance from us; and so he actually is, with respect to his body and human presence. But Paul reminds us, that, while he is removed from us in bodily presence, he fills all things by the power of his Spirit. Wherever the right hand of God, which embraces heaven and earth, is displayed, Christ is spiritually present by his boundless power (Calvin, *Galatians, Ephesians, Philippians and Colossians*, 177).

In contrast, Barth's affirmation of divine spatiality leads him to say something that is more Lutheran than Reformed: he speaks of "Christ's omnipresence even in His human nature" (Barth, *CD* II/1, 489) and even less ambiguously of the "human corporeal omnipresence of Jesus Christ" (Barth, *CD* II/1, 490).

God; that is, whether God has determined himself thus. His being in created space is a predicate of space only in so far as it is first a predicate of God. There is no such thing as a natural theology of space. Divinity is not a natural property of space.[11]

Though perhaps more paradoxical than the claim that God determines himself to be in our time, the claim that he determined himself to be in all presently occurring created spaces is no less consistent. If God determines himself to be this identity then he is this identity! The antecedent of this proposition is, in keeping with the thesis proposed about God's divine action in creation in Chapter 2, both basic and sufficient for it being the case that God is present to our created space.[12]

---

[11] This is undoubtedly the most abstract application of Barth's methodological credo cited in Chapter 2, namely, everything that is said about the world depends absolutely upon this subject, God. The same rule holds always, that all the predicates are determined by him. This holds also for creation. "Fundamentally, what is involved here is the knowledge of the Creator; and after that and from that viewpoint, His Work must be understood" (Barth, *Dogmatics in Outline*, 50). The great problem modernity has with thinking of God in space is that it asks whether it makes sense to say that God is in space (conceptual falsification); whether such a claim is integratable with what we know of space scientifically (shouldn't we be able to detect God in space as a Soviet astronaut once famously implied?) (empirical falsification). In other words, modernity seeks to evaluate the truth of the conclusion "God is in space" by reflecting on the natural properties of space rather than assessing the rationality of the premise "God determines *himself* to be the one who is within the space of the world."

[12] One might go so far as to say that God creates both in space and in time. God possesses uncreated space in the same sense in which he possesses uncreated time. God creates in time presupposes that God possesses time (nonmeasurable time, to be sure). And, possessing time, God is in his own time – is therefore in himself. Likewise, God possesses space implies that God is in space. This implies that God creates in space since, possessing space, God is in his own space – is therefore in himself.

The protological origins of YHWH's soteriological identity in the created world

God does something else on the seventh day of creation. He blesses his resting on the seventh day. In so doing, he, *inter alia*, determines himself to be the one who does not withdraw from being in personal relationship with his human creature. Indeed, this action of blessing is the primal enactment of YHWH's identity as the identity he is – an essentially soteriological identity. As such the action serves to explain why YHWH's personal relationship with Israel is one in which he reveals himself as a judging yet forbearing, desisting divine identity in the exodus narrative and even – it can be argued – in the Deuteronomistic narrative.

Immediately, one can see that to treat the *heptamaeron* as the *hexamaeron* – as Basil of Alexandria, Ambrose of Milan, and Aquinas did – is to eliminate this crucial soteriological dimension from the Priestly creation narrative, a dimension that provides for a continuous trajectory between, on the one hand, the creation history and, on the other, God's action in the historical realm where his identity is revealed as a judging yet desisting forbearing self: YHWH the judging yet desisting forbearing self

"The world is not without the fact that from its beginning in creation the gracious address and lordship and presence of God are concretely true and actual even within its own constitution" (Barth, *CD* III/1, 224). But the first event of the seventh day does not, of itself, preclude God from withdrawing from being in personal relationship, from ceasing to be in continuous (not merely continual) relationship. History might have been otherwise. Clearly, such would have been the case had God ceased to be present within the temporal and spatial constitution of the world and had retired as it were back into eternity.

Therein lies the significance of the second event of the seventh day: *the divine blessing*. God blesses the seventh day on which he rests. It is common for the Bible to refer to the blessing of animate beings – God, humankind, and animals, for example. Why then is the seventh day blessed and sanctified? The connection with the Sabbath cannot be discounted or rejected but it does not have to be to the only sense of the text or even its primary sense. *If we follow the*

text literally, we cannot avoid concluding that what God blesses is pre-
cisely his resting on the seventh day of creation. He could have blessed
the world and sanctified it from outside the world. In particular, he
could have blessed the seventh day (the day after creation) without
having first rested on it! But this is not what he does. Rather, He
blesses and sanctifies it from the context of the seventh day of creation, from the context of his having rested on the seventh day,
from the context of having remained in our time (and space) after
creation. The crucial act is the divine rest. And the fact that, as Von
Rad points out, God blesses the seventh day implies that what God
had previously done on that same day – rest – is also a matter for
the world. That is to say: God blesses the result of his determining
himself to be temporally (and spatially) located within the world
he had previously created. That is: in his self-determination he gets
himself into the time (and space) of his creation, and this is what he
blesses.

God blesses – sanctifies, makes holy, sets apart – his being
present within the constitution of the world. In particular, in the
context of what I said in the previous chapter, God blesses –
sanctifies, makes holy, sets apart – his being in continuous personal relationship with humankind. This means that he wills not
to withdraw from occupying the same temporal and spatial
framework as his human creatures. One can see immediately
that God being in continuous personal relationship with his
human creatures requires as a prerequisite that he belong to the
same time frame as the events that constitute a presently occurring human life, inclusive of the human life of the people of
Israel. This is what he wills not to withdraw from.

To say that God blessed the seventh day is to say that he
blessed the contents of the seventh day, which is to say that he
blessed his being part of, belonging to, coexisting within, his
own creation. He blessed – sanctified – his being present within
the constitution of the world. Von Rad described the divine rest
of the creation history, and the blessing thereof as indicative of a
"third something" between God ("one thing" as it were) and the
world ("another thing").[13] The phrase is an illuminating one

---

[13] Von Rad's comment is of some relevance here: ". . . that God has
'blessed' 'sanctified' . . . this rest, means that P does not consider it as

bringing to mind a third ontological realm which includes God and the world together, and thereby in effect supersedes the previously existing individual independent "atomic" entities of God and world. There is in fact only God together with the world, in the world – God present *in perpetuum* within the constitution of the world.

God blesses – sanctifies – his belonging to the creation. It is ultimately this that God sanctifies – sets aside as "sacred" – the twain never to be cut asunder, come what may. In effect, God's self-determining self-determines himself *not to withdraw* from belonging to – from being alongside and therefore on the same ontic level as – his creation. This has an obvious implication for the fact of God creating humankind "in his own image." God sets aside as "sacred" his determining himself as the creator of a being with whom he is in personal relationship. He wills not to withdraw from being in personal relationship with humankind.

Only in context of YHWH's enacted soteriological identity on the seventh day can it be credible to affirm Israel's experience of being in covenantal relationship with YHWH. For the covenantal relationship in question is a particular example of personal relationship between YHWH and humankind. Suppose that "YHWH wills not to withdraw from being in personal relationship with humankind" is false; in such a context would it make sense to speak of a covenantal relationship in which God says, "I will be your God and you will be my people"?

Hence though Genesis 2:1–3 does not actually employ the term "covenant" (*berith*), it can be argued that the seventh day makes inevitable the kind of "covenantal" history of God's faithfulness within the constitution of the creaturely world to which the Old Testament witnesses. This is why Barth says that "the history of the covenant was really established in the event of the seventh day" (Barth, *CD* III/1, 217). This event, as he puts it, constitutes "the supreme starting-point for all that follows" (Barth,

---

[13] (*continued*) something for God alone but as a concern of the world, almost as a third something that exists between God and the world" (Von Rad, *Genesis*, 62). Again he writes: "'to sanctify' means to separate exclusively for God" (Von Rad, *Genesis*, 62).

CD III / 1, 217). It is in this sense that the seventh day is the beginning of the history of the covenant.

"Covenant" (*berith*), Barth asserts, is the Old Testament term for the basic relationship between the God of Israel – Yahweh – and his people, the people of Israel. Barth uses the term "covenant" to refer to "the historical reality with which the Old Testament is concerned whether it actually uses the word or not: 'I will be your God and you will be my people' (Jer. 7.23, 11.4, 30.22, 31.33, 32.38; Ez. 36.28)" (Barth, *CD* IV / 1, 22). It is "the relationship with God as such which is everywhere presumed in the Old Testament cultus, in the law-giving, the prophecy, the historical and poetical writings . . . It embraces everything that takes place between the two partners" (Barth, *CD* IV / 1, 23). For Barth the covenant is "not a truth which as such has ceased to be an event, the act of God and of Israel. It can of course be thought of as a historical fact. And it can be represented and worked out in institutions. But it is not itself an institution" (Barth, *CD* IV / 1, 23). The ultimate reason that Barth can make these claims about the covenant – and, indeed, speak of God being in covenantal faithfulness with humankind (inclusive, therefore, of the prehistory of Israel) – is because of the truth-claim regarding God's self-determination on the seventh day of creation, in particular, God determining himself as the sanctifier of his personal relationship with humankind

It is only in the context of the second act of the seventh day that one can rationally affirm the historical truth-claim pertaining to the history of God's covenantal faithfulness within "the middle of the creation" itself: the covenant God makes with Noah (Gen. 9:8–17), with Abraham (Gen. 15; 17), and later with the Israelites of the Exodus (Exod. 19 – 24).

Concluding remarks

In contradistinction to the traditional apophatic conception of God's eternity and infinity, I have argued that divine spatiality and divine temporal successiveness make better sense of God's personal and historical relationship with his people "Israel" as witnessed in Scripture. Temporal successiveness conforms more readily than apophatic eternity to the historical trajectory of the formation of Israel's Scriptures, since the former acknowledges that Israel's relationship with YHWH begins in the created *presently occuring* "time frame" common to all creatures. Divine spatiality enables one to conceive of an "eternal" place that makes sense even in a Copernican universe of talk of the risen or resurrected Jesus. It also avoids making God's omnipresence a necessity rather than an act of freedom.

Moreover, if our remit is to affirm the rationality of Israel's experience of YHWH as we find it, for example, in the Yahwist's redactional action in the Pentateuch (inclusive of the Exodus tradition and the primeval history), in the Deuteronomistic history (inclusive of the history of the Judges, and most especially of the historical trajectory leading to the end of the kingdoms of Israel and Judah), then our interest should be very much on the seventh day of creation and the significance the events of this day have for God having created humankind "in our image, after our likeness." Ultimately, the seventh day intimates the beginning of God's presence within the world, a presence necessary for his being in personal relationship with us.

God creating humankind in "our image, after our likeness" principally means that God created a being with whom he can be in personal relationship – so I argued in Chapter 4 (in line with Barth and others). Clearly this does not of itself mean that God *will be* in personal relationship with humankind, nor does it preclude God withdrawing from being in personal relationship were he to have previously determined himself to be as such. But if God is in some kind of continuous personal relationship with humankind then his action toward us must occupy the same temporal framework as the history of humankind. This is what is claimed in the first event of the seventh day of creation, the divine resting.

Bibliography

Anselm, *Monologion*. In *Anselm of Canterbury: The Major Works*, edited by Brian Davies and Gillian Evans, (Oxford: Oxford University Press, 1998) 5–81.

Aquinas, *Summa Theologiae*. In *Basic Writings of Saint Thomas Aquinas*, edited by Anton Pegis (New York: Random House, 1945); *Summa Contra Gentiles*, translated by James F. Anderson (Notre Dame: University of Notre Dame Press, 1975).

Barth, Karl, *Church Dogmatics* II/1, translated by T. F. Torrance and G. Bromiley (Edinburgh: T. &T. Clark, 1957); *Church Dogmatics* III/1, translated by T. F. Torrance and G. Bromiley (Edinburgh: T. &T. Clark, 1958); *Church Dogmatics* IV/1 (Edinburgh: T. &T. Clark, 1956).

Calvin, John, *Galatians, Ephesians, Philippians and Colossians*, New Testament Commentaries, vol. 11 (Grand Rapids: Eerdmans, 1975).

Childs, Brevard, *Introduction to the Old Testament as Scripture* (London: SCM, 1979).

Duhem, Pierre, *Medieval Cosmology*, edited and translated by R. Ariew (Chicago: University of Chicago Press, 1985).

Farrow, Douglas, *Ascension and Ecclesia* (Edinburgh: T. & T. Clark, 1999).

Helm, Paul, "Divine Timeless Eternity." In *God and Time*, edited by G. E. Gassle, 28–91 (Illinois: IVP, 2001); *Eternal God* (Oxford: Oxford University Press, 1988).

Jenson, Robert W., "For Us He Was Made Man," *Nicene Christianity: The Future of a New Ecumenism* edited by Christopher Seitz, 75–86 (Grand Rapids: Brazos Press, 2001); *Systematic Theology*, vol. 2 (Oxford: Oxford University Press, 1999).

Luther, Martin, "Confession Concerning Christ's Supper." In *Martin Luther's Basic Theological Writings*, edited by T. Lull, 375–404 (Minneapolis: Fortress Press, 1989).

Parker, T. H. L., *Calvin's Old Testament Commentaries* (Louisville: Westminster John Knox, 1993).

Pelikan, Jaroslav, *Christianity and Classical Culture: The Metamorphosis of Natural Theology in the Christian Encounter with Hellenism* (New Haven: Yale University Press, 1993); "Creation and Causality in the History of Christian Thought." *Southwestern Journal of Theology* 32 (1990): 10–24.

Rad, Gerhard von, *Genesis*, translated by J. Bowden, 3rd ed. (London: SCM, 1972).

Rowland, Christopher, *The Open Heaven: A Study of Apocalyptic in Judaism and Early Christianity* (London: SPCK, 1982).

Steinmetz, David, "Calvin and His Lutheran Critics." In *Calvin in Context*, edited by David Steinmetz, 172–87 (Oxford: Oxford University Press, 1995); "Scripture and the Lord's Supper in Luther's Theology." In *Luther in Context*, edited by David Steinmetz, 72–84 (Grand Rapids: Baker Academic, 2002).

Swinburne, Richard, *The Christian God* (Oxford: Oxford University Press, 1994).

Torrance, Thomas F., *Space, Time and Incarnation* (Edinburgh: T. & T. Clark, 1997); *Space, Time and Resurrection* (Edinburgh: T. & T. Clark, 1998).

Westermann, Claus, *Genesis 1–11* (Minneapolis: Fortress Press, 1994).

Wierenga, Edward, "Omnipresence. " In *A Companion to the Philosophy of Religion*, edited by Philip L. Quinn and Charles Taliaferro, 286–90 (Oxford: Blackwell, 1997).

Wolterstorff, Nicholas, "God Everlasting." In *God and the Good: Essays in Honor of Henry Stob*, edited by Clifton Orlebeke and Lewis B. Smedes, 77–98 (Grand Rapids: Eerdmans, 1975); "Unqualified Divine Temporality." In *God and Time*, edited by G. E. Gassle, 187–238 (Illinois: IVP, 2001).

Wright, J. Edward, *The Early History of Heaven* (New York: Oxford University Press, 2000).

Zellini, Paolo, *A Brief History of Infinity*, translated by D. Marsh (London: Penguin Books, 2004).

6

The Self-Determining Self and Israel's Historical Experience of YHWH

In Old Testament narrative, the "explanatory concept" of divine self-determination in the world is juxtaposed to another "explanatory concept." This is the people "Israel's" historical experience of YHWH acting in their life. Hence, the totality of Old Testament witness – witness as historical truth-claim – encompassess two fundamental explanatory concepts: first, divine self-determination understood in terms of the divine dynamics of the creation narrative, and which therefore entails reference to a verb ("creates," "releases," etc., as in "the one who created all things" or "the one who releases Israel from the bondage of Eypt"); and second, Israel's historical experience of YHWH acting in her life.

The relation between the two is as follows. The primary datum is an "empirical" one: the historical experience that this YHWH acted in the life of this people Israel. In the Old Testament this experience is explained in terms of the divine initiative. Nothing new in this claim. What is new is to say that in the Old Testament the historical experience of Israel is explained in terms of YHWH determining himself to be the one who acts in the life of his people Israel. YHWH therefore is the one who acts in the life of his people Israel. Crucially, what follows from this explicandum is the fact that the life of the people Israel is one in which YHWH acts. Therefore Israel's historical experience, and her claim thereof, is a rational one.

The Old Testament, and Old Testament narrative in particular, is expressive of Israel's historical experience of YHWH, the God of Israel, acting in, and being in personal relationship with, her life. Von Rad emphasized the essential kerygmatic, confessional nature of this experience. Is the category of "experience" sufficient as an explanatory concept? No. God determines himself to be the creator of all things. He does this essentially through the divine speaking. He ends his creation history with his action of "getting himself" into the world he had previously created. Then, from a location within the world, he determines himself to be the one who releases Israel from the bondage of Egypt. He does not do this without determining himself to be the one who speaks to Israel. He speaks to Israel – this too is Israel's historical experience. If God determines himself to be the one who speaks of his soteriological intention to Moses then he is the one who speaks of his soteriological intention to Moses. And if he determines that Moses hear him then Moses hears him – and Moses hears YHWH speaking to him even were this same Moses deaf ("From heaven he made you hear his voice" [Deut. 4:36]). Therefore the attribution to Moses of the historical experience of YHWH speaking to him – or better, perhaps, his claim that YHWH speaks to him in time – is a valid one. God did speak to Moses. Not one but two categories are necessary and perhaps sufficient to do justice to – to encompass the whole witness of – the Old Testament. Israel's historical experience is expressed in narrative; but narrative also testifies to the divine speaking. Without the latter juxtaposed to the former we gravely underestimate the epistemic sophistication of the Old Testament.

The reintroduction of the concept of experience into biblical and systematic theology

The concept of experience and, in particular, experience of God has not received good press in certain circles in theology in recent years, mainly due to the influence of Karl Barth, Hans Frei and George Lindbeck. I am deeply indebted to all three for my theological orientation but I am of the opinion that the concept of experience of God must be revived within modern theology.

George Lindbeck's *The Nature of Doctrine* offered a taxonomic reading of the options open to modern theology. These were: cognitive-propositional, experiential-expressivist, and cultural-linguistic. Lindbeck himself, as is well-known, favored the latter. My starting-point is to question whether the categories are as mutually exclusive as Lindbeck's taxonomy made them appear to be though, clearly, he had license from the history of modern systematic theology (Barth's narrative emphasis as against either Tillich's broadly experiential approach or an old-fashioned but still sufficiently contemporary propositional approach).

In particular, if one considers the testimony of Old Testament theology as regards the concepts of narrative and experience one can easily come to the conclusion they are not mutually exclusive after all. (Old Testament theologians are ahead of systematic theologians in this respect. Where for example do we find a discussion from a modern systematic theologian similar to the one that Childs embarks on in the section entitled "The History of History" in *Biblical Theology of the Old and New Testaments*, 122ff.?) Although Von Rad did not employ the concept of experience as a formal explanatory category, he did take recourse to using the concept in several places in his magisterial two-volume *Old Testament Theology*. His most formal answer to the question, "What is the subject-matter of the theology of the Old Testament?" comes in the response that the subject-matter is "Israel's own explicit assertions about Jahweh" (Von Rad, *Old Testament Theology*, vol. 1, 105). Von Rad speaks of the "kerygmatic intention" of Old Testament narrative, which he holds to be expressive of "Israel's faith" which "regards itself as based upon historical acts and as shaped and re-shaped by factors in which it saw the hand of Jahweh at work" (Von Rad, *Old Testament Theology*, vol. 1, 106). Though a kerygmatic theology need not be based on one's *experience* of YHWH acting in one's history, Von Rad does speak in this way. Speaking of the exodus from Egypt he writes that "those who were delivered experienced [*Ehrfarung*] something which in its significance far transcended the personal fate of those who at the time shared in it." Elsewhere he speaks of Israel's "historical experience', of "a confessional presentation of . . . historical experience," and of Israel's confidence in YHWH "on the basis of a rich and wide experience, of her history in fact" (Von Rad, *Old Testament Theology*, vol. 2, 476).

In other words, it can said that, according to Von Rad, Old Testament narrative confesses, testifies to, Israel's historical experience of YHWH's acting in its history. In this sense narrative and experience are entirely compatible in Old Testament studies, and not mutually exclusive as has tended to be the case in systematic theology in our times.

Childs concurs with a great proportion of Von Rad's judgements. He too takes Old Testament narrative to be kerygmatic in nature (though he thinks that too much can be made of these theoretical descriptions *per se*). He says that "the object of historical study is Israel's own testimony to God's redemptive activity" (Childs, *Biblical Theology*, 97). This means that it "reflects the perspective from within the community of faith of how Israel understood its relationship with God" (Childs, *Biblical Theology*, 416). The object of historical study is not a historical reconstruction of events independently of Israel's testimony. "In short, a theology of the Old Testament is not to be confused with a description of Israel's religion but is Israel's own testimony, a perspective from within the faith (emic)" (Childs, *Biblical Theology*, 416). "Israel's faith developed from its initial encounter with God as redeemer from Egypt" (Childs, *Biblical Theology*, 110). "Israel became the people of God . . . by its *experience* [my italics] of redemption from Egypt which it understood as an act of divine favour" (Childs, *Biblical Theology*, 138).

Clearly Childs advocates a theology in which both narrative and experience play a role (though the latter firmly anchored as it is to biblical narrative in no way recapitulates Schleiermacher's philosophical turn to the experiential ego in his understanding of theology as a "feeling of absolute dependence on God"). It seems to me that we require both the narrative emphasis and the experiential orientation if we are to reintegrate systematic theology with biblical studies and thereby affirm the rationality of the Bible in this or any other age. Moreover, bringing the concept of experience back into the centre of the theological arena is liable to be greeted with relief from those who believe that their own experience of God being in relationship with them, working in their life, and so on, cannot be shunted off into the periphery of the theological project. (One frequent criticism of Barth's theology was that it made God too transcendent, too much the "wholly other" God. This I believe was a mistaken accusation since Barth said that it was not experience *per se* he was against but, rather, contruing this experience as a norm against which one could measure one's experience of God. Nevertheless, the charge has stuck.)

Childs' critique of Von Rad's approach

But though Childs broadly agrees with Von Rad's kerygmatic approach, focusing as it does on the experience of the people of Israel, he suspects that Von Rad did not think this approach could stand on its own two feet as a rational enterprise. This is why, according to Childs, Von Rad tried to combine this "confessional" approach with the critical-historical method in a way that Childs deems ultimately inconsistent. For Von Rad, historical criticism unavoidably provided the litmus test of the *rationality* of affirming the people of Israel's experience of YHWH as *experience of YHWH.*[1]

Childs may have thought that the rationality of the claim of historical experience could have stood on its own two feet within Von Rad's framework. As noted above, he describes the theology of the Old Testament as "Israel's own testimony, a perspective from within the faith (emic)." In employing the term "emic" Childs speaks the language of the social scientist, of the anthropologist or the psychologist for example. In doing so he makes a significant gesture. When an anthropologist, for

---

[1] Von Rad then it is who is to be credited with bringing to the fore the concept of Israel's historical experience of YHWH as a central methodological category for interpreting the Old Testament. Childs' main criticism of Von Rad is not in fact the latter's commitment to the concept of "the noetic experience of Israel" *per se*, but rather the fact that Von Rad limited his theology in a fundamental way to this concept and sought to undergird the rationality of the concept of Israel's experience by taking recourse to what he thought was rationality's last refuge in this context – historical criticism. As Childs implies, there was something heroic yet tragic – and inconsistent – in Von Rad's inability to break with the assumption that rationality proper could only be catered for by the critical-historical method.

example, uses an "emic" methodology, *he or she accepts the perspective or understanding that an individual has of himself, or group has of itself, as valid in itself as a true representation of reality.* The anthropologist accepts the individual's or group's respective experience to be as the individual or group says it is; she accepts the individual's or group's respective explanation of that exerience to be as the individual or group says it is (or the very least there is suspension of belief that the individual or group experience is not as the individual or group says it is).

So for example: the village shaman of a primitive tribe explains his special powers in terms of the spirit-world to which he has special or intimate access. The "emic" anthropologist will vouchesafe the validity of this subject's experience of his world, the terms in which this subject understands his world and what happens in it. She will understand it from *within* the shaman's *perspective*.

This description dovetails very well with Childs' description of Old Testament theology as "Israel's own testimony, a perspective from within the faith." How Israel understood herself internally – from within its community of faith – was that it had experienced YHWH's saving identity in its history. Such was Israel's historical experience and such was how Israel explained this historical experience. The witness of the Old Testament functioned as an emic description of a theological reality. Childs seems to be saying that the best Old Testament methodology can do is: accept at face value Israel's "phenomenological" historical experience of and witness to YHWH acting in her life.

Or is he? Is there another way of reading Childs? The "emic" viewpoint studies behavior as from "inside the system." It can be described as the attempt to produce as faithfully as possible the subject's own descriptions of behavior, beliefs, etc. In contrast, what is called the "etic viewpoint" studies behavior from "outside the system." An etic description or explanation is the observer's attempt to take the descriptive information they have already gathered from the subject, and organize or systematize that information in terms of a system of their own making.

Crucially, this "external" systematizing may do violence to the subject's explanation, imposing from without what the observer postulates to be the *real and therefore rational* explanation of the subject's experience. That is: the observer's explanation may undermine the *identity* of the experience, disregarding the experiencer's explanation as variously based on an obsolete or primitive worldview; or based on self-interest (economic, ideological, self-seeking, etc.); or based on some kind of psychological mechanism (delusional). This kind of explanation very often reduces the subject's experience to other than what it appears to be.

So, for example: Freud's psychodynamic theory of human behavior concluded that one had to bypass the conscious experience of human beings because it failed to recognize and indeed constantly disguised or misrepresented the person's real desires and needs. Conscious experience had to be explained in terms of the unconscious or subconscious roots of experience, which were not accessible to the person's waking consciousness due to defence mechanisms such as repression, projection, etc.

Yet though an etic perspective may – and very often does – stand in judgement of an emic perspective, it does not necessarily do so. An etic perspective may also *endorse, reinforce even* an emic perspective. Put otherwise: even though we may not want to affirm an emic perspective as the last word of rationality in religion or theology, there is no *a priori* reason why an emic description should not turn out to be a *rational* perspective. There is no *a priori* reason why an etic description could not function as something like a rational justification of an emic perspective. (As someone once said of Kant, just because one views the world through pink spectacles it doesn't follow that the world isn't pink; it may in fact be so.) It may be that one's experiential awareness of God acting in one's life is rational to affirm on the basis of one or another etic perspective on God. It may be that the emic category of Israel's historical experience of YHWH is not without its etic counterpart. It may be that the people "Israel" provided their own etic category Old Testament narrative – in the form of God's speaking as divine action.

Is this what Childs thought? It cannot be gainsaid that Childs criticized Von Rad in other ways that intimated that he thought that the concept of Israel's experience of YHWH was not sufficient in itself for affirming the rationality of Old Testament narrative as historical truth-claim. When Childs criticized his esteemed teacher Von Rad for failing to "do justice to the final effect of the Priestly writer's editing of the Yahwist's material" (Childs, *Biblical Theology*, 120) he implied that one way Von Rad could have moved the rationality of Old Testament theology without the historical-critical method would have been to understand the noetic experience of the people of Israel in the context of the "ontic priority" of the creation history "within the whole book of Genesis," and indeed beyond. The phrase "the ontic priority of God's creation history" is derived from Childs' juxtaposition of "ontic" (God's divine action) and "noetic" (a concept designating the [intellectual] beliefs of the people of Israel as regards their experience of YHWH) in his book, *Biblical Theology of the Old and New Testaments*:

> From a theological perspective it is significant to note that the present canonical shape has subordinated the noetic sequence of Israel's experience of God in her redemptive history to the ontic reality of God as creator. This is to say, although Israel undoubtedly first came to know Yahweh in historical acts of redemption from Egypt, the final form of the tradition gave precedence to God's initial activity in creating the heavens and earth (Childs, *Biblical Theology*, 385).

I think Childs observed something of momentous importance when he perceived that the solution may have lain in the Priestly creation history and the priority canonical shaping has given it *vis-à-vis* Genesis, the Pentateuch, and indeed the rest of the Old Testament. One way of providing for the rationality of the "noetic sequence of Israel's experience of God" would be to juxtapose to it a claim of God's action in creating, being, and acting in the world. The canonical decision to insert the experiential claims regarding YHWH's actions in Israel's life into the creational context of the Priestly narrative is the first necessary step of this theological juxtaposition.

William Alston's philosophy of experience of God

It is perhaps William Alston's work on the rationality of religious experience that provides the best philosophical commentary on the concept of Israel's historical experience of YHWH. In *Perceiving God: the Epistemology of Religious Experience* Alston describes what he calls "manifestation beliefs" as beliefs to the effect that "God is doing something currently *vis-à-vis* the subject – comforting, strengthening, guiding, communicating a message, sustaing the subject in being" (Alston, *Perceiving God*, 1). Alston then, like Wolterstorff, wants to speak in terms of God being in personal relationship not from eternity but there and then with his human creatures. He continues: "The intuitive idea is that by virtue of my being aware of God as sustaining me I can justifiably believe that God *is* sustaining me in being" (Alston, *Perceiving God*, 1). The central thesis of the book is in fact that "experiential awareness of God . . . makes an important contribution to the grounds of religious belief" (Alston, *Perceiving God*, 1).

Alston writes that "the chief value of the experience of God is that it enables us to enter into personal relationships with God; most importantly, it makes it possible for us to enjoy the relation of loving communion with God for which we were created" (Alston, *Perceiving God*, 2). Alston concludes that it is only if we can perceive God – have an experiential awareness of God – that "the distinctively 'personal' relationships of love, friendship, mutual sharing, resentment, delight in each other's company, and self-revelation are possible" (*Perceiving God*, 304).

Alston makes it clear that his project is distinct from that which seeks to prove the existence of God on the basis of experience, that which comes under the rubric of "the experiential proof of the existence of God." Alston claims his project is one in which "we take ourselves, *in* these experiences, to be aware" of God rather than, as in the experiential proof, taking religious experience *per se* as data – and therefore as evidence – for the existence of God acting upon us. He explains the difference between his employment of the concept of experience of God and the experiential proof thus:

> Like the teleological or moral arguments [the experiential proof] begins with certain data, in this case religious experiences; and the question is as to whether an adequate *explanation* of these data requires an appeal to God. That is *not* the way I am thinking of an experiential support for theism. I am thinking of it as analogous to the experiential support all of us have for the existence of the

physical world. Here it is not a matter of gathering data, in the form of sensory experiences, and then claiming that they are best explained by supposing that they are due to the action of the physical world on us. It is rather that we take ourselves, *in* these experiences, to be aware of the physical world. No explanatory issues are involved. To be sure, a few philosophers have attempted to carry through the explanatory argument just mentioned, but they have been conspicuously unsuccessful; and in any event that is not our normal stance. By analogy, I am claiming that a participant in a theistic religion takes herself to be aware of God at various times, that it is rational for her to do so, and that because of this theistic belief is rational for her (Alston, "Experiential Basis of Theism").

There is much in Alston that bears fruitful comparison with Israel's historical experience of YHWH in Old Testament narrative. The people of Israel do not utilize their experience as the premise of an experiential argument for the existence of YHWH. Rather, the people of Israel took their experience in a much more straightforward, direct way to be that of YHWH acting in their life and history. So, for example, the people of Israel took their experience of their exodus to be that of YHWH leading them out of Egypt.

Alston is very much interested in the *rationality* of affirming experience as experience of God. For him, the rationality of affirming experience of God can stand on its own two feet in the sense that experience of God can move the rationality of affirming experiential awareness of God on its own. Alston's philosophical boldness is commendable and might well have constituted a methodological corrective to Von Rad's reliance on the critical-historical method. Alston's project might have allayed Von Rad's fear about the rationality of a purely "internalist" approach. Instead of seeking the sanctuary of rationality in historical criticism, Von Rad could have argued that "Israel's own explicit assertions about Jahweh" was rational in its own right as an agenda for biblical theology. Alston's philosophical position on experience would also have dovetailed extraordinarily well with the position Von Rad took in the 1936 paper where his conclusion is tantamount to the assertion that Israel's foundational experience of God is not of God as creator but of God as soteriological identity in the exodus.

Indeed, in parallel fashion Alston thinks it is also rational to affirm God as creator of the universe though he thinks this a less foundational premise than experiential awareness of God. Though Alston does not jettison natural theology, he is clear that as regards theistic belief it is a less necessary premise for proving rationality. This is why, as he explains, his conception of theistic belief rests on "twin pillars, of unequal strength":

> First, there are the very general considerations of "natural theol-ogy", accessible to any sufficiently intelligent and reflective person; they give some support to the belief. Of the traditional arguments for the existence of God, I take most seriously the cosmological and ontological arguments. Without claiming for them anything like coercive proof, it seems to me that the cosmological argument, properly construed, provides a significant support for the view that the physical universe depends for its existence on a necessarily existing source of all being other than itself. And the ontological argument, properly construed, provides significant support for the view that this necessarily existing source of all being is an absolutely perfect being (Alston, "Experiential Basis of Theism").

The other pillar is, of course, experience of God:

> The other pillar is the experience of God. It is reasonable to believe in the existence of God because we have experienced His presence and activity in our lives. I consider this to be the more massive pillar. As I see it, the proper role of natural theology is not to bear the whole weight, or even most of it, but to provide basis for reassurance, in moments of doubt, that what we take to be our experience of God is not merely a projection of our needs and fears. I am not concerned to argue that a theistic belief resting wholly on natural theology is a rational belief. Because of this, and because I feel that I have some-thing more distinctive to say about the experiential pillar, I will confine my discussion to that side of the matter (Alston, "Experien-tial Basis of Theism").

I remain unconvinced that the category of experience inclusive of historical experience does sufficient justice to the witness of Scripture. In fact, I remain deeply unconvinced that a concept of experience allied to something like the cosmological argument provides rational justification at all. It is not what we find in

Scripture in the sense that Scripture seems to want to juxtapose something more objective to Israel's "subjective" historical experience than simply rely on the latter on its own, as it were. *It wants to juxtapose divine action inclusive of divine speaking to Israel's historical experience of YHWH.*

The project I want to advance is one that takes into account the canonical shape of the Old Testament. The rationality of the claim of experience of YHWH acting in Israel's history rests most heavily – so I will argue – with the biblical writers' decision to give textual priority to God's creation of the world. For the text of God's creation of the world in Genesis 1:1 – 2.4a tells us in effect that God gets himself into our world (is it too colloquial, not to say too profane, to say that he gets himself into our world?) – which is to say that his final act of creation is to determine himself, his personal self as it were, to be present within the constitution of the world. *Which means that he is.* But it does not stop there. Israel's God is in essence not a mute but a speaking God.

Within the temporal constitution of the world (and, in a certain determinate sense, from a place within the world) God determines himself to be the one who leads the people of Israel out of Egypt; therefore he is the one who leads the people of Israel out of Egypt. It is the rationality of this claim – not the mere experience itself – that makes it rational to affirm the people of Israel's experience as that of experience of YHWH leading them out of Egypt. But what is most constitutive of this action is that God speaks to the people "Israel." Biblical narrative, I argue, represents him as acting in the world, quintessentially in the life and history of the people of Israel, by speaking in it (though, of course, in virtue of his omnipotence, he is not restricted to such actions: he can act without speaking). This is as true of Deuteronomic theology and the Deuteronomistic history as it is of the defining moments of Israel's identity in the exodus narrative. How does God do this? He speaks in the world just as he spoke to create it: by an act of self-determination. There is nothing whatsoever anthropomorphic about this (Enlightenment charges of "primitivism" are unjustified; God does not need a mouth or a physical voice-organ of any kind). The only relevant question is whether God can determine himself thus:

determine himself to be "the one" who says what he says, thereby allowing us to say, "Thus saith the Lord."

Concluding remarks

When I speak of the people "Israel" having the historical experience of God acting in their lives, I also include in this category of historical experience, the experience of God speaking to them. Both Old Testament narrative and the prophetical literature testify to this. In principle the matter is no different from what appears to be the rather more straightforward issue of God acting in the world without "opening his mouth" – his "mighty speechless acts" (so to speak). But should we ignore those who claim to experience God speaking to them as irrational or, less euphemistically, mad? Should we dismiss Moses as a "primitive" ancient? And those who say that God has answered their prayers? We may think this is a metaphor for the fact that someone has received what they asked for; but what about those who actually claim that God spoke to them in answer to their prayers? (There is the "insider" claim that God spoke to Moses; and there is the 'outsider' claim that God determined himself to be the one who spoke to him. Therefore God spoke to Moses.)

My answer is simply that there is nothing wrong with saying that God actually spoke to those to whom Old Testament narrative claims he spoke. This is because it is quite rational to say that God determined himself to be the one who, for example, said to Moses: "I will bring you out from under the yoke of the Egyptians. I will free you from being slaves to them" (Exod. 6:6). God said this to Moses, with all the necessary intentionality attendant on speech acts: self-determining action is basic and sufficient for this being the case. Therefore, one can conclude: it is rational for biblical narrative to claim that God spoke to Moses, and also that Moses had the historical experience of being in personal relationship with God.

And that goes for us all. Our historical experience of being in relationship with God now, and especially in our prayers, is rational too. It is rational because of the historical reality of the self-determining divine self.

Bibliography

Alston, William P., "The Experiential Basis of Theism," http://www.origins.org/articles/alston_experientialbasis.html; *Perceiving God: The Epistemology of Religious Experience* (Ithaca: Cornell University Press, 1991).

Childs, Brevard; *Biblical Theology of the Old and New Testaments* (London: SCM, 1992).

Frei, Hans W., *Types of Christian Theology*, edited by G. Hunsinger and W. C. Placher (New Haven: Yale University Press, 1992).

Lindbeck, George, *The Nature of Doctrine* (London: SPCK, 1984).

McCutcheon, Russell T. (ed.), *The Insider-Outsider Problem in the Study of Religion: A Reader* (London: Continuum, 1999).

Rad, Gerhard von, *Old Testament Theology*, vols. 1 and 2 (London: SCM: 1975).

Seitz, Christopher R., "The Historical-Critical Endeavor as Theology." In *Word Without End: The Old Testament as Abiding Theological Witness*, edited by Christopher R. Seitz (Grand Rapids: Eerdmans. 1998): 28–40.

PART TWO

Were the (biblical) narratives written or read as fiction, then God would turn from the lord of history into the creature of the imagination with disastrous effects . . . Hence the Bible's determination to sanctify and compel literal belief in the past.

Meir Sternberg, *The Poetics of Biblical Narrative*

7

YHWH in the Exodus Narrative: the Self-Determining Self Who is also a Desisting, Forbearing Self

Thus far the account has rendered God determining himself to be present within the constitution of the world, and therefore in personal relationship with us, humankind. Employing the ideas of Nicholas Wolterstorff, I argued that this must mean that God is in time – in our time – or, at the very least, coincident with the events that are occurring in the present (and which we experience in the present tense, so to speak). Otherwise, God could not be in personal relationship with us. More controversially, though I argued that the biblical witness of God's determining himself to be present within the constitution of the world implied a temporal contiguity or proximity with us – and cited Wolterstorff's arguments as a means of vouchsafing for the rationality of this temporality – I also argued that it implied that he had determined himself to be in a place within the world. He determined himself to be the creator of heaven and earth – that which constitutes the cosmos in total – and in doing so (on the seventh day of creation), determined himself to be in the place we term "heaven." God is not merely temporally located within our world but also – in the sense in which he determines to be the case – in a place within our world (and acting from this place within our world), though this does not necessarily entail a spatial location that can be defined by geometrical description, be it Euclidean, Riemanian, or whatever. It is enough that "God determines himself to be in a place in this world" – "in the cosmos (all that is)" – is a logically consistent claim, and not a contradictory or impossible claim.

What I now want to do is to turn to the narratives of the Old Testament which make claim to the fact that what Israel was experiencing in her life was precisely YHWH acting in that life, beginning with the exodus from Egypt. I will ask the question, Is it rational to affirm the narrative-claims of such experience as it is narrated in the Old Testament? Can we do this? The basic answer I will give is that we can. It is rational to affirm this experience because what it is experience of is true, and this because God determined himself to be such that it is so, is true. Crucially of course, the last claim has to be rational, which, I will say, it is.

Von Rad published a famous paper in 1936 entitled "The Theological Problem of the Old Testament Doctrine of Creation" in which he argued that the doctrine of creation was ancillary to the doctrine of salvation in Israel's Scriptures and history. Israel first knew of YHWH as a saving identity and only later inferred that this God was the creator of all things. But Von Rad also noted that what was crucial to the identity of this God under both descriptions was that he was not a God who acted without speaking. Von Rad wrote: "Just as this chapter [of Genesis] knows of nature as created by God's word, so the Old Testament knows history also as created by God's word. See Isa. 9.7; 55.10ff; Jer.23.29, but also 1 Kings 2.27 etc." (Von Rad, *Genesis*, 52). If we put this observation in terms of the Priestly writer as the "author" of the Genesis 1 – 2.4a creation narrative, we can say that the Priestly writer can be imagined extrapolating backwards from the characteristic manner of YHWH's action in the world to that of the creation of all things. God's action in the world is never without his locutionary action of speaking; ergo, thought the Priestly writer, God's action of creating the world is never without the locutionary action of speaking. Divine speaking in biblical narrative and in Old Testament narrative in particular is crucial to the identity of God. Without the reference to divine speaking and intention in the Old Testament, what we have there – even with miracles – falls short of a theological conception of history.[1]

---

[1] I am reminded of Aquinas's claim in the *Summa* (Question 178, article 2) that the wicked cannot work miracles; the latter are the province of good and moral agents. One of Aquinas's intentions may be to be able

Israel extrapolated back from her historical experience of YHWH acting as a soteriological identity to YHWH the creator of all things, to YHWH who is God, the creator of all things. In the canonical shape of the Old Testament this is reflected in the Priestly creation narrative of Genesis 1.1 – 2.4a. But what the Priestly narrator saw, in the narrative tradition of YHWH the soteriological identity, was precisely a connection between a God who spoke and a God who acted. Though one might argue that God did not have to speak in order to act (locutionary actions were a contingent means to the illocutionary end), without the concomitant speaking there was only uninterpretable history and uninterpretable "created being." Accordingly, what the Priestly writer produced in his creation narrative was a God who acted through his speaking. That is say, it was precisely through his speaking that God became the creator of all things: "'Let there be light' – and there was light." It was precisely in his speaking that God, in parallel with his action in the world, announced what he was doing and that he was doing it. That is to say: the Priestly narrator is also a redactor of the tradition in which YHWH is narrated as a soteriologcal identity – principally the exodus tradition. It is not an untoward deduction that the creation narrative intimated the way in which God acted in the world, in the life of Israel. God determined himself to be "the one who created all things"; he determined himself to be "the one who released Israel from the bondage of Egypt." Both descriptions are what philosophers call definite descriptions – uniquely identitifying descriptions which uniquely identify the God of Israel. And just as the former description becomes true in virtue of God speaking (as described in Chapters 1 and 2 of this

---

[1] (*continued*) to – as much as is possible – move epistemologically from knowledge of miraculous event to knowledge of God as executor of this miraculous event. I take the view that this cannot be done. In the realm of possible-world semantics it is surely possible to posit a world in which miracles happen without it being the case that this world was created by God (or that these miracles were done by God). What makes the difference is that God speaks in one world (the one he created precisely by speaking) and thereby acts in it, but doesn't in the other (even though this latter world does not exclude the miraculous). See Aquinas, *Summa Theologiae*, Part I, Q178.

book) then so the latter description likewise becomes true, that is also in virtue of God speaking. Without the concomitant speaking there is only uninterpretable history. God determines himself to be the one who released Israel from the bondage of Egypt. And he does this through his speaking, no more but no less. This is not to say that God cannot act without speaking; nor is it to say that he cannot speak without acting (though speaking in the world is always at the very least communicative action: God does not waste words) – but it is to say that there are no actions which emanate from a mute God in all his encounters with Israel. And it is to say that God can act in his speaking if in it he determines himself to be the one who will act in the life of Israel. If God says to Moses at Exodus 6:2–9 ". . . I will bring you out from under the yoke of the Egyptians. I will free you from being slaves to them . . ." then – given that this happens – it can be said that he determines himself to be the one who will rescue them from their labors in Egypt. Therefore he does rescue them from their labors in Egypt.

Who is this God who acts through divine self-determination? The identity of YHWH is a judging yet desisting, forebearing self. He is this throughout Old Testament narrative but he is this principally and foundationally in the exodus narrative.

Hermeneutical contexts: premodern, modern, postcritical

Prior to the Enlightenment, it could be said that the Judeo-Christian tradition read the Old Testament narratives from Genesis through to Ezra for its plain sense and therefore as one continuous historical narrative committed to a sequence of events subsumed under a theological conception of history:

In the beginning God created the world, humankind fell, Abraham was called, Isaac, Jacob, Joseph, the people of Israel in Egypt, Moses, exodus, wilderness, Sinai, settlement in the land of Israel, the time of the judges, the rise of the monarchy, David, Solomon, the united kingdom of north and south, the divided kingdom, the demise of the northern kingdom at the hands of Assyrian conquest in 722 BC, the downfall of the southern kingdom in 587 BC and the exile from Jerusalem signalling the end of the monarchy, finally the return from exile under the beneficence of Cyrus the Great from 536 BC onwards.

A modern commentator (perhaps working with "Ockham's razor") would typically take a different view of the narrative. First, he or she might simply reject the sequence of events narrated before Israel's subjugation to Egypt, especially the primeval history and most especially the mythical history of the genesis of human sin. Second and more crucially for our purposes he or she would eliminate the theological conception of history at work in later Old Testament narrative. Neither the biblical narrator's story of Israel's exodus from Egypt nor the account of the demise and downfall of Israel and Judah respectively should be attributed to a theological conception of history in which YHWH the God of Israel acted in Israel's history. Though the events might be said to have happened (though not necessarily exactly as described in the narratives), they came about without any intentionality on the part of any God of Israel. Hence, they can be explained in accordance with an entirely naturalistic set of assumptions.

Contrary to this view I am going to argue that divine self-determination undergirds the rationality of the claims made in biblical narrative regarding God's action in history. Though I do not want to say that a naturalistic or "secular" understanding is itself irrational, ultimately, what my theory will juxtapose is what I take to be the two fundamental explanatory concepts in Old Testament narrative: on the one hand, YHWH's *divine self-determination* and, on the other, the people of Israel's *historical experience* of YHWH's speaking and acting in the world. Crucially, I do not want to say that "the people of Israel's historical experience of YHWH acting in her life" implies "YHWH acted in the people of Israel's life."[2] I take it to be the case that one can

---

[2] When Brevard Childs focuses on the canonical shape internal to this narrative he means a specific composite nature he identifies as constituted of the individual contributions of the priestly and yahwist versions (and also the Elohist version) of the deliverance at sea. See Childs, *Exodus*, 23. This canonical shaping he would argue alerts one to the presence of different narrative view-points – of different layers of canonical shaping superimposed on one another – concealed as it were within the surface of the continuous narrative. Crucially: the fact that

understand oneself as experiencing something without it necessarily being the case that this something exists. Accordingly, I take the concept of divine self-determination to be the *more* fundamental concept in that it provides for the *greater* rationality of the claim to historical experience of YHWH than does the concept of historical experience on its own.

In the context of the exodus narrative and, in particular, the "deliverance at the Reed Sea" – which is a central subject of this chapter – this means that, as the Priestly writer might have understood it, the J account on its own was not a complete account of "the deliverance at sea." It did not make an explanatory reference to divine action inclusive of the communicative context provided by the divine speaking.[3] It was essentially an

---

[2] *(continued)* the Priestly writer redacts the Yahwist narrative – and not the other way round – means that our understanding of the final form of the text, the canonical text, has to be informed by the redactional history of the historical formation of Old Testament scripture. This seems to me to be the fundamental difference between Childs' canonical approach and the pre-critical tradition of interpretation one finds in Augustine, Thomas and Calvin. I follow Childs' 'post-critical' orientation in stating my case in terms of the P and J sources and redactions. In that sense, my theory is resolutely 'post-critical'. Barth too was post-critical in his approach to the literary sources of the Old Testament. See my book *Karl Barth and the Strange New World within the Bible*, revised edition, chapter 7.

[3] It has to be said that J does not often posit Israel's historical experience of YHWH without also positing the presence of God's speaking as a potential means of explanation of this experience. It would have been a hypothesis of great simplicity had this not been the case: one could then assert that P provided the explanation of the historical experience of Israel affirmed by J. Nevertheless: what P does is articulate in a much more determinate fashion is a theory (insofar as this concept is not anachronistic) connecting divine action with divine speaking. The most important – indeed paradigmatic – example of this is of course the P creation narrative. That is: P understands the creation narrative as paradigmatic for the way that God acts in the world. Hence in the cases where J has omitted – for whatever reason – to include God's speech in the narrative (as in the climactic events in Exodus 14) – P will ensure that the narrative-events are grounded in, and given their meaning by, the divine speaking.

account of Israel's historical *experience* of YHWH – a narrative written from the perspective of the people Israel – rather than from the perspective of YHWH (as P seems to have it). As the J account has it: Israel saw the marvellous work that YHWH did against the Egyptians. The people feared YHWH, and put their faith in YHWH and in his servant Moses. Crucially: it contains no narrative of God speaking. This is not to say that J did not know of its speaking therefore personal God: one only has to look at Exodus 3 to dispel that notion. But, still, it remains true that this God seems to be absent from the J narrative in chapter 14. And it is P who remedies this absence by placing the J account in the context of the speaking God who, I will argue, speaks and hence acts, but who can also in his speaking determine himself to be an identity other than the one literally implied in the action of communicative action (as in Exodus 6:2–9 as cited above).

It should be noted also that, even though P introduces a more supernaturalistic account of the deliverance at sea, the writer is at pains to place even the realm of miraculous event in the context of the divine speaking. A world in which super-naturalistic events are possible is not in itself sufficient to deduce the presence of an acting God. A world with divine speaking is. This is why the Old Testament scholar Claus Westermann described the relation between the word of God and historical event, between the word of God and history, "the basic problem" in the then "present search for understanding the Old Testament" (Westermann, *Essays in Old Testament Interpretation*, 4). Another Old Testament scholar James Barr said much the same thing when he spoke against G. E. Wright's account of divine action in the latter's *God Who Acts* on the grounds that G. E. Wright's God was essentially a God who acted without speaking in history (Barr, *Old and New in Interpretation*, 43). Von Rad also brilliantly characterized the Deuteronomistic history in terms of the relation between word and historical event (Von Rad, "Deuteronomic Theology"). As Childs put it of the Passover pericope in the context of Israel's exodus from Egypt in the following:

> The biblical writer brackets the Exodus event with a preceding and a succeeding interpretation. He does not see the exodus as "an act of

God" distinct from the "word of God" which explains it. In theological terms, the relation between act and interpretation, or event and word, is one that cannot be separated. The biblical writer does not conceive of the event as primary or "objective" from which an inferential, subjective deduction is drawn (*contra* G E Wright, *God Who Acts*, SBT, 8). The event is never uninterpreted. Conversely, a theological interpretation which sees the subjective appropriation – whether described cultically or existentially – as the primary element from which an event can be reconstructed, is again introducing a theological scheme which has no warrant in the theology of the redactor (Childs, *Exodus*, 204).

Childs' point is: to have described the events of Israel's exodus from Egypt outside of the context of God's speaking – without God's speaking to Moses as an intrinsic part of the narrative (and therefore being in personal relationship with Moses) – would have rendered Israel unable to identify who had intervened in their historical life. As we will see, to place the deliverance at sea in the ontic context of divine self-determination through divine speaking is to say precisely that God's word does explain God's act. It does explain *who* is acting.

From exodus to promised land: YHWH the judging yet forbearing divine identity

There is agreement among biblical commentators (Von Rad, Noth, Childs, to name but three) that the traditions in the pentateuchal narrative after the history of the patriarchs (inclusive of the credal statements such as Deut. 26:5ff.) can be assigned to the following individual complexes of tradition: the exodus tradition, the wilderness tradition, the Sinai tradition, the settlement tradition. There is also a consensus that the most important tradition of the Pentateuch and indeed the foundational tradition of the history of the people of Israel and its claim to be in historical relationship with the God of Israel, YHWH, is that of the exodus tradition. This explains why, as Noth puts it, "the expression 'Yahweh who brought Israel out of Egypt' very early became a *fixed formula* which occurs in widely differing contexts." The theme of "guidance out of Egypt" is, according to Noth, *"a primary confession* of Israel." YHWH is "the one who led Israel out of Egypt" (Noth, *History of Pentateuchal Traditions*, 23).

Intrinsic to the narrative presentation of YHWH "guiding Israel out of Egypt" is God's action in delivering Israel from the Reed Sea – the miracle of the Reed Sea – one of God's "great and terrible acts," one of his "signs and wonders." But though Noth argues that the activity of YHWH in this confessional formula originally seems in fact to have referred to "the destruction of the Egyptians in the Sea" (Noth, *Exodus*, 104), there is also evidence in the final form of the text that the theme of deliverance at sea simultaneously functions as the thematic point of departure for the narrative which succeeds it: the "wilderness" narrative culminating in the approach and occupation of the promised land. Indeed this seems to have been its original context within the J (or JE) account.

As this latter narrative presents it, what we have, among other things, is *a saving history which is one and the same event extending from, and beginning with, the deliverance from Egypt at the Reed Sea and ending with the settlement tradition in the land of Canaan* (cf. Von Rad, *Old Testament Theology*, vol. 1, 281).

It is because of this fact that one can argue that the experience Israel has of YHWH acting in this history is precisely of a judging yet forbearing, saving God. The Reed Sea account becomes an act of God's faithfulness toward Israel in the face of Israel's lack of faith in her God. In this sense it can be argued that Israel's lack of faith – intensifying as it does into disobedience and rebellion right up to the approach to the promised land (Num. 21:4) – constitutes the primary hermeneutical context to God's saving action. This is the reason the "murmuring" tradition against YHWH's action of "leading them out of Egypt" is a central datum of the wilderness tradition. What begins as a thematic of faithlessness in God's provision becomes – after the golden calf incident – a thematic of disobedience and (repeated) rebellion against God.

Yet God desists from withdrawing his saving action. Though the wilderness is pictured as "a series of very great crises" in which YHWH has to ponder the nature and continuation of his relationship with Israel in the context of judgement and divine wrath (he refuses to lead Israel any further in person due to the fact that his holiness would result in annihilation for his sinful people), he does not abandon his saving history but sets up mediating institutions (the angel of the Lord, the holy tent, etc.) in order to remain in personal relationship with Israel (Von Rad, *Old Testament Theology* vol. 1, 284; 288).[4]

In the context of the "murmuring" tradition in the wilderness, the occupation tradition – understood from the perspective of Israel's highly theological conception of history – testifies no less unambiguously than the deliverance phenomenon to the

---

[4] Von Rad argues that there are two different traditions present within the Pentateuch and the rest of the Old Testament, e.g., the difference between Jer. 2 and Ezek. 20. The first tradition puts the emphasis on God's marvellous signs and wonders succouring Israel in the desert. In contrast, the second puts the emphasis on Israel's faithlessness and sin (Von Rad, *Old Testament Theology*, vol. 1, 280–89). But, in this context, it is clear that the "murmuring" tradition takes the form of two related but distinct stereotyped patterns (Childs, *Exodus*, 258–62). Pattern 1 takes the form of a genuine need (such as food or water) which is followed by a complaint, then by an intercession on the part of Moses, which issues in the need being met by God's miraculous intervention. Pattern 2 takes the form of an initial complaint (without the basis of a genuine need) which is followed by God's anger and punishment (judgement), then an intercession from Moses, and finally a reprieve of the punishment. The cry of the people of Israel narrated by Exod. 14:11–13 exemplifies the former pattern while their behaviour as they approach the promised land (Num. 21:4) is indicative of the latter pattern. Further evidence of the stereotyped shaping of this material is the fact that the murmuring stories of Pattern 1 before the golden calf incident are all of Pattern 1; whereas the same stories after the great apostasy are all of Pattern 2. Both patterns are equally old. Hence the later commentary on the tradition, notably Jer. 2 (emphasizing Pattern 1 and God's marvellous saving actions); and Pss. 78; 106; 136; Ezek. 20 (emphasizing Pattern 2 and Israel's identity as "a defiant faithless crowd" [Von Rad, *Old Testament Theology*, vol. 1, 283]), are not in any sense incompatible. What we have is the narrators' focus equally on the human actions and the divine. Indeed, Ezekiel's take on the wilderness period as "a type and pattern of the coming judgement" of the Babylonian exile of 586 BC (Von Rad, *Old Testament Theology*, vol. 1, 283), can be understood within the context of the theological conception of history identified in terms of YHWH's judging yet forbearing identity.

judging yet ultimately soteriological identity of the God of Israel. For, ultimately, even in the wake of Israel's disobedience and rebellion and God's reactive judgement, God remains faithful to his people. The crossing of the Reed Sea coalesces in the biblical imagination with the crossing of the Jordan River. In this way the "guidance out of Egypt" theme and the "guidance into the arable land" theme (the settlement or occupation) constitute the *terminus a quo* and the *terminus ad quem* respectively of the one saving historical event in which Israel's experience of its God is the one who shows gracious forbearance to her even in his judgement of her.

The Reed Sea narrative

Nevertheless, as Noth points out, there is a tradition present in Exodus in which the theme of "guidance out of Egypt" does culminate with the "deliverance at the sea" theme (Noth, *History of Pentateuchal Traditions*, 51). In effect, the latter theme is brought – and it is rational to say that it is the work of the Priestly narrator – into closer relationship with the exodus out of Egypt. The P narrative construes the deliverance theme as the culminating event in Israel's exodus from Egypt, recapitulating the great creative acts of redemption out of chaos in the Priestly creation narrative, and in this way placing the emphasis on YHWH's saving divine action at the heart of Israel's earliest tradition. (It might be said that the Priestly narrative puts the emphasis more on the soteriological identity of God than on his judgement *per se*.) Undoubtedly, however, this final form of the narrative affirms a theological conception of history in which God and God alone effects Israel's release from Egypt.

In the J account the crossing of the Reed Sea is depicted as the effect of "natural causes" (strong east wind, dry seabed, panic among the Egyptians). By comparison, the later P account is "supernaturally" orientated (splitting of the sea, wall of water, etc.). This has suggested to the modern critical reader the theory that the original crossing was the result of "a series of natural events, and that the later writer sought to articulate the theological *meaning* of this event by extending the imagery into the supernatural" (Childs, *Exodus*, 228). But since the J account of the crossing is embedded in the extended soteriological narrative of Israel's journey toward the promised land, it is only *relatively* less concerned than P with putting emphasis on the divine action in this event.

The modern account, focusing as it does on a supposed historical development within the text from natural to supernatural, allows "the modern biblical theologian to speak of the great act of God at the exodus in delivering his people while at the same time to regard the event historically as little more than the accidental escape of some slaves across a treacherous marsh" (Childs, *Exodus*, 228). In this account, there is only one event which begins and ends in the realm of natural causes, and which at best is identified wholly with "God's act," and "God's act" wholly with it.

This is not the witness of the final form of the text. It aligns the two levels of divine activity in the final form of the text in a way that combines "ordinary and wonderful elements" (Childs, *Exodus*, 228.) As Childs puts it: "There never was a time when the event was only understood as ordinary, nor was there a time when the supernatural absorbed the natural . . . Israel saw the mighty hand of God at work in both the ordinary and the wonderful, and never sought to fragment the one great act of redemption into parts" (Childs, *Exodus*, 238). We might say that the P narrative is more concerned with narrating the event from God's perspective (from within the narrative context of "God present within the constitution of the world"); whereas the J narrative gives an account of the divine activity from Israel's perspective, and her historical experience thereof. The emphasis in the P narrative on God's perspective coincides with the locus of divine action, which in turn is to be identified among other things with the divine speaking.

Divine self-determination with or without historical supernaturalism!

There is an exact parallel here with what was said in Chapter 2 regarding God determining himself be the creator of all things with or without natural theology. To recapitulate: that God determines himself to be the creator of all things does not rule out the possibility of natural theology since divine self-determination does not rule out God leaving his "fingerprint" on creation. But neither does it entail it; God can determine himself to be the creator of all things without leaving his "fingerprint" on creation. This is because God's self-determining action is basic and sufficient.

Supernatural events in history are the historical counterparts of divine fingerprints in nature. They are not necessary conditions of God determining himself to be the one who acts in the world. Neither are they sufficient conditions; for, according to this account, they do not entail that God has determined himself to be the one who acts in the world. Therefore, it cannot be natural or supernatural categories that make God's act *God's act*; it is God's self-determination that is wholly determinative of God's act. Since divine *self*-determination is sufficient, the former categories, especially the supernatural, are unnecessary; it is not the supernatural *per se* which makes God's act *God's act* (it is God determining himself, thus says the biblical witness).

This cuts the ground away from those who want to argue that God's action in the world is of itself supernatural. This would be the case only were it true that God determining himself to be the one who does this or that action were of itself a supernatural action. But within a doctrine of God in which divine self-determination rules supreme as an expression of God's omnipotence, it would not make sense to describe such self-determination as supernatural; it would be to commit a naïve category-mistake. All God's self-determining actions are equally effortless.

A similar point has been made regarding the comparison between God's creating the world and God acting in the same world he created. There is no conceptual distinction to be made as regards the power and might of God in his creation of the world over that of his soteriological history *vis-à-vis* the people of Israel. From our "all too human" perspective we are naturally inclined to think that the power and energy involved in creating the world – the universe, all that is – is a great deal more than that involved in judging and saving Israel. But in fact as Meir Sternberg points out, the pattern of repetition, and in particular, the laconicism of spoken word and fulfilment, in the Priestly narrative – "and God said, 'Let there be . . .' and there was" – is indicative of the effortless manner ("God need not exert Himself to work wonders" to quote Sternberg) in which God creates the world (Sternberg, *Poetics of Biblical Narrative*, 111). The implication to be drawn from this is that God's self-determination is as sufficient and as effortless in one context as it is in the other.

Accordingly, to say that the manner in which God created the world is qualitatively identical to the way in which he interacts with his people, the people of Israel, and humankind in general, is to say that concepts of might and power – which might well apply in a scientific context – are inapplicable in the context of the doctrine of God in a biblical context (except of course as a description of that very effortlessness).

Divine self-determination in a world with laws of nature!

In the wake of Newton's discovery of mechanical laws of the universe, the Enlightenment (and, in particular, those of a deistic outlook) thought it much easier to conceive of God creating the world than of his acting in the world. God's action in creating the world was free in a fundamental way that his action in the world was not: the former was not faced with the seemingly inflexible unbending obstacle that God himself had imprudently and short-sightedly (so it appeared) placed in his own way when it came to his intention to act in the world. From the vantage point of his own laws of nature, it seemed that his action in the world was constrained in a way that his action to create the world was not. Accordingly, philosophers (and scientists) found the conception of God creating the world rather more tractable than his acting in it. Creating the world didn't require a miraculous deed; acting in the world did. Therein lay the problem.

To begin and end the story of God, as deists did, at the creation of the world ran counter both to Von Rad's insight of the historical formation of Israel's belief about its God and to the history of canonical shaping. Israel first knew its God as "the one who released it from the bondage of Egypt." It first knew its God acting in the world, in its historical life. From its perspective, identifying God of Israel as the creator of all things already presupposed belief that this same God had acted in the people "Israel's" historical life. If attributing the latter action to this God was irrational then the question, whether the former action was rational, could not arise. If it was not rational to affirm this God acting in the world, one could not ask whether this God (the one formerly believed to be "the one who released Israel from the bondage of Egypt") was also the creator of the world itself.

The question, whether laws of nature pose a problem for divine action, obviously doesn't arise in the case of the creation of the world. The question, whether laws of nature pose a problem for divine action in the world, clearly does (unless we reject the claim that such regularities exist).

Divine self-determination is both basic and sufficient for it to be the case that God does what he determines himself to do. This means that it is divine self-determination and divine self-determination alone that determines whether God can do or does this or that action. Divine self-determination is solely a matter of divine omnipotence – of what God "does to himself" (he determines *himself*, nothing else) – and not the laws of nature. The existence of the laws of nature poses no more a constraint on divine action in the world than their non-existence places on divine action in creating the world. With effortless economy, divine self-determination provides a persuasive explanation why this is so. God can certainly observe the laws of nature he has created, but he is not in any way bound by them. The latter would be the case only were such laws or regularities able to interfere with his self-determination. But since this is a matter solely for himself – that is, independent of anything else at all – they cannot. The beauty of the theory is precisely that, if divine self-determination is sufficient in itself, then this must mean that it is so regardless of the nature of created being (regardless, for example, whether there are laws of nature or not).[5]

---

[5] Hence, to take the case of God's resurrection of the man Jesus from the dead: it is often said that is this is a violation of an extremely obvious law of nature, namely: dead men don't rise from the grave. But clearly the more pertinent theological question is, Can God determine himself to be the one who raised Jesus from the dead? And the question then is, Is it any more difficult for God to determine himself to be the

Three modes of divine self-determination in the world

In the exodus narrative God both acts in the world by speaking and by acting in the world without speaking – though the latter never occurs outside of the context of a speaking God. How does this occur? God determines himself to be the one who speaks in the world – God speaking is always God acting in history because it is his determining himself to be the one who says what he says in history. God can also determine himself to be one who does things (speechlessly, as it were) in the world. In order to act in the world other than by speaking in it, God has only to determine himself to be the one who acts in such-and-such a way. These two modes are perhaps the most common ways of God acting in the world.

But I do not rule out the possibility that God speaking in the world can also simultaneously be God determining himself to be this or that personal historical identity, acting in history otherwise than simply in his speaking – precisely to be "the one who releases Israel from the bondage of Egypt." If God says to Moses at Exodus 6.2–9, ". . . I will bring you out from under the yoke of the Egyptians. I will free you from being slaves to them" then – in addition to the fact that he determined himself to be the one who says, ". . . I will bring you out from under the yoke of the Egyptians. I will free you from being slaves to them" – it can be said that he determines himself to be the one who will rescue them from their labors in Egypt. Therefore, he *is* the one who will rescue them from their labors in Egypt. Therefore, he *does* rescue them from their labors in Egypt (if it is true that one *will do* something then it follows that one *does it*). Therefore YHWH *acts* in personal and historical relationship to the people of Israel. And he had done this in this case merely by speaking – no more no less – since his speaking is his determining himself to be this historical-personal self. God's speaking is not mere event, it is also, crucially, action. And we can say that it is action because it is God

---

[5] (*continued*) one who raises Jesus from the dead than it is for him to determine himself to be the one who answers your prayer? Or do anything else for that matter? The answer is that God's action is equally effortless in all cases, inside or outside the ontic context of the regularities of nature.

determining himself to be this or that historical identity. The disanalogy with human speaking is fundamental and complete. My speaking can never be my action in God's sense since if I said what God said, for example, at Exodus 6.2–9 it would *not* be my determining myself to be the one who will lead Israel out of Egypt. And without this implication in operation my words are powerless by comparison. Given the nature of God as divine agent, God's speaking is not meant to be construed as any ordinary human speaking. He doesn't have to do anything other than determine himself to be the one who says what he says (we have to do much else in order to determine ourselves to be the ones who say what we say; our speaking is not a basic action in this sense). To repeat: there is no warrant in biblical narrative for positing an exact analogy between divine and human speaking in the Bible in the context of a theory or doctrine of divine action.

I submit that the simple litmus test of this doctrine of divine action is that if it is a logically consistent explanation as regards the creation of the world, then there is no reason why it should not be equally so in the case of divine action within the world. Just as God's act of self-determination is both basic and sufficient for it to be the case that the world was created by God then so God's self-determination is both basic and sufficient for it to be the case that God acts in the world (what I am in fact doing is transposing this account of the mechanics of God's action in creation to God's action within the constitution of the world). There is the premise that God determined himself to be the one who delivered Israel from the bondage of Egypt and there is the logically deduced conclusion that Israel was delivered from the bondage of Egypt by God. In other words – as in the case of creation – God determining himself to be the one who delivered Israel from Egypt entails that God delivered Israel from Egypt. He is the one who delivered the people "Israel" from the bondage of Egypt. Therefore it is rational for the narrator of the final form of Exodus to affirm that God – YHWH – led the people of Israel out of Egypt.

Is the theory paradoxical? Decidedly, yes – but not I think contradictory. Imagine, not that your actions are the instrumental cause of Israel's release from Egypt, but that you in your actions are in the process of determining yourself to be the one who frees or will free Israel from Egypt, and that therefore you *are* the one who frees or will free Israel from Egypt; and that therefore – as a matter of logic – Israel *has* been delivered from Egypt by you (you cannot be the one who delivered Israel from Egypt and it not be the case that Israel was delivered from Egypt by you). Imagine this and then you may grasp what might be the deepest implication of what it means to say that God determining *himself* to be this historical identity is basic and sufficient for him to be that historical identity. At bottom it may mean that God has no need for the world or Israel or Egypt to exist for it to be the case that he determine himself to be the one who saves the people "Israel" from the labors of Egypt. Of course, given the human condition you can only do it in your imagination. God can do – and did – it in reality.

The normative (philosophical) status of Israel's historical experience of YHWH's identity

Childs' exposition of the relationship between word and event in the context of the exodus narrative can be extended to Israel's experience of YHWH's identity in the wilderness tradition (although Childs is speaking specifically about the exodus above, he argues that there are lessons here for our understanding of the final form of the text writ large). What makes it rational to affirm Israel's historical experience told from this narrative viewpoint? What makes it rational to affirm this theological conception of Israel's history as outlined above? William Alston might say that Israel's experience can be affirmed in and of itself. I want to say that what makes for a more rational story is to understand it within the context of the Priestly creation narrative and what God determines to be true of himself at the culmination of the creation history. God determines himself to remain in personal relationship with humankind in unconditional fashion, from within the constitution of the world, both temporal and locational. The narrative viewpoint delineated in Exodus tells of a God who remains faithful to Israel even in the context of the crisis of judgement brought on by Israel's rebellion. Hence, were Israel to experience judgement – and this is the claim of her Scriptures – it would occur within the final horizon of an ultimately soteriological divine identity.

Next question: What makes it rational to affirm Israel's experience of YHWH's identity as a judging yet desisting forbearing God? The answer is that Israel experiences YHWH as a judging yet desisting forbearing identity because that is what God determines himself to be in this historical-temporal relation. This is what makes the claim true. The modern epistemological question (understood in the context of knowledge defined as true, justified, belief) is, How does Israel know that God determines himself in the way that makes it true that what Israel experiences in the "historical moment" is true? This question is an anachronistic one, biblically speaking. It is not a claim that Scripture recognizes it has to answer, or reckons it has to answer, even.

Rather, the final form of the text – and fundamentally the canonical shaping provided by the Priestly creation narrative – supplied its own answer in the following way. The affirmation of Israel's historical experience of YHWH as experience of YHWH as a judging, desisting, forbearing God is rational because YHWH determined himself to be this self in his historical-temporal relation there and then with Israel. This is the fundamental rationale behind the plain sense of God speaking to Israel, declaring himself to Israel. That is also the fundamental significance of the canonical "ontic priority" of the Priestly creation narrative. We have a way of understanding how (it comes about that) the biblical affirmation of Israel's experience is true. Within the context of having determined himself to be present within the constitution of the world, it would be irrational to think that God would not thereafter *act* within the constitution of the world, act within the context of determining himself to be the creator of the one with whom he could be in personal relationship. It is irrational to think that God would simply "exist" within the world. But what makes it true is that God determines himself to be such that it is true. This is to put it at its most abstract. In its most concrete form we would say that God determines himself to be this judging yet desisting, forbearing God; therefore he is this self, and he is this in temporal-personal relation to the people of Israel.

Not only is it rational to affirm YHWH as "the one who led Israel out of Egypt"; it is also rational to affirm YHWH's identity as the one who is "compassionate and gracious . . . slow to anger, abounding in love and faithfulness, maintaining love to thousands, and forgiving wickedness, rebellion and sin. Yet he does not leave the guilty unpunished" (Exod. 34:6b–7).

Concluding remarks

The precritical tradition *was* rational to affirm a theological conception of history in these narratives. But, among other things, this rationality is based not in terms of the claims in the individual narrative itself (in contradistinction to the premodern tradition), but rather in terms of the canonical shaping that is brought to bear on these narratives in virtue of the redaction of the Pentateuch by the Priestly writer, and in particular the effect the textual priority the Priestly creation narrative has on the rest of the Old Testament. For example, let us suppose that there was a Yahwist who affirmed the theological conception of history at work in the tradition-complex that is the exodus story (Exod. 1 – 14). What makes it *rational* to affirm the Yahwist's affirmation is that Genesis 2:1–3 tells of God determining himself to be present within the temporal constitution of the world such that he is in personal relationship with humankind. Given this action it follows that God is temporally present within the constitution of this world in the sense that he is temporally coincident with all the events that occur in it. He also determines himself to be in a place within the constitution of the world, though not in a place definable by spatial coordinates. It is from this place that he determines himself to be the one who leads the people of Israel out of Egypt; ergo, it is true that he leads the people of Israel out of Egypt. Hence Israel's claim that this is what they experienced in the exodus is a rational claim.

Though it might seem as if any divine intention to act in the world would be frustrated by the unyielding obduracy of the laws of nature – a restriction not imposed upon the creation of the world (for obvious reasons) – this is not so for the very reason that divine self-determination is both basic and sufficient for it to be the case that God does what he determines himself to do. To repeat: the beauty of the theory is precisely that, if divine self-determination is sufficient in itself, then this must mean that it is so regardless of the nature of created being (regardless, for example, whether there are laws of nature or not). Logic is very powerful (to quote the great twentieth-century mathematician Kurt Gödel)! Unifying divine action in creating the world and divine action in the world under the one explanatory concept of divine self-determination enables the systematic theologian to begin his theological reflection at the point at which Von Rad began his theological reflection on the Old Testament. That locus is the exodus narrative, *in medias res*. We begin with God's action in the world.

Bibliography

Aquinas, *The Aquinas Catechism: A Simple Explanation of the Catholic Faith by the Church's Greatest Theologian* (Manchester, New Hampshire: Sophia Institute Press, 2000); *Summa Theologiae*. In *Basic Writings of Saint Thomas Aquinas*, edited by Anton Pegis (New York: Random House, 1945).

Barr, James, *Old and New in Interpretation: A Study of the Two Testaments* (London: SCM, 1982).

Childs, Brevard, *Biblical Theology of the Old and New Testaments: Theological Reflection on the Christian Bible* (London: SCM, 1992); *Exodus, a Commentary* (London: SCM, 1974).

Feynman, Richard P., Robert B. Leighton and Matthew Sands, *The Feynman Lectures on Physics: Vol. III, Quantum Mechanics* (Reading, Massachusetts: Addison-Wesley, 1965).

Jenson, Robert W., *Systematic Theology*, vol. 1 (Oxford: Oxford University Press, 1997).

MacDonald, Neil B., *Karl Barth and the Strange New World within the Bible: Barth, Wittgenstein, and the Metadilemmas of the Enlightenment*, rev. ed. (Carlisle: Paternoster, 2001).

Noth, Martin, *Exodus, a Commentary* (London: SCM, 1962); *A History of Pentateuchal Traditions* (Englewood Cliffs, New Jersey: Prentice-Hall, 1972).

Piaget, Jean, *Genetic Epistemology* (New York: Columbia University Press, 1970).

Rad, Gerhard von, "The Deuteronomic Theology of History in 1 and 2 Kings," *The Problem of the Hexateuch and Other Essays* (London: SCM, 1984), 205–21; *Genesis*, translated by J. Bowden, 3rd ed. (London: SCM, 1972); *Old Testament Theology*, vols. 1 and 2 (London: SCM, 1975); "The Theological Problem of the Old Testament Doctrine of Creation," *The Problem of the Hexateuch and Other Essays* (London: SCM, 1984), 131–42.

Sternberg, Meir, *The Poetics of Biblical Narrative: Ideological Literature and the Drama of Reading* (Bloomington: Indiana Press, 1985).

Westermann, Claus, *Essays in Old Testament Interpretation* (London: SCM, 1963).

Wright, G. Ernest, *God Who Acts: Biblical Theology as Recital* (London: SCM, 1952).

8

God and the Primeval History

In his magisterial *The History of the Pentateuchal Traditions*, Martin Noth wrote that "the entire weight of the theology of J rests upon" his primeval history and that "it sufficed for [J] to have said plainly how he intended to understand everything beyond that" such that "he then held firmly – almost without exception to the received material of the Pentateuchal narrative, without intervening into its content to modify and expand" (Noth, *History*, 239). Von Rad had earlier (1938) concluded that the Yahwist took over an existing sequence of events – divine election of the patriarchs, deliverance from Egypt, and the occupation – and augmented it in three ways: by prefixing the primeval history, by developing the patriarchal history (Deut. 26:5 mentions only one patriarch), and by developing the Sinai tradition (Von Rad, "Form-Critical Problem," 53–74). But Noth argued that two of these additions – the understanding of the patriarchs as a series of generations (Abraham, Isaac, and Jacob) and the linkage of the exodus tradition with the Sinai one – had already been made. Hence, according to Noth, the Yahwist had added one rather than three traditions: precisely the primeval history.

If Noth is right two important points would follow immediately. The first is that if we were to delineate a determinate thematic at work in the primeval history – what might even be called "the theology of the Yahwist" – it would be possible to say that this was the thematic in terms of which he understood those subsequent narrative traditions whose subject-matter was Israel's historical experience of being in personal relationship with YHWH. The most obvious example in this respect is of course the exodus narrative.

The second is that we could be relatively certain that the Yahwist as a "canonical redactor" in this sense had not interpolated into the tradition an alien eisegetical consciousness. His own canonical intentionality had not erased the original intentionality behind the exodus narrative or the wilderness narrative, and so on. The Yahwist had intended the primeval history to have a "forward" trajectory in that it is meant to tell us how he understood the exodus narrative for example; and how we should understand the exodus narrative. But this also meant that the exodus narrative in turn could tell us how the Yahwist understood the primeval history; and how we should understand that same history.

The remarkable intertextual (perhaps intratextual) exegetical fact is that just as the identity of YHWH in the exodus narratives is that of a judging yet desisting, forbearing God then so the identity of YHWH in the primeval history is also that of a judging yet desisting, forbearing God. YHWH is pictured not merely as a judging yet desisting God toward Israel, YHWH is depicted as a judging yet desisting God toward the human race as a whole, toward humankind. His soteriological identity is revealed in its universalist dimensions. God desisted from the beginning.

The theology of J: YHWH, the judging yet desisting, forbearing God of the primeval history

The theme of a judging yet desisting, forbearing divine identity is central to the theological intention of the Yahwist in his redaction and linkage of originally independent traditions into the one primeval history of Genesis 2 – 11. In this respect, Von Rad's majestic characterization of the Yahwistic primeval history is worth quoting at length:

> The Yahwistic narrator has told the story of God and man from the time mankind began, and this story is characterized by an increase in sin to avalanche proportions. The sins of Adam and Eve, Cain, Lamech, the angel marriages, the Tower of Babel – these are stages along that way which has separated man farther and farther from God. This succession of narratives, therefore, points out a

continually widening chasm between God and man. But God reacts to these outbreaks of human sin with severe judgements. The punishment of Adam and Eve was severe; severer still was Cain's. Then follows the Flood, and the final judgement was the Dispersion, the dissolution of mankind's unity. Thus at the end of the primeval history a difficult question is raised: God's future relationship to his rebellious humanity, which is now scattered in fragments. Is the catastrophe of ch. 11.1–9 final? We shall postpone an answer for the moment (Von Rad, *Genesis*, 152).

Yet, this is not the whole or even the primary story for Von Rad:

The Yahwistic narrator shows something else along with the consequences of divine judgement. Adam and Eve remain alive in spite of the threat of death (ch. 2.17); indeed, God has clothed them. Thus, in all the hardship of punishment, God's activity of succour and preservation was revealed. Cain was cursed by God, to be sure, and his relationship to the earth was profoundly disturbed; but the story ends with the establishment of a mysterious protective relationship between God and Cain. He went forth from Yahweh's presence not abandoned by him but watched over and protected against being slain by a barbarous humanity. At the conclusion of the Flood story, God's will to preserve mankind becomes especially clear. God begins with man anew . . . it was almost as though God had given up; at any rate, God transferred man, in spite of his unchanged corruption (ch. 8.21), to a newly ordered world, whose natural order was solemnly guaranteed to endure. We see, therefore (already in primeval history!), that each time, in and after the judgement, God's preserving, forgiving will to save is revealed (Von Rad, *Genesis*, 152–53).

To be sure, though such concepts as "salvation," "grace," and "forgiveness" are not explicitly employed in the narrative, Von Rad does not doubt that they embody accurate discerning judgements as to what is in the text (*Genesis*, 153). He concludes: "What is described, therefore, is a story of God with man, the story of continuously new punishment and at the same time gracious preservation, the story, to be sure, of a way that is distinguished by progressive divine judgement, but that, nevertheless, man could never have travelled without continued divine preservation" (Von Rad, *Genesis*, 153).

Von Rad reads the primeval history as ever-increasing incursion of sin into human life. First there is the relatively "trivial" action of eating of the forbidden fruit; then there is the more serious crime of fratricide; then heavenly disorder; then there is the statement that humankind is evil throughout, bringing in its wake the catastrophe of a flood threatening the continued existence of the whole human race; then there is the story of the Tower of Babel which Child describes as God's threat "to return creation to a primordial chaos" (Childs, *Biblical Theology*, 120). Indeed Childs rightly depicts Von Rad's interpretation of Genesis 1 – 11 as "a history of increasing alienation from God" (Childs, *Biblical Theology*, 120). In contrast, in his *Commentary on Genesis 1 – 11* Westermann wants to argue that the primeval history is extrapolated backward from Israel's present historical experience of the reality of the human condition, and in particular, its trials and tribulations (e.g. in Gen. 3: the great pain and danger of childbirth; the toiling in the field to produce enough to live on). The primeval history is in essence "mythic" time, the events of which constitute an etiology of present human universal experience. Hence though both Von Rad and Westermann will acknowledge that the individual traditions making up the primeval history were originally independent creations from different historical contexts, they differ as regards the writer's intention in linking these distinct traditions into one unified primeval history.

The difference between Von Rad's interpretation and Westermann's can be characterized as one between a "horizontal" and a "vertical" interpretation of the primeval history (Childs, *Biblical Theology*, 120). Von Rad appears to find some temporal structure in the history in the sense that he implies that in the final form of the text one must acknowledge some kind of passage of real historical time between Genesis 1 and Genesis 11. In this sense is it a "horizontal" interpretation; and the claim that it represents an "ever-increasing incursion of human sin before God" only serves to confirm that this is the correct way to understand Von Rad. Westermann on the other hand thinks that the individual stories – Adam and Eve, Cain and Abel, etc. – represent universal humankind and provide etiological explanation of fundamental features of human existence. Hence, Cain and

Abel are really Adam and Eve out of the garden: "'Man' is not just Adam and Eve, but also Cain and Abel" (Westermann, *Genesis 1 – 11*, 318). This implies that Adam and Eve are no more "primeval" than Cain and Abel, the latter no more "primeval" than the former. According to Westermann, the essence of the primeval history is less about temporal structure and more about the origins of the fundamental ontological structures of human existence.

Temporal structure in so far as it forms part of a truth-claiming enterprise must therefore be subject to the criterion of rationality of historical truth-claim. This means treating the narrative of Genesis 2 – 11 as in some sense corresponding to the historical reality of the natural history of humankind. Traditionally of course, this is just how they were treated. The literal sense of these stories was taken to be a description of events that had really happened (Augustine, Aquinas, Luther, Calvin). Even if we feel we cannot endorse the great classical theologians' view on this in the wake of the Enlightenment, modernity can still make sense of Von Rad's claim of an "ever-increasing incursion of sin into human life." Von Rad's interpretation of Genesis 2 – 11 can be said to bear the stamp of historical authenticity in the sense that what it describes is the trajectory of the underlying "dark" centrifugal forces of the human condition that must perforce be given a narrative in time since this "typical" history of ever-increasing misrelation to, and alienation from, God, is something than can only develop in time. When the people "Israel" attributed this shape to the history of the human condition, they did not do anything irrational. The succession of generations begetting a growth in population is a plausible historical narrative; violence at the level of the nuclear family (Cain and Abel) may well have been followed by the wickedness endemic to the human race (the story of the Flood). This is the way it may well have been in the pre-Israelite universal human past. Moreover, if we understand the illocutionary stance of the primeval history as not "the way it was" but rather "the way it might well have been," we have no difficulty in endorsing Von Rad's interpretation. This is what is meant by referring to the narrative as describing a typical history. (See Wolterstorff on the application of this illocutionary stance to the claims of the gospel narratives in *Divine Discourse*, ch. 14, esp. 244–45, 249–50). But even if we were to feel that Von Rad's "historical" interpretation of Genesis 2 – 11 is too ambitious a claim, we might at the very least want to say that each individual tradition within the narrative refers to a typical history. In this sense then the narrative as a whole is not merely as Westermann would have it, "mythic" history beyond real historical time.

Supervening over the history of human alienation is the history of God the judging yet desisting, forbearing self. In the primeval history, notwithstanding their special relationship with YHWH, the people of Israel recognized their solidarity with the rest of the human race, and in particular with their ancestral ancients who populated and made their way in the world. Their external morphology or form is in nowise different from the rest of humankind, nor are their passions and appetites; their genealogies, accordingly, imply a genealogical solidarity with the rest of humankind. Nothing is new under the sun, nothing different under the human skin; what is true regarding Israel's "all too human" life is no less true of their ancestors. Their ancestors too must have been – from the very beginning – susceptible to the less attractive elements of the human condition. There never had been a golden age in the past; nor had these problematic aspects of the human psyche been removed by the passage of time and the development of civilization.

Nevertheless, Israel constituted unambiguous evidence that these same ancestors had survived to reproduce offspring (a geneticist would point out that at some period prior to the existence of the people of Israel, the then gene pool constituted 100 percent of the gene pool of this future Israel). In other words, the God who had led them out of Egypt, desisting from withdrawing his personal relationship from them, had also desisted from bringing to an end the whole human race, actual or potential. He must have done; otherwise the human race would not still be in existence but would have come to an end and Israel, genealogically speaking, could not have come into existence. The genealogies that one finds throughout the Old Testament are not only an expression, or even celebration, of the dogged survival, as it were, of Israel and Israel's ancestors; rather, they are indicative of the fact that Israel and her ancestors have gone on in history solely by the grace of God.

The genealogies of Genesis depict all of humankind as the effect of the creator's blessing, from Adam (Gen. 5), and from Noah (Gen. 10). Westermann writes that God's blessing is "effective in the quiet, steady march of growth, expansion, prosperity, and fertility" of the human race (Westermann, *Genesis 1 – 11*, 17). He notes that the divine blessing is to be "distinguished clearly from God's saving action" (Westermann, *Genesis 1 – 11*, 17). But in the context of God the judging yet desisting, forbearing self the blessings take on an additional function and imply, in the face of human misrelation, a God who wills not to cease in the most final of ways his relationship with humankind.

Just as YHWH had desisted from deserting the people "Israel" then so he had desisted from withdrawing from the human race writ large. The archetypal significance of Adam in Genesis is not that there was a first man but that had God ended this man's life, then – because he is the first man – the human race would have died out there and then. Or better, the archetypal significance of Adam and Eve is not that there was a first human couple but that had God ended their lives, then – because we are speaking of the first couple – the human race would have died out there and then. Notwithstanding the differences in dimensions of evil, the same archetypal resonance occurs in the case of the story of Noah and the flood:

> The LORD saw how great man's wickedness on the earth had become, and that every inclination of the thoughts of his heart was only evil all the time. The LORD was grieved that he had made man on the earth, and his heart was filled with pain. So the LORD said, "I will wipe mankind, whom I have created, from the face of the earth – men and animals, and creatures that move along the ground, and birds of the air – for I am grieved that I have made them." But Noah found favour in the eyes of the LORD (Gen. 6:5–8).

The words of Genesis 6:5–8 have, as Von Rad puts it, "programmatic significance, not only for the understanding of the Flood but also for the entire Yahwistic primeval history" (Von Rad, *Old Testament Theology*, 117). The heart, according to the Old Testament view, is the seat not only of the emotion, but also of the understanding and the will. The statement comprises therefore the entire inner life of humankind. According to the Yahwist it is "only evil all the time." YHWH's initial judgement is to bring to an end this human race whom he had created (as he had Adam) out of the dust of the earth. Yet, though God judges he also shows gracious forbearance. The narrative concludes with "the incomprehensible duration of the natural orders in spite of continuing human sin" (Von Rad, *Old Testament Theology*, 118).

One might also add here that had the first human couple not survived to produce offspring, Israel would not have been. Is this God "YHWH" and therefore the God of the people "Israel" prior to the creation? Is he "YHWH" as it were *ad intra*? Almost certainly the witness of Scripture is that he is.

But this also meant that the primeval history also testified to a "backward" trajectory. The Yahwist is himself one of the people "Israel" – perhaps living in the tenth century BC – and his primeval history conforms to the same divine–human pattern that he sees in action in the narratives that tell of YHWH's covenantal relationship with the people "Israel." The latter is one well described by Barth: "The Israelite who hears and reads about the Creator is to think at once of the One to whom he and his nation owe everything, against who he and his people have sinned a thousand times, but who incomprehensibly has never failed to be faithful to him and his people." (Barth, *CD* III/1, 234).[1] But it is not merely Israelite *qua* Israelite who is rebellious as regards God, it is Israelite *qua* human being who rebels or acts in misrelation toward God. The Israelite knows this in his heart. Hence, the rest of the human race, the other nations, are nowise in a position to say that had it been them instead of Israel with whom YHWH had been in personal relationship, judgement would have thereby been avoided (for we would have been obedient, Lord!). No, this is wishful thinking.

---

[1] The God who is called Yahweh by Israel is also Elohim, the God who is the creator of all things: "Israel – as is emphasized in Genesis 2 – knows and has continually to learn that its God Yahweh . . . the God of Abraham, Isaac and Jacob, is Elohim, God the Almighty Creator" (Barth, *CD* III/1, 240). (One might even say that "the God of the philosophers" biblically construed in the P creation narrative is also Yahweh, "the God of Israel").

The hermeneutics of the subjunctive conditional: the Garden of Eden

If we can say that the primeval history is in some sense "typical" history referring to the historical manifestations of the human condition, can we say the same about Genesis 3, the primal "primeval history" as it were?

I begin with the suspicion that there is a metaphysical or ontological mystery at the core of the story of the Garden of Eden and Adam and Eve's eventual departure (ejection) from it. The ontological mystery is something like the following: even had we begun human life in the most auspicious of environments and even had we been asked not to do something the benefit of which is negligible and the purported cost is infinite (the apparent penalty is death) – we would still have done it. In such a utopian environment we would still be the architects of our own downfall. We would still eat the fruit.

As James Barr has pointed out, the story of Adam and Eve, of "paradise lost", is not one in which Adam and Eve's eating of the fruit in the Garden of Eden is comparable to Prometheus willfully stealing fire from the gods in order to be like the gods.[2] Nor does it endorse the traditional Augustinian interpretation of pride, *superbia*, as the source of Adam and Eve's action (nor, indeed, Tertullian's explanation of "discontent"). Their motivation is more as Barr puts it "a mixture of physical attraction, curiosity, and insouciance or inadvertence" (Barr, *Garden of Eden*, 14). Barr continues:

> It is as if you have in your house a large switch on a wall with a notice saying "This switch must on no account be touched", and then one day there comes an imposing official with a gilded cap,

---

[2] This is one reason that the "Garden of Eden" myth should not be construed as a metaphor for the growth or maturation of humankind and initially painful though consequent and inevitable freedom from God. The Greek myth of Prometheus stealing fire from the gods was employed as a metaphor for Enlightenment freedom (think Beethoven's *Prometheus Unbound*!). The statement "they shall be as gods" seems to me to be utterly ironical; could such "comic' figures become gods!

and you ask about the switch and he says, "Well, of course they say you mustn't touch it, but they are just saying that: of course you can throw the switch, indeed the electricity will probably run all the better if you do." So of course you throw the switch and Bang! Up goes the house in smoke (Barr, *Garden of Eden*, 14).

And yet, though we are not faced with Cain's offence of the murder of his brother Abel (where the term "sin" appears for the first time [Gen. 4:7]), nor with anything like the earth filling with violence – as in the case of the generation before Noah and the flood – we do encounter in this story another example of the profundity of the Yahwist ("that theologian of genius", as Von Rad called him).

Hermeneutically, the "Garden of Eden" story operates as a subjunctive conditional.[3] (It may be said that the natural history of humankind, of the procreation of the species – of the sexes and sexual intercourse, of the passions and the appetites – begins at Genesis with Adam "knowing" his wife in the carnal sense and "begetting" the story of Cain and Abel [cf. Von Rad, *Genesis*, 103–4].[4]) A subjunctive conditional has the grammatical form: "Had p been the case then q would have been the case." So for example: "Had Smith received antibiotics, he would not have died of his infection." Such a grammatical form can also be described as a "counterfactual conditional" since each of its propositions is counterfactual to reality. The facts of the matter are that Smith did not receive antibiotics and, as a result, Smith died. So given these

---

[3] Adam is not created in the Garden. He is created outside the Garden from the dust of the earth. God then places him in the Garden. Indeed, the reference prior to God placing Adam in the Garden to the effect that there was no one to till the ground is indicative of the fact that Adam's – and humankind's – destiny is precisely to till this ground. He is made of the dust of the earth. He will go back to being this dust in death. But at the point when he is placed in the Garden the story goes into the mode of grammar characterized by the subjunctive conditional.

[4] In *Violence and the Sacred* Rene Girard makes the not unrelated point that the primordial myth of the real origins of humankind is to be found in the story of Cain and Abel, and not in Adam and Eve. Moreover, it seems the great sin is in fact violence. God wills to destroy humankind with a great flood because of the wickedness and violence at the heart of his psyche (Gen. 6:13).

facts, the following is a counterfactual conditional: "Had Smith received antibiotics (fact: Smith did not receive antibiotics) then he would not have died (fact: Smith died)."

In what specific way is the story of Adam and Eve in the Garden of Eden a subjunctive conditional? The story is essentially a deflationary tale whose moral is that even had the natural history of humankind begun life in a paradisiacal ideal state (which it did not), it would still have arrived at the less than perfect place it is now. Human pretension to perfectibility would have us believe that had we begun life in such a paradisiacal place as the Garden of Eden we would not have done the things we have done amidst the "blood, sweat, and tears" of the unyielding real world. In the wisdom of what it knows about the human condition, Genesis 3 begs to differ.

Had we found ourselves in the best of all possible worlds, which *pace* Leibniz, we do not, we would like to believe that our inner life and history and destiny would have been strikingly different from what it is in reality. Yet Genesis 3 tells us that, even had we been from the beginning in the most auspicious of environments, and even had we been told by God to forego something the cost of which was negligible if not non-existent to us (there is an abundance of fruit in the garden),[5] we would in a moment of "insouciance or inadvertence" have done the very thing that God had asked us not to do.

Putting it another way: even in the most auspicious of environments humankind could not have kept the most simple command even when it had been informed that the consequence of not doing so was the highest penalty known to it, the forfeiting of human life! There never was a golden age; but more importantly, had there been one, it would have come to an end almost immediately. That is one major moral of the story. God's restriction on the tree of knowledge of good and evil is reminiscent in

---

[5] Augustine notes this feature of the story. In his *The City of God* he writes: "The injunction forbidding the eating of one kind of food, where such an abundant supply of other foods was available, was so easy to observe, so brief to remember . . . Therefore the unrighteousness of violating the prohibition was so much the greater, in proportion to the ease with which it could have been observed and fulfilled" (Augustine, *The City of God*, Bk 14, ch. 12, 571).

its form – "you shall not eat" – of the Decalogue, the Ten Commandments, the Law. One may juxtapose here the observation that Israel's almost unthinking act in the wilderness of molding the golden calf (Exod. 32) immediately follows YHWH's prohibition against Israel having any other gods but him (Exod. 20): "they have been quick to turn away from what I commanded them" says YHWH (Exod. 32:8).

In the context of the Garden of Eden – paradise – one cannot blame the environment for one's actions. That is the simple truth of it. Can one then hold other people responsible for an action whose benefit was negligible and the purported cost infinite? Adam blames Eve, and Eve blames the serpent. At this point the story touches on the margins of the comic impulse, almost ludicrously. In such a perfect environment – when there is no possibility of blaming this best of all possible worlds – the last refuge for a "scoundrel" in this position is to attempt to absolve oneself – get oneself off the hook – by passing the responsibility to others. But in this best of all possible worlds there is no obviously explicable reason why Adam and Eve did as they did. We remain with this great ontological mystery.

One must, of course, temper any conclusion on the comic dimensions of the story with the fact that the focus of Adam and Eve's shame in their nakedness *post facto* is not so much on their action *per se* but rather on shame as "the outward sign of inner dissolution" (Childs, *Old Testament Theology*, 224–25), as "the signal of the loss of an inner unity, an insurmountable contradiction at the basis of our existence" (Von Rad, *Genesis*, 85). (It has little or nothing to do with sex and sexuality; nakedness not nudity is the issue.) One might add to this analysis the observation that shame in this context was the implicit detection of a fundamental disunity at the core of the human condition (whether or not loss coexisted as an element in this experience). Their experience of nakedness is in fact a great anthropological metaphor for a rift in the basic structures of the human ego. It is this to which they respond as in a reflex action in seeking to cover themselves up (regardless of whether they are covering up from each other or from God – though plainly, as the moment has it, it is much more the latter). Their response is plainly not one of seeking to cover up their action *per se*.

Yet if we ask what it is Adam and Eve become aware of in themselves and seek to hide from each other and especially from God, all we can say is: it is *that which was responsible for their action of eating the fruit when the benefit of this action was negligible and its cost infinite.* Put like this, the most obvious candidate of explanation might be stupidity (Adam and Eve are unable to do cost–benefit analysis!). But there is no indication of stupidity in the story – just as there is no indication of this in the story of Israel's "inexplicable" behavior in worshipping an idol immediately after being told not to by God. When Barr says that Adam and Eve's actions are motivated by "a mixture of physical attraction, curiosity, and insouciance or inadvertence" he intimates just an entirely superficial motivation even though he is clear that responsibility for their actions is clearly their own. Nevertheless behind such "trivial" springs of action may lie a more sinister aspect of the human condition which, when operative in other realms of human life, can have calamitous and utterly destructive results.

The Garden of Eden may exist only in the realm of the subjunctive conditional. *But the human beings who are put in it are real human beings; or more precisely: they are expressive of utterly real aspects of the human condition.* It is in relation to this utterly real dimension of the human condition that God demonstrates the reality of his judging yet desisting, forbearing self.

Even though the story is told according to the grammatical mood of the subjunctive conditional, it still narrates God as his characteristic self: as the judging yet desisting, forbearing divine identity. Here I return to Von Rad's insight into the soteriological dimensions of the creation story. Even though God perceives the fundamental disunity in the two who represent the origins of the human race (God does not first note that a fruit is missing from the tree but rather that Adam and Eve are hiding themselves and this because they are aware of their nakedness), he desists from doing what he said he would do at Genesis 2:17.

In 2:17 God issues the threat that were the man to eat from the tree of the knowledge of good and evil, he would – "when you eat of it . . . die." The calamitous event comes to pass but, instead of death, the result is a curse on humanity. God is narrated as declaring that the man will expend great toiling effort to little return tilling the ground for sustenance and survival (Gen. 3:17–19). For example: "By the sweat of your brow you will eat your food until you return to the ground" (Gen. 3:19a–b). The final words of the curse are: "Dust you are and to dust you will return" (Gen. 3.19c). But the curse notwithstanding: by the end of Genesis 3 we can be certain that death has not transpired as God said it would, that God has desisted from carrying out his threat.

Indeed, not only does God desist from carrying out the judgement of death (though there is palpably judgement), he clothes them in a protective manner before they take leave of the "paradisiacal" garden. Milton's description of Adam and Eve at the end of *Paradise Lost* – "through Eden took their solitary way" – must not be understood in a way that severs the pair from continuing providential guidance. YHWH–Elohim remains in personal relationship with humankind even in the face of profound human misrelation.

Excursus: Hannah Arendt and the "Banality of Evil"

In a letter to the American cultural critic Mary McCarthy, the German (naturalized American) philosopher Hannah Arendt wrote that she had written her book, *Eichmann in Jerusalem: A Report on the Banality of Evil* in a state of euphoria. In a letter to a German correspondent she explained why. Twenty years after she had learned of the existence of Auschwitz she experienced a *cura posterior*, which is to say, a healing of her inability to think through to its root the evil of totalitarian criminality. In an earlier and celebrated book, *The Origins of Totalitarianism*, Arendt had employed something akin to Kant's concept of "radical evil" as a basis for explaining evil action. In Kant's moral philosophy, there are three fundamental concepts: will, rules (maxims), and action. The human will made rules for the employment of its freedom in the realm of human action. But what if the "ultimate subjective ground" of making such rules is corrupt such that good maxims cannot be made (the person formulates only bad maxims)? Then, Kant says, radical evil would be *at the root of the human will*, which, because it is free, can be said to be *morally evil*.

It is crucial to see that Kant located radical evil at the locus of the self rather than in human nature *per se*. To seek the explanation of free action as a natural effect of human nature was a contradiction of freedom, and therefore a contradiction of imputing moral character to the doer of such action. Nevertheless, though radical evil was not at the roots of human nature (Kant thought that explaining the origin and propagation of radical evil in terms of an "inheritance from our first parents" particularly inept), radical evil in Kant's thought was something at the "roots" of the will; it was something "deep in the depth of the self." Kant in fact argued that we ought to call what we term "the depravity of human nature" "the perversity of the human heart, which then, because of what follows from it, is also called an evil heart" (Kant, *Religion*, 88). To have an evil or utterly corrupt heart (the point is perhaps better made if we think of what we mean when we say that we to feel something in our hearts) is for this evil to have utterly pervaded the depth of our being, to have reached the roots of our being, to have penetrated our souls, to have permeated our very selves.

Such then was the concept of radical evil that Arendt appropriated in explaining the origins of totalitarianism, the Fascism that was both Nazism and Stalinism. However, much to the dismay of much of the Jewish–American community in the early 1960s, Arendt came to reject "radical evil" as the explanation of the existence of the Nazi death camps. Instead she spoke in terms of a somewhat mystifying concept she called "the banality of evil." What motivated this fundamental change of mind was being sent by the *New York Times* to report on the trial of Adolf Eichmann in Jerusalem in April 1961. Eichmann had been the Nazi in charge of the Gestapo's Jewish section and who had overseen the logistical planning of the "final solution": the mass murder and extermination of millions of Jews during World War II in the gas chambers of the Nazi death camps.

But where she had expected Eichmann to be a monstrous distortion of human nature, she encountered, to her astonishment, a man who was – *nicht einmal unheimlich* – "not even sinister or strange." On the contrary, instead of being monstrous and demonic, Eichmann seemed to be the very epitome of transparent superficiality and mediocrity. He had been neither an ideological anti-Semite nor criminally motivated. He had not thought that Jews were less than human as many of his Nazi colleagues had.

Eichmann's sole objective had been to organize the deportation of millions of Jews to the concentration camps as efficiently as possible (to that end he had promoted the use of gas chambers to maximize the rate of mass extermination in the death camps). As Eichmann had seen it, he simply had a task to do and his job was to do it in as relentlessly meticulous and as functional a manner as possible. Had he been made responsible for the distribution and supply of food to the German army his attitude would have been the same. What had mattered to the exclusion of all else had been doing the task well, to the best of one's abilities. He behaved in the same way in the manufacturing of corpses as he would have had in the manufacture of food. As the philosopher Richard Bernstein put it: "We may find it almost impossible to imagine how someone could "think" (or rather, not think) in this manner, whereby manufacturing food, bombs, or corpses are "in essence the same" (Bernstein, *Hannah Arendt*, 170).

But this is precisely what Eichmann had done. In doing so, he had neglected to reflect on the fact that the effect of his logistical efficiency was to send human beings to their death in the gas chambers daily by their tens of thousands. His focus on the plan in the abstract – on production quotas and efficiency standards – meant that the very idea that his blueprint for mass murder was monstrous had not occurred to him.

What Arendt detected in Eichmann was not stupidity; neither were his actions the expression of absolute evil. Rather, though his actions evinced something entirely negative this was to be understood precisely in terms of absence rather than presence. Instead of plumbing the very depths of evil in the man Adolf Eichmann, Arendt found that his evil had no depths; rather, it was to be explained – or more accurately – described in terms of the entirely superficial phenomenon of "thoughtlessness."

Here was a man who had been responsible for the death of millions of Jews in the gas chambers of the death camps, and it appeared that he had carried his task out not because he hated Jews – not because of an evil will toward Jews – but because he had valued the standard of organizational efficiency above all else. This meant in Arendt's mind that, ultimately, Eichmann had carried out the action of organizing the murder of millions of Jews in the death camps because he had not thought about it; or, had not thought about it at the time of doing it. The "metaphysical" category underlying Eichmann's frightful actions had turned out to be as something as simple and as superficial as "thoughtlessness." She wrote: "However monstrous the deeds were, the doer was neither monstrous nor demonic, and the only specific characteristic one could detect on his part as well as in his behavior during the trial and the preceding police examination was something entirely negative: it was not stupidity but a curious, quite authentic inability to think" (Arendt, *Eichmann in Jerusalem*, 219).

In the wake of this discovery Arendt became famous for another phrase which then passed into cultural currency. "Thoughtlessness was not compatible with any theory or doctrine of radical (in the sense of deep) evil; but it was consistent with the notion of the 'banality of evil'" (Arendt, *Eichmann in Jerusalem*, 219). Proffered at the time as an explanation of the phenomenon of Eichmann, that was not at all what people expected or, indeed – given the appalling nature of the crimes – what they wanted or needed to hear. But the banality of the evil that Arendt saw in Eichmann led her to revise the conclusions she had reached in *The Origins of Totalitarianism*. Instead of postulating an evil that originated in or went to the deepest essence of the human being – as theologians and philosophers were wont to do in the past – Arendt now affirmed the opposite: "the phenomenon of evil deeds, committed on grand scale, which could not be traced to any particularity of wickedness, pathology, or ideological conviction in the doer, whose only personal distinction was perhaps extraordinary shallowness" (Arendt, "Thinking and Moral Considerations," 417).

Instead of the radical depth of evil at the heart of the human condition, Arendt postulated the "extraordinary shallowness" of evil, the "superficiality of evil." Evil was not deep, it was shallow; evil had no roots, it was rootless. Arendt emphasized that banality meant: "'No roots', not rooted in 'evil motives' or 'urges' or strength of 'temptation' (human nature)" (Arendt,

"Thinking and Moral Considerations," 418). The "banality of evil" was not radical in that it was "root-less." And where one expected to find "demonic forces", far less "evil motives" at work, there were none. In *The Life of the Mind* Arendt wrote: "what I was confronted with was utterly different and still undeniably factual. I was struck by a manifest shallowness in the doer that made it impossible to trace the incontestable evil of his deeds to any deeper level of roots *or* motives" (p. 3). Evil is a "surface" not a "depth" phenomenon, and therefore cannot be radical evil. In a letter she wrote in 1963 Arendt emphasized that evil as a "surface" phenomenon nevertheless could spread "like a fungus" because it has no depth:

> It is indeed my opinion now that evil is never "radical", that it is only extreme, and that it possesses neither depth nor demonic dimension. It can overgrow and lay waste the whole world because it spreads like a fungus on the surface. It is "thought-defying," as I said, because thought tries to reach some depth, and the moment it concerns itself with evil, it is frustrated because there is nothing. That is its "banality." Only the good has depth and can be radical (Arendt, *Encounter*, 56).

Nietzsche once said that the Greeks were superficial out of a sense of profundity; Arendt might have said that the banality of evil implies that superficiality goes to the very depths of our all too human self. Perhaps the first falling away from God is the precursor all that is to follow, as Von Rad insinuated: "sin can spread like a fungus." Ultimately the multifaceted connotations of the story of what is narrated happening in the Garden of Eden may have this to tell us about the human condition: that were we (in some ideal experimental research environment) to factor genes and environment out of the equation purporting to explain why people do this or that during their lives, it is not impossible that we would find that they would have done what they did, anyway, regardless, in the bright light of day. Each individual *as an individual* is responsible and culpable before God. But this is a theological conclusion not a social-scientific one.[6]

---

[6] It is not of course that "Adam and Eve's" action in the Garden is evil in the same sense as Eichmann's. Such a claim is preposterous. Nevertheless, the description that might be most appropriate for such as

Concluding remarks

The judging yet desisting, forbearing God of the exodus narratives is reciprocated by the judging yet desisting, forbearing identity narrated in the primeval history. The Yahwist as a redactor of the biblical text writing from within the history of Israel itself appends the primeval history, Genesis 2 – 11, to an already extant tradition that includes the exodus narrative inclusive of the wilderness tradition. His canonical redaction of the primeval history (as Von Rad and Westermann understand it) extrapolates from the Israelite to the human condition writ large. The most famous story of the primeval history – the story of the expulsion of the first man and the first woman, "Adam" and "Eve," from the Garden of Eden in Genesis 3 – is a "myth" of great ontological profundity. Genesis 2 – 3 is quite clear that the etiological source of the couple's expulsion is to be traced back to them and them alone – indeed, to the man, really, if we follow the literal sense of the "legend." (Augustine's understanding of original sin was that prior to "the fall" Adam possessed the possibility of sinning but also the possibility of not sinning. After the fall he lost the latter capacity, and henceforth was powerless to do anything else other than sin. But it was a choice he made, not God.) God tells the man that if they eat from "the tree of the knowledge of good and evil" they will suffer death ("on that same day"). But they go ahead, even when the cost is infinite (purportedly death) and the benefit negligible: they eat the fruit

---

[6] (*continued*) Adam and Eve's actions is, according to James Barr, something like "thoughtlessness." "Thoughtlessness" in this context means something akin to "empty-headedness," which can have a decided moral dimension depending on the context. To "empty one's head" may be to empty oneself of one's self, the self who knows in the context of the Garden of Eden that the benefit is negligible and the cost infinite. Such "thoughtlessness" can be described as a freely willed "cessation of self" – a ceasing to be one's self, a "going on holiday" from one's self. It is therefore not a question of human nature or of the nature of the human animal. It is a question of the self and freedom as opposed to human nature and determinism. It can lead to the most innocuous of consequences or it can lead to the most heinous of consequences. That the same phenomenon can be behind both implies nothing less than the "banality of evil."

from this one particular tree when fruit itself is abundantly available and accessible everywhere else. The Israelite who narrates this story of humankind's protological past "in the grammatical mood of the subjunctive conditional" is certain that the responsibility for our action in the Garden lies squarely on our own shoulders. There is no ambiguity that for him this is the etiological "given" of the story. What perplexes him – and compels him to want to return to "the scene of the crime" as if in the guise of a coroner relentlessly holding an inquest into his own conduct – is the "ontic" inexplicableness of the action. In telling the story of the expulsion from the Garden, the Yahwist confesses to God that he is at a loss to explain himself other than in terms of "thoughtlessness." That is the moral of the story. God (as in the case of the book of Job) may know the reason, but he does not say, preferring to hear what we have to say for ourselves.

Bibliography

Arendt, Hannah, *Eichmann in Jerusalem: A Report on the Banality of Evil*, rev. and enlarged ed. (New York: Penguin Books, 1977); *Encounter*, 22 (January 1964), 56; *The Life of the Mind* (New York: Harcourt Brace Jovanovich, 1978); *The Origins of Totalitarianism* (New York: Harcourt, Brace, 1951); "Thinking and Moral Considerations: A Lecture." Social Research, 38 (1971): 411–21.

Augustine, *The City of God*, translated by Henry Bettenson (London: Penguin, 2003).

Barr, James, *The Garden of Eden and the Hope of Immortality* (London: SCM, 1992).

Barth, Karl, *Church Dogmatics III/1*, translated by T. F. Torrance and G. Bromiley (Edinburgh: T. & T. Clark, 1958).

Bernstein, Richard, *Hannah Arendt and the Jewish Question* (Cambridge: MIT Press, 1996); *Radical Evil: A Philosophical Interrogation* (Oxford: Blackwell, 2002).

Childs, Brevard, *Biblical Theology of the Old and New Testaments: Theological Reflection on the Christian Bible* (London: SCM, 1992).

Childs, Brevard, *Old Testament Theology in a Canonical Context* (London: SCM, 1986).

Girard, René, *Violence and the Sacred*, translated by P. Gregory (Baltimore: The Johns Hopkins University Press, 1977).

Kant, Immanuel, *Religion within the Limits of Reason Alone*, translated by Theodore M. Greene and Hoyt H. Hudson (New York: Harper, 1960).

Noth, Martin, *A History of Pentateuchal Traditions* (Englewood Cliffs, New Jersey: Prentice-Hall, 1972).

Rad, Gerhard von, "The Form-Critical Problem of the Hexateuch," *The Problem of the Hexateuch and Other Essays*, 1–78 (London: SCM, 1966); *Genesis*, translated by J. Bowden, 3rd ed. (London: SCM, 1972).

Westermann, Claus, *Genesis 1–11* (Minneapolis: Fortress Press, 1994).

Wolterstorff, Nicholas, *Divine Discourse* (Cambridge: Cambridge University Press, 1995).

9

God and the Deuteronomistic History

There is a glaring lacuna as regards the church's take on the plain sense of the intervening history between creation and christological redemption. Christian theology's preoccupation with a "creation–fall–redemption" framework has condemned the historical narratives of Israel's personal and historical relationship with YHWH to the margins of contemporary Christian theology. Yet if the exodus narrative was at the very least appropriated (rightly or wrongly) as a typological or even allegorical precursor to Christ, the Deuteronomistic history has fared worse in this respect. There are, I think, two reasons for this. The first is undoubtedly to do with the disastrous cleavage between systematic theology and biblical studies. The Deuteronomistic history is the territory of biblical studies; ergo, it is not suitable subject-matter for the theologian! Hence the almost complete absence of reference to these narratives in the standard theological textbooks (e.g. Daniel Migliore's *Faith Seeking Understanding*, 2nd ed.; Alister McGrath's *Christian Theology: An Introduction*, 3rd ed.). The second is that, compared to the exodus story, the demise of the northern kingdom and the disastrous defeat of the southern kingdom were, prima facie at least, less easy to fit into the Christian narrative. As regards the second reason, I argue – in conformity to the line taken by Childs and Seitz (and one must mention Von Campenhausen here) – that this is to put theological matters the wrong way round. One must start with the Old Testament – the narrative of the historical relationship between YHWH and the people "Israel" – and read the Christian narrative, the New Testament, in terms of it. Such arguments it seems to me are important if we are to restore narratives central to the

Old Testament to our spoken liturgy and the many church hymnaries that make a quantum leap from creation to redemption without dealing with "the middle of the biblical thing." I speak of those narratives which are essential to the identification of YHWH's identity, one of which is the Deuteronomistic history.

Is it possible to do for biblical narrative from Deuteronomy to 2 Kings – from Moses' valedictory speech to Israel, just before she enters the promised land, to the destruction of Jerusalem and the end of the monarchy in 587 – as I have sought to do for fundamental aspects of the exodus narrative? Two features connected to the Priestly creation narrative are again intrinsic to my purpose. Both again come under the rubric of God the self-determining divine self. The first is the thesis that God determines himself to be (present) within the constitution of the world in such a way that he can be in personal relationship with Israel. The second is the thesis that, having gotten into the world, so to speak, God acts in it in a way that parallels his creation of it. That is, just as he determines himself to be the creator of all things then so he determines himself to be the one who e.g. leads Israel out of Egypt. The Priestly writer in effect continues and reinforces the tradition that the way in which God creates the world is fundamentally similar to the way in which he acts in it. He determines himself to be this or that personal identity. And the Bible quintessentially represents this personhood in terms of God's speaking. As was shown in Chapter 7 Childs demonstrated how one could employ the concept of God speaking in the context of his action as the one who led Israel out of Egypt. Similarly in this chapter I will develop what Von Rad argued was one of the central themes of Deuteronomic theology and, indeed, the Deuteronomistic history: God's creative word as the power behind his historical identity which is that of a judging yet desisting, forbearing self.

It may be argued that the Deuteronomistic history cannot come under the intentionality of the Priestly creation narrative for the simple reason that unlike the Yahwist's conception of history, it escapes the intentionality of the Priestly creation narrative. But since the Deuteronomist may be "in receipt" of the Priestly creation narrative it may be that it is this that influences him to conclude that there is an intrinsic and irresistible connection between God's word and historical event in the life of Israel: "'Let there be light' – and there was light" (see Childs, *Introduction*, 131ff.).

Ultimately once more what undergirds the rationality of the Deuteronomistic historian's theological conception of history is God the self-determining self who can be rationally said to speak and rationally said to act. It is this divine self who also provides for the rationality of affirming the people "Israel's" historical experience at this time, namely that God was acting in the disaster of defeat and exile.

The identity of YHWH in the Deuteronomistic history

What is the identity of YHWH in the Deuteronomistic history? There is distinct evidence to say that we are dealing again with YHWH's soteriological identity as a judging yet desisting, forbearing God. The biblical narrative from the book of Joshua to 2 Kings encompasses the history of the occupation of the land to the exile and downfall of Jerusalem, 597–587 BC. The theological crisis that Israel faced was not only one of exile; it was also one of how to square this catastrophic historical fact with the identity of one who had been understood as essentially a saving identity, precisely he who was known as "the one who released Israel from the bondage of Egypt."

In 597 BC Ezekiel, the son of Buzi, was deported from Jerusalem to Babylon by Nebuchadnezzar. Those exiled along with him included not only the king, Jehoiachin, and his court, but also members of the upper class and of the artisan class. From this perspective – thought most plausibly to be before the outright destruction of Jerusalem in 587 BC – Ezekiel surmises that the rebellion of Israel which has brought exile can be traced back to Israel's protohistory with YHWH in the wilderness toward the time of the exodus (before Israel had occupied the land):

"On the day I chose Israel, I swore with uplifted hand to the descendants of the house of Jacob and revealed myself to them in Egypt. With uplifted hand I said to them, 'I am the LORD your God' . . . Yet the people of Israel rebelled against me in the desert . . . So I said I

would pour out my wrath on them and destroy them in the desert"
(Ezek. 20: 5, 13).

The disaster of the Babylonian exile is upon Judah, upon the
people "Israel." In a pitch of rage and anger Ezekiel postulates
the theory that even in the early days of Israel's youth – or at least
after Sinai – the writing was on the wall for his own people. Even
then there were intimations of the future disaster. As Von Rad
puts it, the wilderness period narrated in Exodus is according to
Ezekiel to be perceived as "a type and pattern of the coming
judgement," of the coming destruction of Jerusalem (Von Rad,
Old Testament Theology, 283). But if YHWH's ultimate action in
the Deuteronomistic history is to do the very opposite of what he
did earlier in fulfilling the promise of the land – namely, sending
Israel into exile and latterly destroying Jerusalem – in what sense
can YHWH be a desisting, forbearing God in this history? For as
Ezekiel tells us, in the case of the promised land YHWH's mercy
wins out: "Yet I looked on them with pity and did not destroy
them or put an end to them in the desert" (Ezek. 20:17). To be
sure, subsequent to the account of the Deuteronomistic historian, the Chronicler – and Nehemiah and Ezra too – witness once
more to God's judging yet forbearing identity in the return of the
people "Israel" to their land under the beneficent hand of Cyrus
the Great (Ezra 9:13). So God's soteriological identity at work in
the history of Israel does not come to an end with the fall of Jerusalem in 587 BC (and how can it if it is to include Jesus of Nazareth
in this divine identity?). But the question is, specifically, Does the
Deuteronomistic historian *per se* witness to a judging yet desisting God?

The conception of the "Deuteronomistic history" was in fact
Martin Noth's most brilliant achievement (Noth, *Deuteronomistic History*). It was a conception that he juxtaposed in
opposition to the earlier documentary source-hypothesis, which
sought to treat the history that encompassed the kings of Judah
and of Israel and told the story of exile and downfall as a product
of the same documentary sources that had explained the Pentateuch ultimately in terms of a hexateuch. Instead, the Deuteronomistic history or redaction linked together originally
independent individual traditions in order to explain the course

of approximately seven centuries of Israelite history from the time of the death of Moses to the Babylonian exile in terms of a specific theological conception of history. That is, the Deuteronomistic historian did not "write a history to provide entertainment in hours of leisure or to satisfy a curiosity about national history," but to teach the true meaning of the history of Israel from the occupation of the land to the exile, culminating in the destruction of Jerusalem in 587 BC (Noth, *Deuteronomistic History*, 89). What was this meaning? According to Noth the meaning of this history was that: "God was recognisably at work in this history, continuously meeting the accelerating moral decline with warnings and punishments, and finally when these prove fruitless, with total annihilation. The Deuteronomist, then, perceives a just divine retribution in the history of the people . . . He sees this as the great unifying factor in the course of events" (Noth, *Deuteronomistic History*, 89).

Von Rad does not entirely agree with Noth on this: "the shadow of which the Deuteronomist wrote were the catastrophes of 721 and 586 BCE, which for him were heavy with theological import. They expressed YHWH's sentence of condemnation, following which the redemptive history of Israel had come to a halt" (Von Rad, "Deuteronomic Theology," 207).

Where Noth and Von Rad disagreed was on the issue of whether the Deuteronomist saw the halt of Israel's redemptive history as a final irrevocable termination or whether the writer (or school or movement) conceived the end latent with the hope that Israel still had a redemptive history in front of her. Noth's conclusion is clear: the theme of this Deuteronomist was "the past and, from his point of view, now finished history of his people" (Noth, *Deuteronomistic History*, 107f.). On the other hand Von Rad, ever alive to the idea that biblical narrative pointed beyond itself as a promise that other saving events were on the horizon, saw in the Deuteronomist's reference to Jehoichin's release from prison in 561 BC and his subsequent "rehabilitation" at the court and table of Evil-merodach, king of Babylon – "a regular daily allowance was given him by the king as long as he lived" (see 2 Kgs. 25:27–30) – an indication that the history was not necessarily at an end. Rather, the somewhat elegiac epilogue we have to the history would at the very least be read by its readers as insinuating that the Davidic line had not come to an end (Von Rad, "Deuteronomic Theology," 219–20).

The question for me is whether we can see a particular theological conception of history in this epilogue. In other words, is the point of the story merely that YHWH's providential guiding hand is involved in leading the line of Jehoichin toward a benign ineffectual end or is the implication that here is the person or his office from whom YHWH can in some sense resume his saving history with Israel? There is a parallel to the story of the Babylonian king's treatment of Jehoichin and that is David's treatment of Jonathan's crippled son, Mephibosheth (2 Samuel 9). It is unlikely we are meant to read the latter story as indicative of some kind of promise in Saul's dynasty. *Ceteris paribus*, one might say the same is true of the subsequent course of a pensioner's life – as Jehoichin is described – at the table of the royal court. The modern artistic parallel to my mind is Bertolucci's epic film *The Last Emperor*, which ends with the last emperor of China facing a similar benign fate in communist China with no hope of restoration.

Jehoichin's story may or may not signal for the Deuteronomist final closure for the Davidic dynasty (note Von Rad's point that the Deuteronomist could not accept that YHWH's word had not fulfilled itself);[1] but surely one would not want to say that either way it closes shut YHWH's saving history with Israel. In fact my thesis is that the answer to this question is whether YHWH continues as a judging yet desisting God toward Israel beyond 587 BC. But this of course presupposes that he was this during the history depicted by the Deuteronomist. Was he?

---

[1] Frank Moore Cross took the view that the Deuteronomist thought that the promises to the Davidic dynasty had been realized in Josiah which implied a preexilic date for this particular sequence of the Deuteronomistic history. This means that the conclusion to the Deuteronomistic history – the fall of Judah and Jerusalem – is the work of an exilic redactor. We have a double redaction as opposed to Noth's single redaction. See Cross, "Themes," 274–89.

The judging yet desisting, forbearing God in the Deuteronomistic history

It is to Von Rad that I am indebted for the answer to this question. It is my submission that he brilliantly showed, both in the case of the end of the northern kingdom of Israel in 722 BC and in the exile and downfall of Jerusalem that befell the southern kingdom of Judah, the soteriological identity of a judging yet desisting God at work in the Deuteronomist's theological conception of history.

According to Von Rad, the Deuteronomist is "concerned only with the theological significance of the disasters which had befallen the two kingdoms" (Von Rad, "Deuteronomic Theology," 207). The question is whether this theological significance is to found simply in the form of a wrathful and vengeful God intent on destruction such that the God of Israel had relinquished his primal identity as essentially a soteriological identity or whether this identity remained in force. The other possibility, that YHWH had been defeated by a superior divine power or powers – and driven from the Temple – is not seriously countenanced (though it is a perspective that requires address in the wake of the foreign domination of the land by subsequent empires – Persian, Greek, Seluceid, and Roman – even when the people "Israel" have returned to the land).

The Deuteronomist is relentless in his answer: the catastrophe "was not Yahweh's fault. Generation after generation of Israel had piled up an ever heavier burden of guilt and perfidy, and in the end Yahweh could do no other than reject his people" (Von Rad, "Deuteronomic Theology," 207–8). In *Old Testament Theology*, Von Rad was to write that, according to the Deuteronomist's "theological explanation" the disaster was "not due to YHWH or to the failure of his patience or of his readiness to forgive. On the contrary, Israel had rejected YHWH and his commandments" (Von Rad, *Old Testament Theology*, vol. 1, 332).

This is why the Deuteronomist prefixes the substance of the book of Deuteronomy – the fifth book of the Pentateuch – to his history (Deut. 1 – 4 and Deut. 31:1ff. are thought to be the hand of the Deuteronomist who takes a pre-existing Deuteronomic document and thereby links it up to his history of the kings of Israel and Judah in 1 and 2 Kings). In doing this, he means to employ Deuteronomy as the essential interpretative framework through which the demise of Israel and the destruction and exile of Judah should be understood. In narrative terms Deuteronomy casts a long despairing shadow over the events that befall Israel and Judah at the conclusion of the Deuteronomistic history.[2] Israel and Judah did not keep the statutes and laws of God as delineated in Deuteronomy. In particular, they did not observe the demand that YHWH "should be worshipped only at the one legitimate sanctuary at which he put his name" (Von Rad, *Old Testament Theology*, vol. 1, 336).[3] As Childs points out, even though the centralization of worship at Deuteronomy 12 is "a

---

[2] Nevertheless, this does not render the valedictory speeches of Moses to his people as irremediable past event and therefore irrelevant or unrelated to the present needs of a people in exile. In this respect Von Rad's comment on the "Janus-like" quality of Deuteronomy is extremely apposite: Deuteronomy is the first book of the Deuteronomistic history but it is also the final book of the Pentateuch. This is why though incorporated into an exilic perspective, it makes "every generation analogous to the generation at Sinai, the historical qualities recede before an ideal of faith. But this does not mean that Deuteronomy is 'a post-exilic projection which was devoid of all historical reality'" (Childs, *Introduction*, 222). It was rather "part of a historical process of rendering ancient tradition accessible to future generations" (Childs, *Introduction*, 222) – including the landless in exile in Babylon. In particular, "to the landless community of Babylon possession of the land was not constitutive of Jewish faith, but of a promise yet to be realized" (Childs, *Introduction*, 131).

[3] Deuteronomy demands:

> that YHWH should be worshipped only at the one legitimate sacrifice. This demand had been building at a time which had become conscious in all its magnitude of the difference between historically-based Jahwism and the Canaanite nature cult, and had grasped that worship of YHWH, that is, mingled with the Baal cult, eliminated that which was distinctive in Jahwism. The recognition that one had to choose between the two worships had come, through Deuteronomy, to be the *status confessionis* at this later period. Now, the Deuteronomistic theology of history too holds this very radical standpoint, because, as is well known, it measures the kings of Israel and Judah according to whether they recognised the Temple in Jerusalem as the one legitimate place of worship, or sacrificed on the "high places" (Von Rad, *Old Testament Theology*, vol. 1, 336).

relatively late entry" into the "Deuteronomic corpus," it has been "expanded into a major force within the canonical shape of the book" (Childs, *Introduction*, 219). Indeed as he says, "the stress of ch.12 on centralization as a means of both the unity and purity of Israel's worship now functions as a prism through which the whole legal collection is viewed" (Childs, *Introduction*, 218). YHWH is to be worshipped only in "the place [he] will choose . . . to put his Name there for his dwelling" (Deut. 12.5). The divine name dwells only in the temple that Solomon built in Jerusalem and therefore it was "the place where YHWH was present for Israel and where he spoke to and had cultic dealings with her" (Von Rad, *Old Testament Theology*, vol. 1, 337). To worship elsewhere was tantamount to worshipping other gods or posed the potential threat that other gods would be the focus of worship. Hence the injunction to centralize worship can be understood within the context of the first commandment: "Thou shalt have no gods beside me." (However, centralization of worship did not in itself exclude the possibility of impurity of worship. "Contamination" of the temple with the presence of images of other gods did take place, infamously in the case of one of the kings of Judah, Manasseh [2 Kgs. 21:3–9].)

Accordingly, those kings who built or maintained other "high places" for the people to worship and to sacrifice were in direct breach of the will of God and were guilty of leading the people into sin (1 Kgs. 16:13, 19, 26). It is from this perspective that all the kings of Israel are judged. As Von Rad put it:

> The judgements which are passed on the kings are arrived at solely in the light of this decision. From this standpoint the kings of Israel are condemned out of hand, for they all "walked in the sin of Jeroboam." But even of the kings of Judah only two – Hezekiah and Josiah – are given unqualified praise. Six are approved conditionally (Asa, Jehoshaphat, Joash, Amaziah, Azaraiah, and Jotham): all the rest are reproached with having done "what was evil in the sight of YHWH" (Von Rad, *Old Testament Theology*, vol. 1, 337).

Specifically then, in the case of the northern kingdom, the prophets foretell destruction because of the people's disobedience. The fate of this kingdom, according to the Deuteronomist, is sealed by the first sin, the apostasy of Jeroboam I. The particular sin of the later kings is expressed in the stereotyped comment that all "walked in the sin of Jeroboam." All the kings of Israel fall under condemnation because they "walked in the way of Jeroboam, son of Nebat", which is to say, among other things, they worshipped "other gods" at other "high places" (1 Kgs. 12:25–33).

Yet the matter was not quite so simple for the Deuteronomist, since YHWH had spared the northern kingdom for a further two hundred years. Though the destruction finally came, the Deuteronomist had to explain why YHWH had postponed it for so many generations. In other words, the Deuteronomist "was only confronted with the task, admittedly none too easy a one of explaining why it lasted as one long as it did" (Von Rad, *Old Testament Theology*, vol. 1, 340). According to Von Rad, the Deuteronomist explained this

> in terms of the mercy of YHWH, who does not overlook the comparative goodness found event in reprobate kings. Ahab humbled himself before the sentence of punishment and for this reason the sentence on his house was not executed in his lifetime (1 Kings 21.29), Jehu performed certain acts which were pleasing to YHWH and thus his descendants were to occupy the throne for four generations (2 Kings 10.30; 15.12) (Von Rad, "Deuteronomic Theology," 213).

As Von Rad put it later in his *Old Testament Theology*, YHWH "did not overlook the slightest amount of good there was even in rejected kings" (Von Rad, *Old Testament Theology*, vol. 1, 340). It is submitted that the one who behaves in such a way, the one who delays or postpones divine judgement for this particular reason, is no less than a forbearing, desisting identity. In this lies the continuity between the identity who is said to act in the exodus narrative and the one who is found in the Deuteronomistic history.

The situation with regard to the history of the kingdom of Judah is more complicated. Here again the situation is "presented primarily as the history of human disobedience and steadily mounting divine disapproval. But what has to be explained is God's patient forbearance over a much longer period" (Von Rad, "Deuteronomic Theology," 214). The explanation the Deuteronomist gave was that God desisted from his judgement on Judah and Jerusalem on account of "his promise to establish and uphold the Davidic dynasty given in the prophecy of Nathan in 2 Samuel 7" (Von Rad, "Deuteronomic Theology," 215). The divine promises to the Davidic dynasty are employed to explain the difference in duration between Judah and the northern kingdom.

However, it remained for the Deuteronomist to give an account of the fact that the great catastrophe of 587 closed in over Judah almost immediately after the reign of Josiah, who was the best of all the house of David. How could one rationally affirm the historical conception of a judging yet desisting God if there was no sign of forbearance in the wake of Josiah's obedience, reflected, for example in his reforms? The reason the Deuteronomist gave for YHWH's judgement was that YHWH "had already resolved to pass sentence on Judah because of the sins of Manasseh, which had broken all bounds. Even Josiah's behaviour could avert it no longer. Thus over Judah YHWH's patience had long held even though the judgement had been long-due" (Von Rad, *Old Testament Theology*, vol. 1, 341).

Manasseh had succeeded his father Hezekiah to the throne of Judah and had restored every aspect of idolatry that Hezekiah had rejected and eliminated in the course of his centralized worship focused on the temple in Jerusalem. Such was the apostasy of Manasseh that even Josiah's implementation of reform centred on the book of the law found in the temple in 621 BC (2 Kgs. 22ff.) was not sufficient to persuade YHWH to desist from his course of action as narrated at 2 Kings 21:10–14. Josiah does not live to see the disaster that YHWH visits upon Jerusalem and Judah (2 Kgs. 22:20).

Word and event in the Deuteronomistic history

Thus far I have presented a case for understanding the God evidenced in the text of the Deuteronomistic history as a judging yet desisting, forbearing self. Whether or not one wants to accept Von Rad's thesis that the Davidic promises explain YHWH's relatively "favourable" treatment of Judah by comparison with the northern kingdom – and Von Rad argues that in order to do this, the Deuteronomist has to make David himself a "model" of

Deuteronomic obedience[4] – the fact of the divine forbearance still remains in the history. But Von Rad found another thematic at work in the Deuteronomistic history. This was that God brought about his actions in this history through his word. He writes:

> The Deuteronomic view of the matter is evidently that God had revealed his commandments to Israel, and has threatened to deal with this disobedience by means of heavy punishments, and even by condemning the nation to extinction. This has now come about. YHWH's words had fulfilled themselves in history and had not failed, as the Deuteronomist puts it. The word of YHWH is thus related to historical events by the fact that once he has spoken, his word always and invariably achieves its purposes in history by virtue of its own inherent power (Von Rad, "Deuteronomic Theology," 208).

Again, Von Rad writes that the Deuteronomistic history is therefore "the history of YHWH's creative word" ("Deuteronomic Theology," 220). According to the Deuteronomist, "Israel's history depends upon a few quite simple theological and prophetical propositions concerning the nature of the divine word. It is this word of YHWH, and it alone which gives the phenomena of history a purpose and a meaning, so binding together into a single whole in the eyes of God its manifold and diverse elements" (Von Rad, "Deuteronomic Theology," 220–1).

And in his conclusion to his essay he writes: "Thus the Deuteronomist shows by a wholly valid process, just what redemptive history is within the context of the Old Testament: it is a course of events shaped by the word of YHWH, continually intervening to direct and deliver, and so steadily pressing these events toward their fulfilment in history" (Von Rad, "Deuteronomic Theology," 221).

---

[4] As a character in the Deuteronomistic history he too is subordinated to the book of Deuteronomy. This may mean, as Von Rad points out, that his character is "purged of all dross" in order that it fit in with the moral remit of Deuteronomy (Von Rad, "Deuteronomic Theology," 218). But though it might be said that even the greatest of kings was no less susceptible to the murderous (sexual?) impulses of the human condition, should this necessarily preclude David in the eyes of the Deuteronomist from "walking in the ways of YHWH"?

Later on, in his magisterial *Old Testament Theology*, Von Rad was to espouse the same view: "According to the Deuteronomist it is YHWH's word which has brought Israel to judgement in the catastrophe of 722" (Von Rad, *Old Testament Theology*, vol. 1, 339). More fulsomely:

> It can actually be said that the Deuteronomist gives the historical course of events which he describes its inner rhythm and its theological proof precisely by means of a whole structure of constantly promulgated prophetic predictions and their corresponding fulfilments, of which exact note is generally made. It is here that we get a correct perspective for this view of history. Everything that Ahijah of Shiloh, Jehu ben Hanani, Micaiah ben Imlah, Elijah, Elisha, Huldah, etc. prophesied became history. The history of Israel is a course of events which receives its own peculiar dramatic quality from the tension between constantly promulgated prophecies and their corresponding fulfilment (Von Rad, *Old Testament Theology*, vol. 1, 340)[5].

And finally and most tellingly:

> For the Deuteronomist the divine guidance of history is established beyond all doubt: but it is by his word that JHWH directs history, this is practically hammered into the reader. At the same time the author of the succession document shows that he himself understood this history as the fulfilment of an explicit word of YHWH, since he sets the whole complex in the shadow of the Nathan prophecy (2 Samuel 7). (Von Rad, *Old Testament Theology*, vol. 1, 342; cf. 314, 316).

The question is, Is it rational to affirm this theological conception of history? It may be that from the "inside" or "internal" perspective the Deuteronomist believed quite adamantly that God acted in his word but is there also an "outside" or "external" perspective that endorses the former viewpoint, that vouchsafes for its rationality? Let me answer this question by reference to passages toward the end of 2 Kings central to the explanation of respectively Israel's demise and the Babylonian exile. My

---

[5] Von Rad lists no fewer than eleven prophecies which are subsequently fulfilled by YHWH in the course of the history of Israel and Judah in this period. See Von Rad, "Deuteronomic Theology," 208–11.

answer will, as it did in the case of the exodus narrative, involve God's self-determination in both speaking and acting.

Divine self-determination in the Deuteronomistic history

The Deuteronomist describes the downfall of the northern kingdom in the following way:

> In the twelfth year of Ahaz king of Judah, Hoshea son of Elah became king of Israel in Samaria, and he reigned for nine years. He did evil in the eyes of the LORD, but not like the kings of Israel who preceded him. Shalmaneser king of Assyria came up to attack Hoshea, who had been Shalmaneser's vassal and had paid him tribute. But the king of Assyria discovered that Hoshea was a traitor, for he had sent envoys to So king of Egypt, and he no longer paid tribute to the king of Assyria, as he had done year by year. Therefore Shalmaneser seized him and put him in prison. The king of Assyria invaded the entire land, marched against Samaria and laid seige to it for three years. In the ninth year of Hoshea, the king of Assyria captured Samaria and deported the Israelites to Assyria. He settled them in Halah, in Gozan on the Habor River and in the towns of the Medes (2 Kgs. 17:1–6).

This is a wholly "nontheological" historical description of events, which is to say, one in which human beings and institutions seem to be the sole agencies behind the history. But given that the Deuteronomist views this particular history through a theological lens in which God is the ultimate agency behind the downfall of the northern kingdom, (YHWH the "Lord of history"), this cannot be the whole story. And it is not. He continues: "All this took place because the Israelites had sinned against the LORD their God, who had brought them up out of Egypt . . . So the LORD was very angry with Israel and removed them from his presence. Only the tribe of Judah was left" (2 Kgs. 17:7, 18).

However, Judah and Jerusalem suffer a not dissimilar fate. Why? For the same reason. The Deuteronomist continues: "Judah did not keep the commands of the LORD their God. They followed the practices Israel had introduced. Therefore the LORD rejected all the people of Israel; he afflicted them and gave them into the hands of plunderers, until he thrust them from his presence" (2 Kgs. 17:19–20).

And crucially, God's word itself appears in the text. God speaks:

> The LORD said through his servants the prophets: "Manasseh king of Judah has committed these detestable sins. He has done more evil than the Amorites who preceded him and has led Judah into sin with his idols. Therefore this is what the LORD, the God of Israel, says: I am going to bring such disaster on Jerusalem and Judah that the ears of everyone who hears of it will tingle. I will stretch out over Jerusalem the measuring line used against Samaria and the plumb-line used against the house of Ahab. I will wipe out Jerusalem as one wipes out a dish, wiping it and turning it upside-down. I will forsake the remnant of my inheritance and hand them over to their enemies. They will be looted and plundered by all their foes, because they have done evil in my eyes and have provoked me to anger from the day their forefathers came out of Egypt until this day." Moreover, Manasseh also shed so much innocent blood that he filled Jerusalem from end to end – besides the sin that he had caused Judah to commit, so that they did evil in the sight of the LORD (2 Kgs. 21:10–16).

We can parallel this passage in which God speaks judgement to an earlier one in which God speaks salvation, namely the one already referred to (in Chapter 7) in which God says to Moses, ". . . I will bring you out from under the yoke of the Egyptians. I will free you from being slaves to them . . ." (Exod. 6:2–9). How did I say in Chapter 7 that it was rational to affirm that God spoke to Moses as narrated in Exodus 6:2–9? The answer was that he determined himself to be the one who said these words, with their intended meaning to Moses. (You can affirm whatever philosophy of language is sufficient for God to have satisfied the criterion of having spoken meaningfully to Moses. He does not simply determine himself to be the one who strings some random words together in his speaking, but acquires obligations to mean what he says. But whatever philosophy of language it is, God fulfils it through divine self-determination.)

This applies similarly in the case of 2 Kings 21:10–16. And indeed, as Von Rad puts it: "The Deuteronomist makes Solomon give very clear expression to this correspondence which exists between God's word and the course of history: 'Thou didst speak with thy *mouth* and with thy *hand* hast fulfilled it this day' (1 Kings 8:24)" (Von Rad, "Deuteronomic Theology," 220). God not only determines himself to be the one who says what he says (and therefore truly says it), he also determines himself to act (independently of the speaking, as it were) in a separate act in which he determines himself to be the one who does in the present – at the time of the Babylonian exile, for example – what he said in the past he would do. To paraphrase what was said of the saving history of the exodus in Chapter 7: God determines himself to be the one who will employ the might of the Babylonian empire to judge and exile Jerusalem; then he is the one who will employ the might of the Babylonian empire to judge and exile Jerusalem. Therefore, he *does* employ the might of the Babylonian empire to judge and exile Jerusalem. (if it is true that one *will do* something then it follows that one *does it*). God acts in the world, and specifically acts in the history of his people "Israel," by determining himself to be the one who acts in it; therefore he acts in it.

Clearly then, divine action at the culmination of the Deuteronomistic history comes under the auspices of "divine self-determination without natural theology." Not only is an entirely nontheological description of history narrated – as at 2 Kings above; had one actually been at the scene of the event to witness the destruction of Jerusalem, the only empirical description one could have given would have been a purely human affair taking place between Jerusalem and the Babylonian Empire – because this is all that one would have seen and heard. As Von Rad put it, the Deuteronomist conceives of a *concursus divinus* as the operative principle at work in the history of the monarchy. The Deuteronomist:

> depicts a succession of occurrences in which the chain of cause and effect is firmly knit up – so firmly indeed that human eye discerns no point at which God could have put in his hand. Yet secretly it is he who has brought all to pass; all the threads are in his hands; his activity embraces the great political events no less than the hidden counsels of human hearts. All human affairs are the sphere of God's providential working (Von Rad, "Historical Writing," 201).

In other words: though there is no claim to the unusual or the miraculous – to signs of God's wondrous presence as there may be in the exodus narrative – the Deuteronomist wants to claim that the fall of Jerusalem and the First Temple is God's own action. What would make it rational for him to do so is the mechanics of "divine self-determination without natural theology." The logic of the case is entirely as in Chapter 2 and I will not rehearse all the arguments here once again – except to say that if God determines himself to be the one who does what he does to Jerusalem in 587 BC then this is basic and sufficient for it to be the case that what happened to Jerusalem in 587 BC is designated by the predicate "action of God."

God is in history – within the temporal and spatial constitution of the world – acting in history "then and there" as explained in Chapter 5. He is acting in that he speaks and he is acting in that he acts, as in speech acts and deed acts. This is all rational to affirm. Therefore, in so far as the Deuteronomist characterizes "Israel's" historical experience of the Babylonian exile as that of YHWH acting in her life then this experience is likewise rational to affirm. Am I claiming that if it were rational to say both that God speaks to Israel (through for example the prophets) and acts in the life of Israel, then it would be rational to affirm Israel's historical experience as that of God speaking to Israel and of God acting in the life of Israel? I am to the extent that when we transpose this question to the personal level, we seem to get the same answer: if it were rational to say that God both speaks to me and acts in my life then it would be rational to affirm my experience of God speaking to me (answering my prayers, say), and of God acting in my life.

Concluding remarks

What I have attempted in this chapter is to endorse the rationality of a theological interpretation of the Bible as regards the Deuteronomistic history. It has been pointed out that by the standards of modern historiography – and even by the standards of the fifth-century Greek historians, Herodotus and Thucydides – the Deuteronomist did not produce a historiographical work but rather a "theodicy" (Nicholson, "Story," 135–50). Even though the consensus is that there are three historical sources of the Deuteronomistic narrative:

(1) "the book of the acts of Solomon" (1 Kgs. 11:41);
(2) the "book of the chronicles of the kings of Judah" (14:29; 15:7, 23, etc.);
(3) the "book of the chronicles of the kings of Israel" (14:19; 15:31; 16:14, 20, 27, etc.).

– there is no question but that the Deuteronomist did not set himself the task of checking the reliability of these sources. They are a means to an end which is precisely the story of the downfall of Israel and Judah brought about by YHWH. If the Deuteronomistic history corresponds in any way to Johannes Huizinga's definition of history as "the intellectual form in which a nation renders an account of itself to itself" (Huizinga, "Definition," 9), it is only in so far as this history renders an account of its God as the Lord of history. But does this imply that such an account is necessarily beyond the pale as regards rationality? No. Let us suppose that counterfactually the Deuteronomist had critically checked his sources as regards the nontheological historical claims – the succession of the kings, and each individual king's actions as regards the worship in the temple and "the high places." The aim of the Deuteronomist is not to present an empirically attested account of the monarchy from the time of the divided kingdom in the tenth century to the pardoning of Jehoiachin (2 Kgs. 25:27–30) in 562 BC. It is an account to show that the identity of the God of the Deuteronomistic history remains, and is therefore compatible with, the same divine identity manifest in the saving history of the exodus: "the one who released Israel from the bondage of Egypt." It is crucial for the Deuteronomist that it is God's hand that was at work in the event of the destruction of the temple and the Babylonian exile. Moreover, of the specific explanation the Deuteronomist provides for divine action in 587 BC, one can say that canonical shaping, neither theologically nor philosophically, excludes the possibility that other factors, perhaps more social and economic, came into play.[6]

---

[6] I am thinking of a passage such as we find in Jer. 22:1–9:

> This is what the LORD says: "Go down to the palace of the king of Judah and proclaim this message there: "Hear the word of the LORD, O king of Judah,

---

[6] (*continued*) you who sit on David's throne – you, your officials and your people who come through these gates. This is what the LORD says: Do what is just and right. Rescue from the hand of his oppressor the one who has been robbed. Do no wrong or violence to the alien, the father-less or the widow, and do not shed innocent blood in this place. For if you are careful to carry out these commands, then kings who sit on David's throne will come through the gates of this palace, riding in chariots and on horses, accompanied by their officials and their people. But if you do not obey these commands, declares the LORD, I swear by myself that this palace will become a ruin. For this is what the LORD says about the palace of the king of Judah: "Though you are like Gilead to me, like the summit of Lebanon, I will surely make you a desert, like towns not inhabited. I will send destroyers against you, each man with his weapons, and they will cut up your fine cedar beams and throw them into the fire. People from many nations will pass by this city and will ask one another, 'Why has the LORD done such a thing to this great city?' And the answer will be: 'Because they have forsaken the cove-nant of the LORD their God and have worshipped and served other gods'."

Bibliography

Childs, Brevard, *Introduction to the Old Testament as Scripture* (London: SCM, 1979).

Cross, Frank M., "The Themes of the Book of Kings and the Structure of the Deuteronomistic History." In *Canaanite Myth and Hebrew Epic*, edited by Frank M. Cross, 274–89 (Massachusetts: Cambridge University Press, 1973).

Huizinga, Johannes, "A Definition of the Concept of History." In *Philosophy and History: Essays Presented to Ernst Cassirer*, edited by R. Kiblansky and H. J. Paton, 1–10 (Oxford: Clarendon Press, 1936), reprinted (New York: Harper Torchbooks, 1963).

Mayes, G. A., *The Story of Israel between Settlement and Exile: A Redactional Study of the Deuteronomistic History* (London: SCM, 1984).

McGrath, Alister, *Christian Theology: An Introduction*, 3rd ed.. (Oxford: Blackwell, 2003).

Migliore, Daniel, *Faith Seeking Understanding*, 2nd ed. (Grand Rapids: Eerdmans, 1995).

Nelson, R. D., *The Double Redaction of the Deuteronomistic History* (Sheffield: JSOT Press, 1981).

Nicholson, Ernest, "Story and History in the Old Testament." In *Language, Theology and the Bible*, edited by S. E. Balentine and J. Barton, (Oxford: Oxford University Press, 1994), 135–50.

Noth, Martin, *The Deuteronomistic History* (Sheffield: JSOT Press, 1991).

Rad, Gerhard von, *Old Testament Theology*, vols. 1 and 2 (London: SCM, 1975); "The Deuteronomic Theology of History of 1 and 2 Kings," *The Problem of the Hexateuch and Other Essays* (London: SCM, 1984), 205–21; "Historical Writing in Ancient Israel," *The Problem of the Hexateuch and Other Essays* (London: SCM, 1984), 166–204.

Seters, John van, *In Search of History: Historiography in the Ancient World and the Origins of Biblical History* (New Haven: Yale University, 1983).

PART THREE

The problem of the early Church was not what to do with Old Testament in the light of the Gospel, which was Luther's concern, but rather the reverse. In the light of the Jewish scriptures which were acknowledged to be the true oracles of God, how were Christians to understand the good news of Jesus Christ?

Hans von Campenhausen, *The Formation of the Christian Bible*

The Old Testament functioned as a coherent whole in shaping the Christology of the New Testament, and its influence cannot be restricted to single verses or to exact linguistic parallels.

Brevard Childs, *Isaiah*

10

The Gospel Narrative, Substitutionary Atonement, and the "Directorial Eye" of the Evangelist

This chapter intends to put the case for an understanding of systematic theology that respects a plain-sense reading of both the Old and New Testaments as against the conventional tendency to reread the Old in terms of the New. Accordingly, the identity of YHWH as a judging yet desisting, forbearing self continues to be fundamental to a plain-sense reading of the gospel narrative (especially the Synoptic Gospels); but, somewhat remarkably, in such a way as to affirm the doctrine of substitutionary atonement as the central doctrine of the New Testament. I hold that this particular version of the doctrine – presupposing as it does a plain-sense unity of Old and New Testament – is to be preferred over the classical versions as proposed by the patristic, medieval, Reformation, and modern interpretations of the doctrine. Fundamental to this new version – inspired as it is by the work of Karl Barth in *Church Dogmatics* IV/1 – is the literary and explanatory device of the "directorial eye" of the evangelist, which I argue is at work in the passion narrative at the locus of Pontius Pilate's judgement on Jesus of Nazareth. The real theological identity of Pilate's judgement is in fact YHWH's judgement on Jesus. In this sense is there a doctrine of substitutionary atonement objectively present in the synoptic narratives in which ultimately it is YHWH who takes his own judgement on himself in the form of his Son, Jesus of Nazareth. Soteriology is to be understood in terms of the soteriological identity of the God of Israel. Jesus of Nazareth is to be understood in terms of the soteriological identity of the God of Israel. In this sense is Christology subordinate to objective soteriology. But note well: the first and last and therefore prevailing word of God is not divine judgement but divine love. God takes this particular judgement on himself because it is eschatological judgement (as the judgements in Old Testament narrative are not). Such judgement – were it to have fallen on Israel and by extension the world – would have meant not merely dying and death, but dying and death apart from God, who had finally and eternally turned his back on his personal and historical relationship with Israel and humankind, and "left us to it." But he did not do this. Because this judgement would mean utter end – and there is no desistance or forbearance possible with such a judgement – God takes it on himself, in the form of his Son, Jesus of Nazareth. Ultimately, he does not "pour his wrath out on his Son" in a sense apart from himself; in so far as such language is to be used, he "poured it out on himself" – took it upon himself.

The fundamental motif of the gospel narrative: YHWH, the God of Israel who takes his own judgement on himself – in the form of his Son, Jesus of Nazareth

Let me start the substance of this penultimate and central chapter with what I think is the fundamental thematic of the gospel narrative. It is the story of YHWH, the God of Israel who takes his own judgement on himself – in the form of his Son, Jesus of Nazareth. I want to say that the evangelists recognized that this God was precisely the one identified in the Old Testament, and principally in Old Testament narrative, as essentially a *soteriological* identity. The God of Israel reveals himself to be a judging yet desisting, forbearing, and saving historical identity. To be sure, he is "the one who releases Israel from the bondage of Egypt" in the exodus narrative, and as we know "the one who released Israel from the bondage of Egypt" is a key identifying description of the God of Israel in the Old Testament. Nevertheless this definite description is not sufficiently comprehensive to be descriptive of his identity in the later narratives. It does of course remain true of him at the time of the

Deuteronomistic history and the Babylonian exile. He remains the "one who released Israel from the bondage of Egypt" in 587 BC. In other words: the uniquely identifying description is not merely true of him as past truth (as something he has done in the past); rather, the description is indicative of his present identity continuous with his past actions. This explains why Israel sought an understanding of the exile that remained characteristic of the action of a God who had released Israel from bondage.

Nevertheless, it is not the identity that ties all these narratives together in terms of the sameness of divine identity. The divine identity that does this is precisely the God of Israel understood as a *judging yet (ultimately) desisting, forbearing, saving God*. The God of Israel is this in the exodus narrative. But he is also this – paradoxically – in the narrative that in modern times goes by the name of the Deuteronomistic history and which culminates in the downfall of the (southern) kingdom of Judah and Babylonian exile early in the sixth century BC, having already testified to the demise of the (northern) kingdom of Israel in 772 BC. YHWH is also this in the postexilic period. And most pointedly, he is this in the very words of Ezra who, when speaking of the return from exile under the beneficence of Cyrus the Great from 536 BC onwards, experiences YHWH as having "punished us less than our iniquities deserved and have given us such a remnant as this" (Ezra 9:13). Even though Judah is to be no more a kingdom, the return from exile is still the action of a gracious and merciful God who saves his people Israel more than they deserve. And Ezra recognizes this.

It is this personal historical identity that the evangelist sees at work in the gospel narrative. *The God of Israel who takes his own judgement on himself in the form of his Son in the gospel narrative is the judging, yet desisting and forbearing historical identity identified in Old Testament narrative as this personal identity.*

I recognize that to say YHWH takes his judgement on himself, and then to add – "in the form of his Son" – is to court semantic anomaly if not downright inconsistency and contradiction. (How can YHWH really take his own judgement on himself if it is in fact taken on the shoulders of his Son?) It is a question – one that recurs in different forms throughout the history of doctrine – that discerns an apparent tension inherent in speaking of a

monotheism which yet includes the man Jesus. But let me put
this historic critique to one side for the moment and consider
another criticism of this thematic, which comes from yet another
angle. This criticism goes as follows. Whatever else the gospel
narrative is about, isn't it much more about Jesus Christ (also of
course Jesus of Nazareth) and less about YHWH, the God of
Israel? To be sure, Jesus speaks of God all through the gospel but,
still, it is Jesus and not this God who is the central figure in the
narrative. The Old Testament is about YHWH the God of Israel,
yes, but the New Testament, like the new covenant, is about
Jesus Christ, his only Son. A straightforward and simple
demarcation!

I would argue that this demarcation is too simple, especially if
it is employed as a framework with which to view the relation
between the Old and New Testament. To be sure, the demarcation is undergirded by a very venerable tradition that has Jesus
or Christology writ large, as it were, interpret the Old Testament.
Jesus or Christology interprets the Old Testament as a book of
typology or prophecy or even allegory. One may read the Old
Testament for its plain sense as it were, as one's first hermeneutic; but then, in the light of one's reading of the New Testament,
one rereads the former for its christological sense, the second
and primary hermeneutic.[1] As regards the primary hermeneutic,
one may describe the relation between the two testaments as a
"front-to-back" model in the sense that one reads the New Testament first, then "reads" the Old Testament as it were behind it
rather than the other way around. One may also describe the
relation of New to Old by an automobile metaphor, as a "front-
wheel drive" model. One reads the Old Testament from the
context or perspective of the New Testament and, in particular,
the Christ event, and in the light of this, one deems to pull the
Old Testament along, behind you as it were. (Someone like
Marcion might be described as one who didn't want to pull
much of this part of Scripture along with him, didn't think there

---

[1] Francis Watson's *Text and Truth: Redefining Biblical Theology* (Edinburgh: T. & T. Clark, 1997) is a pre-eminent example of this kind of
"trinitarian-christological" rereading of the Old Testament in terms of
the New Testament.

was much point in wasting time pulling along what wasn't necessary for his and the church's spiritual journey.)

Now as I say this is a most venerable tradition. It informed the patristic period, dominated medieval theology (especially with its tendency toward the allegorical mode of biblical interpretation), and remains – even given the emphasis on the plain sense of Scripture – the prevalent mode of biblical interpretation today. Yet – to my mind – it poses something of an obstruction to stating the doctrine of atonement in its most cogent form, that which I have outlined above in which the primary agent is YHWH the God of Israel. The alternative position, which I should say has been gaining currency in recent times – and arguably has a precedent in the apostolic fathers and the early church (see Von Campenhausen, *The Formation of the Christian Bible*) – is one I describe in an opposite manner to this "front-to-back" or "front-wheel drive" model. It is a *"back-to-front"* model or a *"back-wheel drive"* model; one reads the Old Testament for its plain sense in order to identify who the God of Israel is: who it is that acts in Israel's history, his divine identity, as it were, construable as a historical identity. One then attempts to read the gospel narrative as the story of this same divine identity. Clearly, to the extent that the narrative can be read as this story, it is read in terms of one's plain-sense reading of Old Testament narrative. The New Testament is, as it were, read from the context or perspective of the Old Testament, rather than as Christian convention has it (though not necessarily the Scripture principle) the other way round. It is not then that Jesus interprets the Old Testament; rather, he or his story is interpreted in terms of the Old Testament. In particular, the Jesus of Nazareth as rendered in the gospel narratives – especially the synoptic narratives – is read in terms of the divine identity of YHWH as rendered in Old Testament narrative. He is read in terms of that identity as it is manifest: initially in the exodus narrative, centrally in the Deuteronomistic narrative, but also before and after these narratives – in both the primeval and in the postexilic history. As Brevard Childs puts it, paraphrasing some of the seminal work of Hans von Campenhausen, "the problem of the early church was not what to do with the Old Testament in the light of the Gospel, which was Luther's concern, but rather the reverse. In the light of the Jewish scriptures which were acknowledged to be the true oracles of God, how were Christians to understand the good news of Jesus Christ?" (Childs, *Biblical Theology*, 226).

The "directorial eye" of the evangelist

Why then has the tradition on the whole not viewed the synoptic narratives in terms of YHWH, preferring to put the focus entirely if not completely on Jesus of Nazareth? The answer at bottom is that it has failed to perceive what I call "the directorial eye of the evangelist." What do I mean? Let me explain with the help, appropriately, of what Graham Greene called the most important art-form of the twentieth century: cinematic film.

If I were to write the screenplay or (even less realistically!) direct the next movie on Jesus of Nazareth I would do it quite differently from the way it has been done before. This is for the simple reason that none of the previous films have quite succeeded (and some have failed quite strikingly) to portray Jesus of Nazareth as he is depicted in the Gospels. Nicholas Ray's *The King of Kings*, George Stevens' *The Greatest Story Ever Told*, Pier Paulo Pasolini's *The Gospel According to St. Matthew*, Franco Zefferelli's *Jesus of Nazareth*, Martin Scorsese's *The Last Temptation of Christ*, Mel Gibson's *The Passion*, a number of animated films (for example, *The Miracle-Maker*) – my perception of each of them is this. They have all fallen short if measured by what I call the "'directorial eye' of the evangelist." All in some way or another fail to recognize and include the "directorial eye" of the evangelist in the Synoptic Gospels.

It is therefore not merely that some have failed to be faithful to what is on the page of the gospel if measured by the key events of the gospel story. To be sure, when measured by the criterion of verisimilitude to the narrative in this sense, some of the films have exhibited quite striking disparities. Moreover, in these cases, the explanation is quite obvious. Scorsese's film *The Last Temptation of Christ* is based on Kazanzakisis' novel of the same name. But as Hans Frei pointed out almost thirty years ago in *The Identity of Jesus Christ*, this novel is not really about the personal identity of Jesus Christ as identified in the Gospels at all. By this he meant that the Jesus rendered in Kazanzakisis' novel – no less than some kind of Nietzschean superman – contradicts the Jesus rendered in the Gospels. Excepting some kind of exceptionally sophisticated harmonization tantamount in fact to sophistry, the two accounts cannot meaningfully be reconciled. But this means that Scorsese's film – in so far as it is a faithful account of Kazanzakisis' novel – cannot be a faithful account of the gospel story. Pasolini's *The Gospel According to St. Matthew* is also susceptible to a similar kind of judgement in that its Marxist-motivated/inspired presentation leaves us with a Christ selectively seen through the eyes of a director who has revolution and perhaps the Beatitudes continually to mind. Notwithstanding the cinematic esthetic beauty of this film – in the realm of religious film-making, Pasolini's comes to mind immediately as a masterpiece – its vision of Christ is more Pasolini than the gospel.

It may be said that, granted Scorsese's and Pasolini's films owe more to extraneous artistic and political sources than to the Gospels for their respective visions, surely many of the other films are direct accounts of the Gospels? Whatever the personal or idiosyncratic sensibilities or intentions of the director, surely Ray's film, Stevens' film, and even more plainly Zefferelli's film, are faithful renderings of the gospel as we have it? Both Stevens' and Zefferelli's respective films for example have not excised the resurrection from their cinematic accounts in the supposed name of realism or credibility but have unashamedly included reference to it. Indeed, they include most if not all of the key events of the gospel history. But this is not my criticism. Nor is it that the films have failed – or omitted – to depict what we understand as Jesus' divinity. There are a number of animated versions of the gospel story – most recently the *Miracle-Maker* – directed from an unashamedly Christian and proselytizing perspective that clearly emphasize this aspect of Jesus' identity.

Yet I would argue that none of these features are in themselves sufficient to guarantee a faithful rendering of the synoptic narrative. Ironically, faithfulness in the strict sense exclusively to what is communicated or told us directly by what is "on the page" is not enough. Indeed, I would say that the great irony at work is that in all the cases where the director's primary concern is getting the ostensive reference of the Gospels – resurrection included –

on to the screen, the consequence will be a vision cut asunder from that of the "directorial eye" of the evangelist. This is because it is to present us with a vision that is *ultimately at odds with the gospel. It is to create a film that, though not without great emotional content, will focus on the key events of the narrative – cross, resurrection – without any kind of sensitivity to those details in the narrative which, though less directly communicated than these key events, provide for the narrative's deepest interpretative key.* Unless one includes in one's cinematic vision what is communicated merely indirectly, or only subtly insinuated, or in a word, *shown* by the narrative – and not only what is directly communicated or unequivocally said – *theological discrepancy will have intruded to vitiate the fundamental objective of the gospel's own vision.* For if one merely depicts what is *unequivocally* stated on the page, one will omit what is merely "*equivocally*" conveyed on the page – which is to say, one will be retelling the narrative without looking at it through the directorial lens of the evangelist.[2]

And this means that you would not see that the gospel narrative is the story of YHWH – precisely the judging yet desisting forbearing self identified in the previous chapters of this book – who takes his own judgement on himself in the form of his Son, Jesus of Nazareth. You would not see this because you would not see what the evangelist sees through his directorial lens. He sees that *Pontius Pilate's judgement on Jesus in the passion narrative leading inexorably to death on the cross is in fact YHWH's own judgement on Jesus.* This is what the evangelist perceives is the real theological identity of Pilate's judgement.

---

[2] If one so wishes, one could think of the "directorial eye" of the evangelist as a species of illocutionary stance in the manner in which Wolterstorff has it in his book *Divine Discourse*. The illocutionary stance could be understood in terms of the use to which the writer puts the meaning of the text. It is quite unambiguously "off the page" but is necessary to distinguish e.g. fiction-telling from historical truth-claiming. It is within the latter category that the "directorial eye" of the evangelist as regards Pontius Pilate is to be sought. Donald Davidson is perhaps the primary origin of the necessity of introducing the distinction between use (construed in his terms as "belief") and meaning into semantics on the grounds that meaning on its own cannot but underdetermine interpretation. See his *Inquiries into Truth and Interpretation*.

Here is the crucial question, Why *did* the evangelist take recourse to employing the literary device of the "directorial lens"? In the very part of the synoptic narrative in which YHWH seemed most absent – the passion narrative – he was in fact most present (though he is also present – again "invisibly" but most potently – in the raising of Jesus). But this could only be perceived through, as it were, the "directorial eye" of the evangelist. It was not something that was said explicitly in the course of events related in the narrative; rather it was intimated indirectly, insinuated, indirectly communicated. To use a Wittgensteinian concept, it was shown, not said. Why?

On the one hand, the evangelist wanted to say that Pilate's judgement on Jesus belonged to the very essence of YHWH's history with Israel. In seeing Pilate's judgement as YHWH's judgement, the evangelist meant to incorporate it into a history of Israel that crucially encompasses the Babylonian destruction and exile of the southern kingdom of Judah in 587 BC and the demise of the northern kingdom of Israel in 722 BC. In the context of the resurrection appearances, the evangelist's "great idea," even vision, is that the judgement that YHWH executes on Jesus in the passion narrative is of the same generic kind (order) that he had previously executed on Judah in 587 BC and on Israel in 722 BC. Just as Scripture has it that both the Babylonian and Assyrian defeat of each kingdom is in fact identical with the judgement of the God of Israel, then so the "directorial eye" of the evangelist has it that Pilate's judgment of Jesus is also the judgement of God on Jesus.

On the other hand, the synoptic narratives were most probably conceived and written in their final form before the tension between the Christian community and the Jewish authorities reached such a level that those Jews who confessed Christ were eventually excommunicated from the synagogue (ca. 85–90 AD). In contradistinction from John's Gospel,[3] the Synoptic Gospels

---

[3] All four gospels of course also aim to proselytize gentiles. With the excommunication from the synagogue of those Jews who confessed Christ (ca. 85–90 AD), it is likely that Christians and Jews had gone their separate ways into two distinct and antagonistic social groups by the time the history of tradition had produced John's Gospel (see Dunn, *Partings of the Ways*). Israel was no longer being asked to decide for or

bear witness to the efforts of those Jews, who will subsequently be excommunicated from the synagogue, to proselytize those Jews of the synagogue who may or may not be excommunicated from the synagogue – who may or may not come to accept Jesus as the Messiah. "Israel" has not yet bifurcated into its two great historic religious communities – rabbinic Judaism and Christianity. Jewish Christianity could still hope to become the mainstream Jewish identity. In such a context, what made the synoptic *narrative* a *gospel* narrative is a crucial *kerygmatic* dimension. This kerygmatic dimension calls for a *faith-decision* of a certain kind on the part of the listener or audience.

Old Testament narrative such as the Deuteronomistic history did not evince this kerygmatic property. It was completely uninterested in asking the people of Israel to make a faith-decision regarding the theological identity of the Assyrian and Babylonian conquests. Almost certainly there was reflection on the nature of these calamities as regards their theological identity, and in particular, how the "one who had released Israel from the bondage of Egypt" could have visited such catastrophes on his people. But once the theological explanation had been determined – "written in stone" – in the form of sacred writing, Scripture even, the appropriate response to the genre was not one of "conversion" to or "faith" in Judaism. The people of Israel were not seeking new adherents to their faith; what they wanted was entirely to do with themselves, and that was to adjust or augment their belief-system in order to arrive at a constant, in the sense of consonant, *internal* self-identity as regards their covenant relationship with YHWH.

This explains why the Deuteronomistic narrative makes it quite clear that these events are God's judgement on Judah and Israel respectively. Scripture tells us quite clearly that YHWH acted against the northern kingdom (2 Kgs. 17:18–23) and, even more pointedly, *YHWH himself tells us in Scripture what he will do to Judah* (2 Kgs. 20:16–19; 21:10–16). There are no "degrees of

---

[3] (*continued*) against the gospel as the continuation or the concluding chapter of YHWH's story. The claim is now "fixed in stone" just as it is in the case of the Deuteronomistic history even though there is no real narrative presentation of the atonement in John's Gospel (although the truth-claim is made).

freedom" in this biblical narrative. To affirm the narrative "on the page" is to affirm that Babylon's and Assyria's actions against Judah and Israel respectively were identical with YHWH's judgement and actions against Judah and Israel respectively. It is intrinsic to the identity of *remaining* a member of the people of Israel.

In contrast, one *became* a Jewish Christian, a Gentile Christian. One made a faith-decision; one responded to the synoptic narrative as kerygma. Even within the context of the resurrection appearances, one made a faith-decision that Pilate's judgement belonged to the same theological-historical genus of action as the Babylonian and Assyrian conquests.

Whose do you say Pilate's judgement on Jesus is? Is it merely his own, so that Jesus' death is a consequence of the power of the secular and religious authorities alone. Or is it in reality – though physically embodied in individuals such as Pontius Pilate – really YHWH acting in history and therefore YHWH's own judgement on Jesus?

YHWH is not narrated as speaking either in the passion narrative or in the resurrection narrative as he is, say, toward the end of 2 Kings. (Intriguingly, Barth used the phrase "the language of facts" [*der Sprache der Tatsachen*], Barth *CD* IV/1.) In that sense, it is *left open* for the Gentile or Jewish reader or listener of the word to respond to the kerygma – make a faith-decision – for or against the theological identity of Pilate's judgement. But what a momentous decision it is; for if we decide that Pilate's judgement is the God of Israel's judgement on Jesus then we are in effect claiming that this narrative belongs to the history of YHWH's personal relationship with his people, Israel, as depicted in Old Testament narrative. We may even claim that it is – in some sense or another – the concluding chapter (and what a chapter!) of the history of YHWH with his people Israel, as depicted in Old Testament narrative.

The God of Israel identifying himself with Pilate's judgement in the narrative is precisely the God of Israel who had judged Israel earlier – quintessentially in the Babylonian exile of Judah in 587 BC but also in 722 BC with the fall of the northern kingdom. Old Testament Scripture makes it quite clear that the actions of, respectively, Babylonian military might as regards Judah, and Assyrian ascendancy as regards Israel are to be identified with

YHWH's judgement on Judah and Israel respectively. The parallel is clear. Pilate as representative of the Roman Empire in Palestine stands in this respect in a one-to-one relation with the Babylonian and Assyrian empires. All are to be identified with YHWH's judgement.

Moreover, in affirming what the evangelist perceived through his "directorial lens", the Jewish or Gentile Christian had responded to what was the essential and objective *kerygmatic locus* in the synoptic narrative. *Their faith-decision constituted an actual participation in the story itself.* The Jewish or Gentile Christian who perceived along with the evangelist that Pilate's judgement was really YHWH's judgement effectively *defined themselves as one of those who had been saved by Jesus' substitutionary action.* (In this sense it can be said the synoptic narrative indirectly communicated a doctrine of substitutionary atonement which had within itself the potential to inspire an unrivalled "pulpit performance" of "preaching the gospel" as a triumph of dialectic and imagination.)

In his book *The Genesis of Secrecy* the literary critic Frank Kermode uses the language of "insiders" and "outsiders" in the context of the question Jesus asks Peter at Caesarea Philippi (Mark 8.31–33) (Kermode, *Genesis of Secrecy*, 112). One's answer to the question, "Who do you say I am?" effectively defines one as an insider – in so far as one repeats Peter's answer (the Messiah, the Son of God, etc.) – or as an "outsider" if one rejects Peter's answer. Exactly the same logic operates in the question the evangelist asks about Pilate's judgement. The question whether Pilate's judgement in the narrative is in fact also God's judgement leading to "judicial" execution by crucifixion, or whether what we have here is a purely human tragedy of an innocent man sentenced to death – will define whether you are an "insider" and therefore Judeo-Christian, or an "outsider" who rejects this kind of theological conception of history at work in the narrative.

Just as YHWH *the judging yet desisting, forbearing divine identity* is in fact manifest in these two great crises – for reasons I have specified in Chapters 7 and 9 – then so he is also manifest as this historical identity in the gospel narrative. YHWH the judging yet desisting, forbearing identity is equally present in gospel narrative. He is the one identity holding to two Testaments in one unity while allowing the independent "plain-sense" voice of each to have its say.

But the judgement Jesus of Nazareth proclaims on Israel and the world is precisely *eschatological* judgement. It is of such a nature that if "this strange judgement had not taken place, there would be only a lost world and lost men" (Barth, *CD* IV/1, 222). Accordingly, YHWH the God of Israel takes this judgement – his own judgement – *on himself* in the form of his Son, Jesus of Nazareth. Crucially, the way in which this happens in the narrative implies that the gospel story objectively contains a doctrine of substitutionary atonement that *involves most intimately Jesus of Nazareth substituting himself in place of Israel and the world, and undergoing YHWH's judgement in their stead.*

The breakthrough: Barth's "narrative" doctrine of substitutionary atonement

It was in fact Barth who made the decisive breakthrough toward moving the conclusion that the gospel could be understood as the story of YHWH in the above sense. I say "decisive break-through *toward* moving this conclusion" because I do not think that Barth himself ultimately understood the gospel narrative in terms of YHWH the God of Israel who takes his own judgement on himself in the form of his Son, Jesus of Nazareth. I am inclined to think that his "christocentric concentration" (as it was called by Von Balthasar) led him to a overly christocentric conception of the God of Israel whose "refusal to give His name"[4] is finally known only in the revealed identity of Jesus Christ. Barth to my mind put insufficient emphasis on the fact that the God of Israel has a *prior* identity to that of Jesus of Nazareth (in the exodus and Deuteronomistic narratives, for example!). Instead of understanding Jesus in terms of the prior identity of YHWH the God of Israel, Barth's christocentric focus reversed the relation and subordinated the identity of the latter to that of the former. This is

---

[4] For some sterling criticism of the evacuation of the identity of the God of Israel from Christian doctrine in modern times, see Soulen, "YHWH the Triune God," 37–39. See also Soulen, *Christian Theology and the God of Israel*.

why it may be said that Barth offers no substantial interpretation of the plain sense of Old Testament narrative. He has no theology of the plain sense of the exodus narrative or of the Deuteronomistic history, for example.

But paradoxically, though Barth puts too light a stress on the independent witness and plain sense of the Old Testament as regards his conception of the identity of YHWH, he was almost unerringly right when it came to the relation between Jesus and YHWH in the New Testament, and the plain sense of the synoptic narratives in particular. Any judgement of Barth as a "front-wheel drive" theologian must be tempered by this observation. As regards the synoptic narratives, Barth was a "back-wheel drive" theologian in the sense that *he puts much more emphasis on the presence of YHWH in the Synoptic Gospels than is customary for a theologian of his christocentric orientation.* Though the gospel narrative does in fact appear to be much more about Jesus of Nazareth and less about YHWH, the God of Israel, this is not in the least incompatible with the view that the narrative is in fact about YHWH taking his own judgement on himself. It was Barth who made the crucial breakthrough as regards how the narrative could be understood in this way.

The most powerful version of the atonement is one that understands Jesus of Nazareth in terms of the identity of YHWH, the God of Israel, not the other way round. *But the precise way in which YHWH does this involves most intimately Jesus of Nazareth substituting himself in place of Israel and the world, and undergoing YHWH's judgement in their stead.* Barth's careful formulation of the mechanics of this substitution is in fact his signal contribution to the doctrine of atonement.

There are four crucial steps to understanding Barth's doctrine of substitutionary atonement. The first two steps are to do with literary form and content. The *first* focuses on Barth's preference in this respect for the synoptic narratives over the Johannine one. The *second* draws attention to the essential three-part structure of the literary shape of the synoptic narrative. The *third* step involves foregrounding what Barth calls the "judicial framework" of the first two parts of this narrative. Jesus declares the eschatological judgement of God in the first part of the narrative and is himself judged by the ruling Jewish body, the Sanhedrin, and then most decisively by the governor and procurator of Judea, Pontius Pilate. As Barth puts it, the passion narrative is best described within a judicial framework: "an arrest, a hearing, a prosecution in various courts, a torturing, and then an execution and burial" (Barth, *CD* IV/1, 226). The *fourth* step is the really significant one. In the light of Jesus' resurrection appearances after his death on the cross, the evangelist invites his "readers" or "audience" to discern in Pontius Pilate's judgement the divine judgement at work. In this way is the merely human judicial framework transformed into a theological drama of substitutionary atonement.

The question is this, Is the story simply about a man who proclaimed the judgement of God on Israel and the world and then died an inglorious failure on a cross outside the gates of Jerusalem at the hands of the ruling Roman authorities? Was Pilate's judgement on Jesus merely the judgement of one man (no matter how powerful) on another? Or is the narrative about YHWH taking his own judgement on himself in the form of his Son, Jesus of Nazareth? In other words, is the narrative about inglorious failure or is it about substitutionary atonement? Let me take these four steps in turn.

The locus of Barth's doctrine is the synoptic narratives

The locus of Barth's doctrine of substitutionary atonement is in fact the gospel narratives at the head of the canonical shape of the New Testament, the synoptic narratives: Matthew, Mark, and Luke. For Barth this locus is evidence that substitutionary atonement is in fact the most important doctrine of the New Testament.

A short historical note would be worthwhile at this juncture. In *Church Dogmatics* IV/1, Barth notes how Luther's preference was for the Johannine Gospel over the synoptics. In making this preference Luther belonged to a tradition that stretched pre-eminently back to Origen and continued up from Augustine through the medieval period to Luther's own time, and beyond.[5]

---

[5] Indeed John's Gospel only cedes its pre-eminence in this respect in the wake of the results of historical- and source-criticism, and, in particular – in the course of the nineteenth century – the general

The reason for this is precisely the overtly "pedagogical" or "doctrinal" nature of the figure of Jesus in John's Gospel, which makes the gospel a different genre of narrative. This is why Calvin thought that one should read John's Gospel first and then turn to the synoptics afterwards. He writes that the Gospel of John is "a key to open the door to the understanding of the others. For whoever grasps the power of Christ as it is here graphically portrayed, will afterwards read with advantage what the others relate about the manifested Redeemer" (Calvin, *Gospel of John*, 6). And later in the same paragraph he writes: "As to John being put fourth in order, it was done because of his order in time. In reading them a different order will be better" (Calvin, *Gospel of John*, 6). As is known, Calvin took his own advice when it came to exegesis, the commentary on John appearing in 1553, followed by the harmony of the Synoptic Gospels in 1555. Calvin sums up the difference between the two genres in a way that is characteristic of how the whole classical tradition viewed the difference. John's Gospel "emphasised more the doctrine in which Christ's office and the power of His death and resurrection are explained" than the synoptics which simply "narrate the life and death of Christ" but as it were "more fully" (Calvin, *Gospel of John*, 6).

Now, in the paragraph in *CD* IV/1 in which Luther's preference is noted, Barth expresses his agreement with the judgement of tradition on the synoptic narratives. He writes: "It is obvious in these Gospels there is little express mention of the significance of the Christ event which took place there and then" (Barth, *CD* IV/1, 224). Instead, it "is content simply to tell the story – this is how it was, this is how it happened. There is interpretation only in the lightest and sometimes rather alien strokes" (Barth, *CD* IV/1, 227). And later on in IV/1 he says: "The Gospel story [expressed in the synoptics] . . . does not offer any theological explanation. It says hardly anything about the significance of the event" (Barth, *CD* IV/1, 239).

---

[5] (*continued*) acceptance of the historical priority of Mark. Hitherto, a great nineteenth-century theologian like Schleiermacher had taken the view that this gospel carried the greatest historical weight due to the fact it had been written by "the beloved disciple," John himself – unlike Mark's Gospel.

Yet the strange fact presents itself to us that it was in the synoptic narratives – where just the kind of "doctrinal explanation" of which Calvin spoke was precisely lacking – that Barth found his doctrine of substitutionary atonement. He persevered to find it precisely in the historicity of the narrative itself rather than being content with the more doctrinal affirmations of John 1:29 or 3:16; passages that, as we know, speak more directly of atonement or reconciliation. Utterly paradoxically, it is the narrative's very reticence bordering on silence as regards *the presence of YHWH in the passion narrative* that is *indicative* of the very doctrine of substitutionary atonement that Barth is after. I mention this now because this feature is of seminal importance when we come to step four.

The literary shape of the synoptic narrative: the three essential parts

The early twentieth-century German theologian Martin Kähler famously characterized Mark's Gospel as a passion narrative with an extended introduction. This description is now taken to be too simplistic a characterization of the gospel; and one implication would be that one has to give *equal* weight to both Jesus' ministry and his passion history, instead of "privileging" the latter at the expense of the former. What has not been rejected is something like a consensus view to the effect that Mark's Gospel has three essential parts to it when the sequel to Jesus' death on the cross – the resurrection-appearances history – is added. (We might add to this the contemporary view that Mark is made of two essential sources [when we set aside the resurrection tradition]: units of tradition arranged by the evangelist constitutive of Jesus' ministry; and a pre-Markan passion narrative which achieved a self-contained literary form at an early stage in the tradition.)

We therefore have three parts if we restrict ourselves to the Synoptic Gospel that is Mark's. To be sure, both Matthew and Luke prefix an infancy narrative to their gospels; hence, we cannot conclude without qualification that the literary shape of the synoptic narrative *per se* is three-part in structure. Notwithstanding this however, *in the context of Barth's doctrine of substitutionary atonement*, there are three essential parts to the synoptic narrative.

Discernment of literary shape is a literary matter and not a matter of faith as it were. It comes as no real surprise therefore that – whatever fundamental disagreement existed between, on the one hand, Barth, and, on the other, the modern critical (liberal) tradition of David Friedrich Strauss to Albert Schweitzer to Rudolf Bultmann and beyond – there is no fundamental disagreement on the question of the narrative structure of the Synoptic Gospel. All agreed that the final form of the narrative could be broken down into three essential parts. The first part corresponded to Jesus proclaiming the eschatological judgement of the God of Israel on Israel and the world in Galilee. The second part was the passion narrative culminating in Jesus' death on the cross. The third was the sequel to the first two parts, the Easter narrative: the resurrection-appearances history or encounters between the risen Jesus and his followers.

Barth locates the division between the first part and the second part in the following way: "The sections from the record of the entry into Jerusalem up to and including the last supper can be regarded as belonging to the first or the second part, or as the transition from the one to the other. But from the description of Gethsemane [onwards] at any rate the second part forms a self-contained whole" (Barth, *CD* IV/1, 226).

Jesus' agony in the Garden of Gethsemane is in fact the key moment in the narrative when the man who had hitherto proclaimed the eschatological judgement of YHWH's kingdom now himself begins to undergo the judgement of the religious and civil authorities (the Jewish and Roman authorities respectively) culminating in his execution on the cross. Judgement takes place in the first part of the synoptic narrative and judgement takes place in the second part of the synoptic narrative. For this reason Barth provides an exposition of the first two parts of the historicity of the synoptic narrative in terms of a *judicial framework*.

In other words, mere literary appreciation of the synoptic narrative as *narrative* does not suffice. It does not suffice because we must come to terms with the *historicity* of the first two parts of the narrative. The judicial framework does just that; and in doing so brings us a step nearer *divine* substitutionary atonement, which is the fundamental theme of the gospel. So Barth.

The first two parts are to be understood in terms of a judicial framework

It is a commonplace observation of New Testament scholars that Paul's letters evince very little interest in the historical Jesus, preferring to know Jesus Christ "after the flesh." Bultmann saw in Paul's remark (as he saw in John's Gospel) the first stage in the process of demythologizing the mythical Jesus into a Christ-figure accessible to modern philosophical if not theological categories.

In contrast, Barth sees in Paul's lack of concern with the historical Jesus precisely a *lack of reference to the historical contents outlined in the first part of the synoptic narrative*. Since Barth understands Paul as offering essentially a theological interpretation of the passion narrative – the second part of the narrative – in terms of a "theology of the cross," this is not of itself a major shortcoming. For one thing it dovetails perfectly with Barth's understanding of the canonical shape of the New Testament where Paul provides, among other things, a commentary on Jesus' death on the cross (Barth, *CD* IV/1, 313).

Yet as a child of the nineteenth century, Barth knew that the great book which had brought to an end the first quest for the historical Jesus – Albert Schweitzer's *The Quest of the Historical Jesus* – had made a great deal of *the Jesus of the first part of the synoptic narrative*. By the end of the nineteenth century the historical priority of Mark had superseded the earlier traditional belief that this status be awarded to John, the gospel of the "beloved disciple" who had known Jesus personally (as opposed to the other evangelists) and therefore had first-hand knowledge of Jesus' life. Schweitzer's book reflected this reversal of priority. More importantly, Schweitzer detected in the first part of Mark – and therefore in Matthew and Luke (both of whom he rightly thought reliant on Mark) – a Jesus-figure who remains a pivotal influence on New Testament studies even today.[6] The Jesus

---

[6] I speak most obviously of N. T. Wright's *Jesus and the Victory of God*, more of which will be said at the end of the chapter.

Schweitzer discerned in the first part of the synoptic narratives was no less than *an eschatological Jesus who had declared God's final judgement on Israel and the world*. Not for Schweitzer the picture of Jesus as a mere teacher of ethics for a future world religion!

Barth was not unaware of the rationality, even probable historicity, of Schweitzer's apocalyptic Jesus. Paradoxically, he had no compunction in concurring with Schweitzer's depiction of Jesus since it is essentially what he too discerned in the first part of the synoptic narrative, *reading it as a theologian reading Scripture. Barth agreed that something like Schweitzer's Jesus was a valid reading of the first part of the synoptic narrative*. Moreover, he agreed that the first part must be just as determinative for the identity of Jesus of Nazareth as the second part, the passion narrative; the part traditionally taken since Paul to be in the end the sole criterion of the identity of Jesus. As Barth put it, we "must understand the first part of the story as a commentary on the second, and *vice-versa*" (Barth, *CD* IV/1, 235) This stress on the first part of the synoptic narrative as equally important in the determination of a doctrine of substitutionary atonement was a new phenomenon in the history of systematic and dogmatic theology and heralded Barth's desire to play the critical-historical school at its own game!

Ironically, it is precisely because of this demand (of reciprocity of commentary) that Barth had other ideas than the ones proffered by Schweitzer as regards the passion narrative. Paradoxically, where Schweitzer saw nothing but a romantic, tragic hero dying an inglorious and deluded death on a cross (Jesus had proclaimed the end of the world but had died an unfulfilled failure in this respect), Barth discerned a certain commonality of motif in the passion narrative corresponding precisely to the motif of judgement implicit in the first part of the narrative, to Jesus' proclamation of the eschatological judgement of YHWH on Israel and the world. Just as Jesus judges in the first part then so he is judged in the second part. The passion narrative corresponds to a sequence of events Barth describes as: "an arrest, a hearing, a prosecution in various courts, a torturing, and then an execution and burial" (Barth, *CD* IV/1, 226). In other words, Jesus judges in the first part of the narrative and he is judged in a judicial context – first by the Jewish authority in Jerusalem, the

Sanhedrin – and then most importantly by Pontius Pilate, the governor and procurator of Judea.[7] As we will see, Pilate's judgement is most important – not merely because his is the judgement that leads inexorably to Jesus' execution on the cross, but because it is the locus of the real identity the evangelist perceives at work in the narrative: YHWH's judgement on Israel and the world falling instead on Jesus himself.

There is no doubt that the judicial framework that Barth employed to great effect in his exegesis of the literary structure of the synoptic narrative was inspired by the Reformed doctrine of the judicial work of Christ, and by Calvin's version of this doctrine in particular. I have dealt with the historical roots of this aspect of Barth's doctrine of substitutionary atonement at some length in Chapter 11 of my book, *Karl Barth and the Strange New World within the Bible: Barth, Wittgenstein, and the Metadilemmas of the Enlightenment.* Suffice to say that Barth chose the "forensic" framework over the traditional patristic and medieval understandings of Christ's death of the cross – sacrificial or cultic, military, financial or feudal – because, as he put it himself, he found that he was able to see the narrative "better and more distinctly and more comprehensively" under the judicial framework than would be possible had he committed himself radically, for example, to the priestly framework (Barth, *CD* IV/1, 275). The reason Barth is so intent on emphasizing the judicial framework of the passion narrative – in preference to the presence of the priestly or sacrificial work of Jesus – is that it in turn corresponds to the larger judicial framework that also encompasses the first part of the synoptic narrative. In contrast, the "priestly" or "sacrificial" motif is largely if not completely limited to the passion narrative, the second part. Hence in the context of narrative historicity it is not able to construe the passion narrative as a commentary on the first part of the narrative. The great strength of the judicial framework is that it does.

---

[7] Conversely, though Pilate's judgement on Jesus occurs in the nexus of the events leading from Gethsemane to the cross, it also has a context beyond the passion narrative itself. This context is precisely the *first part* of the narrative. Pilate's judgement on Jesus does not take place in a vacuum. It takes place precisely in a narrative context in which Jesus has previously – already – proclaimed YHWH's own judgement on Israel and, by extension, on the world.

Moreover, the manner in which it delivers a doctrine of substitutionary atonement to the church in nowise depends on the believer's subjective act of faith that Jesus' death on the cross was a sacrifice. To be sure, Jesus did die for us on the cross as Paul explicitly says, but the grounds for this assertion emerge at bottom from the objective truth-claims one finds in the judicial framework of the synoptic narrative itself. The assertion is not based, as it were, exclusively on the ingenious theological meaning which Paul provides in his epistles as an interpretation of Jesus' death on the cross. Indeed, Barth would say that Paul's sacrificial metaphors can be understood only with the context of the canonical shape of the New Testament. Only if we observe the canonical priority of the synoptic narrative in this sense are we able to see that the concept of sacrifice constitutes a commentary on the judicial work of Jesus of Nazareth narrated in the passion rather than vice versa.

Before we proceed to the crucial fourth step in the exposition of Barth's doctrine of substitutionary atonement, let me recapitulate the three steps that we have just covered. First, we noted that Barth's preference is for the synoptic narratives over the Johannine one. Next, we drew attention to Barth's emphasis on the essential three-part structure of the literary shape of the synoptic narrative. The *third* step foregrounds what Barth calls the "judicial framework or shape" of the first two parts of this narrative. Jesus declares the eschatological judgement of God in the first part of the narrative and is himself judged by the ruling Jewish body, the Sanhedrin, and then most decisively by the governor and procurator of Judea, Pontius Pilate: the passion narrative is best described within a judicial framework: "an arrest, a hearing, a prosecution in various courts, a torturing, and then an execution and burial" (Barth, *CD* IV/1, 226)

What is common to each of these steps is that none of them presupposes any kind of faith-stance or extra-naturalistic assumption on the part of the reader of Scripture. This observation is especially pertinent to the third step – the most controversial as far as biblical scholars would be concerned. Though there are biblical scholars such as Dominic Crossan who argue that it is circumstantially, historically unlikely that an encounter between Pontius Pilate and Jesus actually took place – far less that this encounter took the form of the dialogue narrated in the gospels – equally there are biblical scholars who, again on historical grounds, want to affirm just this historical truth-claim. N. T. Wright for example implies that it is just as rational to affirm that the encounter took place as to say it didn't. Whether one wants to query the accuracy of the gospel account of the actual words they spoke to each other, one would at the very least hold that, whatever happened, Pilate did issue a judgment on Jesus that led to Jesus' execution by crucifixion. The latter to Wright's mind is a rational claim to make.

But note well: a biblical scholar like Crossan isn't arguing a point about theology. In particular, he isn't arguing a point about whether substitutionary atonement is true or rational to believe. He is arguing over the strictly naturalistic-historical point about whether Jesus ever stood in front of the governor of Judea, Pontius Pilate. In so far as he rejects the latter, he rejects the validity of the judicial framework as a means of understanding the synoptic narrative. But it seems – if we take another biblical scholar like N. T. Wright as our guide – that it is just as rational to affirm the judicial framework as it is to reject it.[8] Barth would agree. But, again, *note well*: the affirmation of the judicial framework, inclusive of the encounter between Pilate's judgment and Jesus' execution, is entirely compatible with Schweitzer's view of Jesus' passion and death as expressive of tragic and essentially ignoble failure. Neither God nor theology necessarily belong in the judicial framework that Barth discerns in the synoptic narrative.

The resurrection and the identity of Jesus of Nazareth

What makes the decisive difference is seeing the judicial framework in the light of the resurrection appearances. The first two parts must be

---

[8] The following point cannot be made sufficiently often. Though it is not rational for one person to affirm both p and not-p, it is not inconsistent to say that, on the one hand Barth affirms p and, on the other, another person, say, Crossan, affirms not-p. Though p and not-p cannot both be historically true – and therefore it would be inconsistent to claim this – it is rational for one person to affirm p and another to affirm not-p. Theology is essentially about the rationality of historical truth-claims.

understood from the perspective of the third part, Jesus' appearances after his death on the cross to those who had known him during his pre-Easter life. Barth takes the view that, outside of the context of the resurrection appearances, Jesus' life did indeed end in failure on the cross, no matter the presence of a judicial thematic across the first two parts of the narrative. The synoptic witness in the passion narrative is that the disciples were completely at sea, unable to comprehend what was at work in what was happening to Jesus after Gethsemane (and indeed largely oblivious to his words at the Last Supper); accordingly, Peter denied, Judas betrayed, and every last one of the disciples scattered after the crucifixion.[9]

But inside the context of the resurrection-appearances history, Jesus of Nazareth reveals himself to be included within the identity of YHWH, the God of Israel. For Barth it is not coincidental that the New Testament's confession of Jesus' divinity or his inclusion within the divine name of YHWH is always coupled with reference to his exaltation in his resurrection from the dead (Matt. 28:19).[10] In particular, the New Testament's confession at John 20:28 may be understood in this way, and Philippians 2:9–11 that Jesus is to be included within the divine name of YHWH.

But as Barth says of these witnesses [of the apostolic church], "it is not they who have given him this name, but God" (Barth, *CD* III/2, 450). And Barth goes on to say: "God has given him this name by exalting him above all things . . . (Phil. 2.9) out of and after his death on the cross" (Barth, *CD* III/2, 450). That is: YHWH has included Jesus in his own divine identity, his own divine soteriological identity by giving Jesus his own name *by* exalting or *in that* he exalted Jesus above all things through resurrecting him from the dead. YHWH is the one who raised Jesus by raising him from dead *and thus* exalting him above all things.[11] How it is rational to claim this, Barth would say, is because of Jesus of Nazareth's resurrection appearances as

---

[9] See Kümmel, *Theology of the New Testament*, 68–69.

[10] The name of the Father, the Son and the Holy Spirit is the New Testament counterpart to the name of YHWH in the Old Testament.

[11] In this context it is not difficult to deduce the significance Anselm's revealed name for God "that than which a *greater* [my italics] cannot be conceived" had for Barth. "Greater" is almost a synonym for "higher."

narrated in the gospel narratives. The resurrection-appearances history *presupposes* Jesus' resurrection from the dead (Barth, *CD* III/2, 447). I have dealt with Barth's exegesis of this history elsewhere and in particular how it is rational to affirm its historicity without falling foul of Troeltschian rationality as manifested, for example, in Troeltsch's famous principle of analogy.[12]

What Barth is effectively saying is that YHWH includes Jesus within his own divine soteriological identity *by* giving Jesus his own name. And he gives him this name precisely *by* raising him from the dead, which is to say, exalting him above all things in heaven and on earth.[13]

The implication is to be drawn: outside the resurrection-appearances history, the first two parts of the synoptic narrative – even inclusive of a compelling judicial pattern of motif – end

---

[11] (*continued*) Jesus effectively reveals himself to have this name – which proves his existence within the divine existence – in his resurrection appearances from the dead.

[12] I again refer to my book *Karl Barth and the Strange New World within the Bible* and, in particular, Chapter 8 though see also Chapter 6, 116–26. The key passage in this respect in the *Church Dogmatics* is *CD* IV/2, 144–48.

[13] It is clear that the resurrection stories are comprised of two essential motifs. The first is the empty tomb tradition witnessing to the claim that the God of Israel has raised Jesus from the dead. But the claim is not merely that Jesus has been raised from the dead, but that Jesus has been raised to heaven. This, I would submit, is the reason the angelic figures play a crucial role in the tradition: "He has risen! He is not here" (Mark 16:6). The second tradition is the appearances tradition, presupposing *the resurrection itself* – in the sense that Jesus *appears from heaven* (see Jenson, *Systematic Theology*, vol. 1, 194–201). But, as was said in Chapter 5, God raises Jesus from the dead in the sense that he determines himself to be the one who has the crucified one in the space peculiar and exclusive to God. This is the divine action underlying the resurrection of Jesus of Nazareth. Clearly the empty tomb tradition allows for the general resurrection from the dead, which can also be understood under the auspices of the act of divine self-determination in which God determines himself to be the one who raises us all from the dead. Jesus is already in heaven and we await a similar such act of self-determination which means that we too will exist in the space of God. To be raised from the dead is to be in the space of God peculiar and exclusive to him. That is the hope and the promise.

in inglorious, unfulfilled, deluded failure with the man Jesus' death on a cross. Inside their context, however, *the first two parts – inclusive of the same judicial framework – are to be included within the divine soteriological identity of YHWH.*[14] *In other words, the judicial framework itself is to be understood within the soteriological identity of YHWH.*

Barth's theological move: the judicial framework as substitutionary atonement

The crucial step in Barth's doctrine of substitutionary atonement is upon us. The question is this, How is the judicial framework of the synoptic narrative to be understood within the soteriological identity of YHWH? Barth understands the Easter story as "the commentary on the Gospel story in the unity and completeness of its first two parts" (Barth, *CD* IV/1, 228). In this context, Barth says, we "must understand the first part of the story as a commentary on the second, and *vice-versa*" (Barth, *CD* IV/1, 235). In other words: unless we affirm the resurrection-appearances history then we cannot understand the first two parts – Jesus proclaiming the eschatological judgement of God in Galilee and being judged and executed in and around Jerusalem – to be the *theological* unity that the evangelists understand them to be.

The corollary of this question is, How is someone like Schweitzer's Jesus – the Jesus of *the first part of the judicial*

---

[14] The resurrection appearances confer on Jesus' person or identity inclusion in the divine soteriological identity of YHWH. But Jesus' appearances also reveal that the risen Jesus is the same person as the one the disciples had encountered in his pre-Easter existence and history: "Jesus' resurrection appearances reveal that the risen Jesus declares himself to those who had known him in his identity with the one previously followed and had died on the cross and been buried" (Barth, *CD* IV/2, 144), who this person is in continuity. This is why Barth says that an alternative way of saying the same thing is to say that the name "YHWH" is "inseparable from [Jesus'] person, and His person inseparable from his name" (Barth, *CD* III/2, 450). The resurrection appearances tell us that the Jesus of the first two parts of the synoptic narrative is no less to be included in the divine soteriological identity of YHWH.

framework – to be understood within the divine identity of YHWH? For as we have noted, this Jesus who in Schweitzer's view declared the eschatological judgment of YHWH on Israel and the world *is* himself precisely the one who is to be included in the soteriological identity of YHWH. This means that Jesus is to be understood as included in the soteriological identity of YHWH even as he declares YHWH's own eschatological judgement on Israel and the world.

For Schweitzer, Jesus' life ends in tragic, vain death on a cross. And this remains true; even if Jesus' proclamation of YHWH's judgement in the first part of the narrative corresponds in particular to the Roman procurator Pontius Pilate's judgement of Jesus which leads ultimately to his execution on the cross as an "enemy of Rome"; even if the passion story culminating in Jesus' death is best described within the judicial framework of: "an arrest, a hearing, a prosecution in various courts, a torturing, and then an execution and burial" (Barth, *CD* IV/1, 226).

But what if, Barth asks, the evangelist wants to say that what is perhaps the most famous encounter between two people in western civilization, story, and history *was in fact really an encounter between Jesus and YHWH, the God of Israel*? What if the evangelist wanted to say that the judgement of Pilate on Jesus that had ultimately led to his execution on the cross *was in fact YHWH's own judgement on Jesus*?

Then, Barth said, we would not be reflecting on the historically insignificant datum of a Jewish man's death on a cross, but rather on a theological drama of substitutionary atonement, which involves *most intimately Jesus of Nazareth substituting himself in place of Israel and the world, and undergoing YHWH's judgement in their stead.* And we would be reflecting on this not as mere (subjective) interpretation of the narrative but as a historical truth-claim *objectively present in the narrative.*

The theological identity of Pilate's judgement: YHWH's judgement on Jesus

Before I proceed to the explanation of how the strictly theological identity of Pilate's judgement on Jesus could motivate the conclusion of a narrative "doctrine" of substitutionary atonement, I want to say something about the *historical* source of Barth's claim. It is most likely that the inspiration as regards the theological identity of Pilate's judgement was from Calvin. Barth lectured on the 1536 *Institutes* in his 1922 lectures on the theology of Calvin, and he was also extremely well acquainted with the 1559 edition. In both places Calvin construes Pilate's judgement of Jesus from his judgement seat (John 19:13) as a prefiguration of the judgement that would have awaited us at God's heavenly judgement seat on the last day had Jesus not substituted himself in place of us and taken on our impending judgement in his way to the cross. In the 1536 edition Calvin writes: "He suffered . . . under Pontius Pilate, condemned indeed by the judge's sentence, as a criminal and wrongdoer, in order that we might, by his condemnation, be absolved before the judgement seat of the highest Judge" (Calvin, *Institutes*, 1536 ed., 54).

And more expansively in the 1559 edition, Calvin writes:

> The curse caused by our guilt was awaiting us at God's heavenly judgement seat. Accordingly Scripture first relates Christ's condemnation before Pontius Pilate, governor of Judea, to teach us that the penalty to which we were subject had been imposed upon this righteous man. We could not escape God's dreadful judgement. To deliver us from it, Christ allowed himself to be condemned before a mortal man – even a wicked and profane one (Calvin, *Institutes*, 1559 ed., 509).

He continues:

> To take away our condemnation, it was not enough for him to suffer any kind of death: to make satisfaction for our redemption a form of death had to be chosen in which he might free us both by transferring our condemnation to himself and by taking our guilt on himself. If he had been murdered by thieves or slain in an insurrection by a raging mob, in such a death there would be no evidence of satisfaction. But when he was arraigned before the judgement seat as a criminal, accused and pressed by testimony, and condemned by the mouth of the judge to die – we know by these proofs that he took the role of a guilty man and evildoer (Calvin, *Institutes*, 1559 ed., 509).[15]

---

[15] It is also worth pointing out that a similar idea is expressed in his 1555 *Harmony of the Gospels*. Calvin describes the encounter between Jesus and Pilate in these terms: "The Son of God wished to stand bound

If we look at Barth's exegesis on Pilate's judgement we see that he follows Calvin's emphasis on the importance of the "judicial" aspects in the details of the narrative. Like Calvin, Barth foregrounds the significance of the "narrative" fact that Pilate acts as a judge sentencing a man as in a court of law. Barth would agree with Calvin that, had Jesus been "murdered by thieves, or slain in an insurrection by a raging mob" the theological interpretation of his death would have to be quite different from the one generated in a judicial context. In other words, *Barth's perception that the synoptic evangelists wanted to identify Pilate's judgement on Jesus as God's judgement on Jesus is very probably to be traced to Calvin.*

There is, however, a very significant and very interesting difference. This difference, in my opinion, made a decisive contribution to Barth's claim that substitutionary atonement was objectively in the synoptic narrative. It is not merely that Calvin thought God had providentially predestinated this most famous encounter in human history, nor that he thought God had done this from eternity.[16] To be sure, according to Calvin and indeed the whole classical tradition from Augustine to Aquinas, God acted in history from eternity as it were. *But this did not of itself preclude the possibility that God had decreed from eternity that Pilate's judgement of Jesus be his own judgement.* Such a position was clearly conceivable even given Calvin's understanding of God's

---

[15] (*continued*) before an earthly judge and therefore submit to the death sentence, that we might not doubt that we are freed from guilt and free to approach the heavenly throne of God . . . God's Son stood trial before a mortal man and suffered accusation and condemnation, that we might stand without fear in the presence of God" (Calvin, *Harmony of the Gospels*, vol. 3, 179).

[16] This is effectively what he says in his 1553 commentary on John's Gospel:

> if we want to read the story of Christ's death with profit, the chief point is to look to Christ's eternal counsel. The Son of God is before the judgement seat of a mortal man. If we think this was done by men's will and do not raise our eyes to God, our faith must needs be put to shame and confounded. But when we realise that our condemnation is blotted out by Christ's because it pleased the heavenly Father thus to reconcile mankind to himself, we . . . glory even in Christ's ignominy (Calvin, *Commentary on John's Gospel*, 165).

relation to time. But Calvin did not draw this conclusion. Rather, he drew the conclusion from the plain sense of Scripture that Jesus' encounter with Pilate remains merely and unalterably *an encounter between Christ and a mere man*. To be sure, the encounter constituted both a prefigurement of Jesus' intercession for us before the heavenly judgement seat of God; and of our standing before the same judgement but without fear of judgement since Jesus had taken it on himself in our stead. But Pilate's judgement is never in Calvin the presence of God's judgement then and there – whether real and *de facto* or providentially predestinated from God's vantage point in eternity.

It is quite otherwise with Barth. In contrast to Calvin, Barth thought that Pilate's judgement was *actually and really* God's judgement on Jesus then and there, occurring then and there in time, in historical time.[17] It was this insight that enabled him to make the seminal breakthrough to the idea of a doctrine of substitutionary atonement right there at the centre of the synoptic narratives. He realized that if Pilate's judgement then and there was in fact YHWH's judgement then and there – that this was what was narrated in the second part of the narrative – then he effectively had a doctrine of substitutionary atonement. How did he come to see this? *The answer is to do with how Barth interpreted the first part of the narrative.*

The two narrative conditions of substitutionary atonement

Barth asked two crucial questions. He asked the question, *What if the narrative is saying that YHWH's judgement on Jesus executed through Pilate in the passion narrative is the self-same judgement that Jesus declared on Israel and the world in the first part of the narrative?*

---

[17] According to Barth, God was in history acting in history. He had been in history ever since "the seventh day of creation" when he had determined himself to be within the spatial and temporal constitution of the world, the very same world he had created beforehand. For Barth this self-determination was sufficient for it to be true that God had spatially located himself within the world. This was what was meant by speaking of "God in heaven." Heaven was no mere mythological conception for Barth! See Chapter 5 of this book.

And he asked the question, What if the narrative is saying that
this is true because YHWH *made it true,* made his own judgement
– Pilate's judgement – on Jesus *the very same* judgement that Jesus
himself had previously declared in Galilee? In other words:
what if it were the case that not only is Pilate's judgement on
Jesus God's own judgement on Jesus, but also that this judgement of God's – expressed through Pilate's – is the very same
judgement that Jesus declared in the first part? And that both
were true because God made it so?

*Then, Barth says: we have a doctrine of substitutionary atonement
in the first three gospels at the head of the New Testament canon.*
It is there objectively in the narrative. As he puts it in *Church Dogmatics* IV the gospel story in its "unity and completeness" narrates a story in which:

> the divine subject of the judgement on man as which Jesus appears
> in the first part of the evangelical record becomes the object of this
> judgement from the episode of Gethsemane onwards. If this judge-
> ment is fulfilled at all – and that is what the Evangelists seem to be
> trying to say in the second part of their account – then it is with this
> reversal (Barth, *CD* IV/1, 238).

Barth indeed calls this reversal of judged and judge (the judge of
the first part of the narrative becoming the judge in the passion
narrative) a "curious reversal of fortune." Implicit in the above
passage is the fact that Jesus becomes the object of the *self-same*
eschatological judgement in the second part of the gospel story
that he issued in the first part of the gospel story. But he can only
become the subject of the same judgement if his own judgement
(God's judgement) coincides with Pilate's judgement (God's
judgement). This is indeed what Barth says. According to Barth,
the rationale behind the narration of Jesus' agony in Gethsemane
is precisely that the good will of God is absolutely at one with the
evil will of the Sanhedrin and of Pilate. Gethsemane marks the
beginning of the forsakenness of God that culminates in Jesus'
cry of dereliction on the cross. "The Lordship of God is concealed
under the lordship of evil and evil men" (Barth, *CD* IV/1, 269).
When Jesus utters the words: "Abba, Father, everything is possible for you. Take this cup from me. Yet not what I will, but what
you will" (Mark 14:36), what he is painfully and sorrowfully

aware of is the awful imminence of God's will identified with the evil that is acting against him even unto death on the cross. And indeed, it is God's will, concealed under what it is supremely *not*, that will bear down on Jesus once the sequence of events are set in motion by his arrest in Gethsemane.

It is because the above is true that Barth can make a claim regarding the relation of God's judgement in the second part of the narrative to Jesus' own declaration of God's judgement in the first part. Once again the "judicial" context inclusive of the first part of the gospel narrative is to the foreground. Barth writes: "It was a matter of the divine judgement being taken out of the hands of Jesus and placed in those of His supremely unrighteous judges and executed by them upon Him" (Barth, *CD* IV/1, 271).[18]

This is a crucial claim. The self-same judgement that Jesus had declared in the first part of the gospel narrative is "taken out of the hands of Jesus" and placed pre-eminently in the hands of Pilate. Since the identity of Jesus' judgement is precisely "the divine judgement" then so too is Pilate's judgement identical with "the divine judgement." Pilate's judgement on Jesus coincides with God's judgement – Jesus' eschatological judgement – exercised in the first part of the gospel story. Or more precisely perhaps: Pilate's judgement in the second part *is* Jesus' judgement in the first part.

The divine judgement therefore remains constant, remains the same across the first two parts of the synoptic narrative. What changes across the two parts is the object of judgement. In the first part Israel and the world constitute the object of judgement. In the second part, Jesus constitutes the object of judgement. It is because this truth holds that Jesus comes to be in the passion story the *object of his own judgement – his own judgement being the one that he had declared on Israel and the world in the first part of the narrative*. This is because the God of Israel had made *his* judgement on Jesus – identical with Pilate's judgement on Jesus – also identical with Jesus'

---

[18] What makes these people sinners – the Sanhedrin, Pilate, etc. – is the brute fact that they act against God in the person of Jesus. See Barth, *CD* IV/1, 499. Jesus, remember, reveals himself as God through the resurrection, and in the subsequent resurrection-appearances history.

judgement.[19] Therefore, I repeat: *Jesus becomes the object of his own judgement.* Were it not the self-same judgement, Jesus – God – could not have taken our place. For then it would be the case that Jesus had suffered a different judgement. And if he suffered a different judgement he could not have taken our place as the object of the judgement declared in the first part of the gospel story. This is the deep literal sense of the story of Barabbas' release (Mark 15:6–15). As Barth puts it: "a murderer is in every respect acquitted instead of Jesus, and Jesus is condemned to be crucified in his place" (Barth, *CD* IV/1, 224). More expansively, Barth writes: "the accusation, condemnation, and punishment to which [the second part of the Gospel story] refers all fall on the very One on whom they ought to fall least, and not at all on those on whom they ought to fall" (Barth, *CD* IV/1, 224). But Barth can say this only because he understands Pilate's judgement on Jesus as identical to – continuous with – the eschatological judgement that Jesus proclaims in Galilee.

Same judgement, different object of judgement equals *substitutionary atonement.* Jesus takes the place of Israel and the world. Jesus takes *our* place, whether Jew or Gentile.

There is an oft-quoted passage in *Church Dogmatics* IV/1 in which Barth writes: "The atonement is, noetically, the history about Jesus Christ, and ontically, Jesus Christ's own history. To say atonement is to say Jesus Christ. To speak of it is to speak of

---

[19] Note also it is not *Jesus* who makes Pilate's judgement his own judgement. Whether or not he could have done this given his divine status, he did not. It is YHWH the God of Israel who did. But there is an obvious distinction between Jesus and Pilate that points to the distinction between "ontic" and "functional" Christology. Jesus is God proclaiming God's judgement. That is ontic Christology (Jesus is not merely a prophet declaring God's judgement). To be sure, Pilate's judgement on Jesus is in reality God's judgement on Jesus but that does not make Pilate God proclaiming God's judgement. He is the instrument of the divine will. No matter it is Pilate, this is a "functional" Christology. That the gospel narrative makes this distinction between Jesus and Pilate is one more (literary) reason for thinking that this realistic narrative intends to make a distinction between its leading character or "hero" and the other secondary characters who surround him (and who appear to usher in his fate on a purely human level).

his history" (Barth, *CD* IV/1, 158). I contend that the exposition that I have provided of Barth's doctrine of substitutionary atonement constitutes the fundamental reason behind that claim. The identity of Jesus of Nazareth is precisely the self-realization of his historical identity in the encountering of the circumstances that happen upon him in the form of the Jewish authorities and, most especially, in his "judicial" encounter with Pontius Pilate. These circumstances are best interpreted in terms of Jesus the divine bearer of YHWH's judgement who (freely) becomes the object of his own judgement. Accordingly, atonement is itself objectively in the historical event that corresponds to the identity of Jesus of Nazareth; it is not a matter of the subjective interpretation of Jesus' death.

Jesus takes his own eschatological judgement on himself

But the judgement Jesus takes on himself in the passion is not just any kind of judgement; it is *eschatological* judgement that he takes on himself, the self-same judgement that he had declared on Israel and the world in his ministry. Barth utterly ironically concurs with the critical-historical tradition that follows in the wake of Weiss and Schweitzer (and in our own time, N. T. Wright). Jesus declares eschatological judgement on Israel and the world in the first part of the synoptic narrative and he becomes the object of this same judgement in the second part. Pilate's judgement is not merely God's judgement, it is God's eschatological judgement on Jesus.

What does it mean to be the object of eschatological judgement? The central theme is this. For Jesus to be the object of eschatological judgement in place of Israel and the world – us – is not merely to undergo death; it is to undergo *eschatological death* as in the *deuteros thanatos*, the "second death" referred to in Revelation 20:14.[20] Hence, not only is God's will indistinguishable

---

[20] Indeed, it is often overlooked that in Barth's later theology, Jesus is not merely resurrected from the dead, but from the "second death." Jesus dies the *deuteros thanatos* in place of us so that we do not die *this* particular death.

from the will of evil people, the will of God is "indistinguishably one with the evil will of men and the world and Satan. It was a matter of the triumph of God being concealed under that of His adversary, of that which is not, of that which is supremely not" (Barth, *CD* IV/1, 271). This is precisely why Barth perceives that what is bearing down on Jesus at Gethemane, pre-eminently in the form of Pilate's judgement and execution of Jesus by crucifixion, must also be expressed in terms of satanic will or radical evil.

To suffer God's eschatological judgement is to live and die *apart from God*, or YHWH, the God of Israel, precisely because God has turned away from us.[21] This is the central meaning of the cry of dereliction on the cross: "My God, my God, why have you forsaken me?" For God to turn away from Jesus in his death on the cross *is what it means to say* that Jesus in death has "descended into hell."

Ordinary death is a death that does not separate us from the love of God (and therefore does not involve the concept of "hell"): "If we live, we live to the Lord; and if we die, we die to the Lord. So, whether we live or die, we belong to the Lord. For this very reason, Christ died and returned to life so that he might be the Lord of both the dead and the living" (Rom. 14:8–9). One might think that this is cold comfort: death is still death. But Barth would say that it is Jesus' death – the "second death" – that

---

[21] I am inclined to think that this concept of "turning away" is fundamental to Barth's conception of *das Nichtige* as he understands it in the context of Gen. 1:2. For Barth seems to want to understand 1:2 retrospectively from the perspective of 1:3. It is God's *turning away* from the chaos described by 1:2 that is constitutive of the reality of *das Nichtige*. In other words, his utterance of the words "Let there be light" constitutes a turning away from chaos. See also Barth's discussion in *CD* IV/1, 253 where he says: "My turning from God is followed by God's annihilating turning from me." Any attempt to evaluate Barth's understanding on these points must pay attention to Barth's conception of divine epistemology in *CD* II/1 and, in particular, his view that God's knowledge does not depend on there being, as it were, independent objects of knowledge. See Barth, *CD* II/1, 543–60. Putting it in the language of divine self-determination: to say that God determines himself to be the one who rejects *das Nichtige* does not presuppose the existence of *das Nichtige* but implies it. Therefore, its existence depends solely on God's self-determination to be the one who rejects it.

constitutes the criterion of *what it is* ordinary death is. This death
– the death that Jesus died – is indeed a "casting into outer darkness" since it is a dying *apart from God*. This "withdrawal" of the
divine self is achieved by the simple yet devastating "apocalyptic" action of God determining himself to be the one who with-
draws, who sets himself apart, from Jesus. Eschatological death
is a privative concept: it is the absence of God. "Hell" and
"Satan" ("the Satan") are also representative of privative concepts in this sense. God's judgement on Jesus is precisely that he
wills Jesus to be apart from him – not to be in personal relationship with him – during the passion and pre-eminently in his
death.

Again, as in the case of the theological identity of Pilate's
judgement, it was Calvin who had the greatest influence on
Barth's thinking about eschatological death. Almost certainly
it was Calvin's exposition of Christ's descent into hell in the
apostle's creed that provided the essential impetus to Barth's
thought. As Calvin says: "we ought not to omit [Christ's] descent
into hell, a matter of no small moment in bringing about redemption" (1559 *Institutes*, 512). Barth would have agreed wholeheart-
edly; and he would have done so on behalf of the historical
figure of Jesus who declared God's eschatological judgement on
Israel and the world, and became the object of this same judgement culminating in the cross.

Calvin noted that: "there are some who think that nothing
new is spoken of in this article, but that it repeats in other words
what had previously been said of his burial, the word 'hell' often
being used in Scripture to denote a grave" (1559 *Institutes*, 513).
(This view was held by Bucer and apparently by Beza.) The best
reason that Calvin gives for thinking such a position untenable is
the simple one to the effect: "it is not likely that a useless repetition could have crept into this summary [the creed]" (1559 *Institutes*, 513). Instead, he proposes the following interpretation.
The death that Jesus submitted to in place of us is one in which he
had to "bear and suffer all the punishments that they ought to
have sustained . . . No wonder that he is said to have descended
into hell, for he suffered the death that God in his wrath had
inflicted on the wicked" (1559 *Institutes*, 515–16). Calvin
continues:

The point is that the Creed sets forth what Christ suffered in the sight of men, and then appositely speaks of that invisible and incomprehensible judgement which he underwent in the sight of God in order that we might know not only that Christ's body was given as the price of our redemption, but that he paid a greater and more excellent price in suffering in his soul the terrible torments of a condemned and forsaken man (1559 *Institutes*, 516).

Concluding remarks

Kant articulated a famous objection to theories of atonement that have substitutionary atonement at their core. It was obvious that one person could take on another's financial debt and pay the debt for this person. A financial debt was transferable. In this sense, one person could take another's place. But a debt of sin or a moral debt was quite another thing. Speaking of the latter kind of debt Kant writes:

> This debt which is original, or prior to all the good a man may do – this, and no more, is what we referred to in Book One as the radical evil in man – this debt can never be discharged by another person, so far as we can judge according to the justice of our human reason. For this is no transmissible liability which can be made over to another like a financial indebtedness (where it is all one to the creditor whether the debtor himself pays the debt or whether some one else pays it for him); rather is it the most personal of all debts, namely a debt of sins, which only the culprit can bear and which no innocent person can assume even though he be magnanimous enough to wish to take it upon himself for the sake of another (Kant, *Religion* 101).

It seems to me that Kant's criticism is repudiated by theories of atonement that put God's omnipotence at the centre of their respective accounts. Calvin's theory of atonement is that the death to which Jesus submitted in our place is one in which he had to "bear and suffer all the punishments that they ought to have sustained" (Calvin, *Institutes*, vol. 1, 515 [Bk. 2, 12.1–3]). There is an Anselmic impulse at work in his view that a "God-man" is required "to present our flesh as the price of satisfaction to God's righteous judgement" (Calvin, *Institutes*, vol. 1, 464–67). Since God is the one who predestines that Jesus should take the punishment that ought to have been borne by the elect (those saved by Jesus' act on the cross), he can be the one who makes Jesus bear the moral culpability. It is not fundamentally a question about whether one person can take on himself the moral guilt of another, but rather whether God can bring this about. Substitutionary atonement means in Calvin that instead of humankind it is Jesus who undergoes God's wrath. Crucially, it is God who brings this about.

God also brings about substitutionary atonement in the theory espoused in this chapter. Owing much to Barth, it holds that divine judgement remains constant – remains the same – across the first two parts of the gospel narrative. What changes across the two parts is the *object of judgement* (in Calvin what changes, more specifically, is the *object of punishment*). Same judgement, different object of judgement equals substitutionary atonement. Jesus takes the place of Israel and the world. Jesus takes *our* place. Divine action occurs in the passion of Jesus then and there such that God makes it the case that Jesus becomes the object of the very same judgement he issued during his ministry.[22]

---

[22] It would be worthwhile to carry out a comparative study of the relative strengths of the theory of atonement endorsed in this chapter and the view advocated by N. T. Wright in *Jesus and the Victory of God*. I take the view that the account of substitutionary atonement presented in this book, owing much as it does to Barth, is preferable to Calvin's view of atonement principally because the narrative historicity it presupposes is rational to affirm by the standards of the Enlightenment. For Calvin, the atonement is concentrated on the cross interpreted as the wrath of God poured out on the man Jesus. Barth, writing this side of the Enlightenment, develops an account which subversively takes advantage of the Enlightenment's advocacy of the eschatological, apocalyptic Jesus as the real historical person. But even though Wright too affirms Jesus as an eschatological figure, this would not seem to stop him putting all atonement theories in one basket:

> the categories of the sixth or fifth or fourth centuries BCE, and those of the sixteenth or subsequent centuries CE, are not necessarily good guides for our understanding of Jesus. Listening to the debate between substitution and representation, in however a sophisticated and nuanced fashion it may be carried on, leaves me as a historian with the same feeling I have when I meet people – as I don't, fortunately, very often – for whom the key question

22 *(continued)*

in the New Testament is whether the Rapture comes before or after the Tribulation (Wright, "The Servant and Jesus," 295).

I reject the implicit claim that all accounts of substitutionary atonement are necessarily nonhistorical accounts. This is because I have argued that central to the historical Jesus is substitutionary atonement as a rational, historical truth-claim. Indeed, my account is ironically decidedly more skeptical than Wright's regarding Jesus' intentions in his ministry even though it advocates a "classical" theory of atonement involving a claim to divine action. According to Wright, Jesus saw his own coming to Jerusalem as YHWH's long awaited return to Zion as king. In his person he enacted the "forgiveness of sins" as the return from exile, which latter had been longed for since the exile in 587 BC. Jesus sees his final journey as the return of YHWH as king involving the messianic woes akin to the suffering servant of Isa. 52:13 – 53.10 (Wright, *Jesus and the Victory of God*, 651). In keeping with this view, Wright holds that "Jesus . . . went up to Jerusalem not just to preach, but to die . . . Jesus believed that the messianic woes were about to burst upon Israel, and that he had to take them upon himself, solo" (Wright, *Jesus and the Victory of God*, 609). In other words, there is a continuity of intention between Jesus' ministry and passion: Jesus goes to Jerusalem to die, and does. In contrast, the view espoused here – which agrees with Barth on many of these matters (Barth is surprisingly modern!) – is that Jesus went up to proclaim the imminence of God's direct reign (YHWH as king: "Your God reigns!" Isa. 52:7). Jesus goes up to preach, not necessarily to die; he identifies himself as "the Son of Man" who will be eschatological judge and ruler (see Theissen and Merz, *Historical Jesus*, 553) vouchsafed by the irresistible reign of God, "coming with the clouds of heaven" (Dan. 7:13). But events take a different turn from his "triumphal entry into Jerusalem" such that the self-realization of Jesus' identity is as a different self-determining subject who understands that what is bearing down on him – in the form of the evil people who will judge and execute him – is really God's judgement. This is what he perceives to be the true nature of the events from Gethsemane onwards ("Abba, Father . . . not what I will, but what you will" [Mark 14:36]), and perhaps indeed from the Last Supper onwards. This is what he submits to as a self-determining subject in the encountering of the historical circumstances that constitute the passion. Bultmann writes that the "Son of Man" motif in the earliest tradition did not speak of a "Son of Man" who would come as in a second coming, *deutera parousia*, after death and resurrection (see Bultmann, *Theology of the New Testament*, vol. 1,

But there is a difference between Barth and Calvin. Though Calvin holds that it is God who brings about (penal) substitutionary atonement, he affirms it in such a way that God might have decided not to will Jesus' passion and death on the cross to be atonement. Calvin writes that God was free to have rejected Jesus' sacrificial death on the cross:

> Christ could not merit anything save by the good pleasure of God, but only inasmuch as he was destined to appease the wrath of God by his sacrifice, and wipe away our transgressions by his obedience: in one word, since the merit of Christ depends entirely on the grace of God, (which provided this mode of salvation for us), the latter is no less appropriately opposed to all righteousness of men than is the former (Calvin, 1559 *Institutes* [Book 2, Chapter 17.1], 334).

This of course is true if the gospel narrative is not about God *himself* – as if God were not necessarily involved in the passion history. But he is. He is necessarily involved because the passion – and the gospel narrative as a whole – is about God taking his own judgement on himself, in the form of Jesus of Nazareth. If Jesus' passion is to be identified with God's self-reflexive judgement then it must be the case that we are speaking of God's ontic self. God is not merely "pouring out his wrath on Jesus"; he is ultimately (in so far as we were to use this kind of language), "pouring his wrath out on himself." Self-differentiation in the divine triunity presupposes the divine unity.

---

[22] (*continued*) 29). Rather, the Son of Man is one who would rule and judge (from Jerusalem) under the aegis of a new dawn and age, precisely God's direct reign. This is utterly consonant with a Jesus who, self-determining subject that he is, goes to the cross in such a way that substitutionary atonement is at the heart of the historical Jesus: YHWH takes his own eschatological judgement on himself – in the form of Jesus of Nazareth. YHWH the king. YHWH the Messiah (Jesus the Messiah).

Bibliography

Anselm, *Cur Deus Homo*. In *Anselm of Canterbury: The Major Works*, edited by Brian Davies and Gillian Evans, 260–356 (Oxford: Oxford University Press, 1998).

Barth, Karl, *Church Dogmatics* IV/1 (Edinburgh: T. &T. Clark, 1956); *Church Dogmatics* IV/2 (Edinburgh: T. &T. Clark, 1958).

Bellinger, Jr., William H. and William R. Farmer (eds.), *Jesus and the Suffering Servant: Isaiah 53 and Christian Origins* (Harrisburg: Trinity Press International, 1998).

Bornkamm, Gunther, *Jesus of Nazareth*, translated by F. McLuskey, I. McLuskey, and J. M. Robinson (London: Hodder & Stoughton, 1960).

Bultmann, Rudolf, *Theology of the New Testament*, vol. 1 (London: SCM, 1952).

Calvin, John, *Gospel of John, 11 – 21*, translated by T. H. L. Parker, edited by D. W. Torrance and T. F. Torrance (Edinburgh: Oliver & Boyd, 1961); *A Harmony of the Gospels, Matthew, Mark, Luke*, vols. 1–3, translated by A. W. Morrison, edited by David F. Torrance and Thomas F. Torrance, (Edinburgh: St. Andrew Press, 1972); *Institutes of the Christian Religion* (1536 ed.) edited by L. Battles (Atlanta: John Knox, 1975); *Institutes of the Christian Religion* (1559 ed.) edited by J. T. McNeill, translated by L. Battles (Philadelphia: Westminster Press, 1960).

Campenhausen, Hans von, *The Formation of the Christian Bible* (London: SCM, 1971).

Crossan, Dominic, *The Historical Jesus: The Life of a Mediterranean Jewish Peasant* (Edinburgh: T. & T. Clark and San Francisco: Harper-Collins, 1991).

Davidson, Donald, *Inquiries into Truth and Interpretation* (Oxford: Oxford University Press, 1984).

Dunn, J. G. D., *The Partings of the Ways Between Christianity and Judaism and their Significance for the Character of Christianity* (London: SCM / Philadelphia: Trinity Press International, 1991).

Frei, Hans W., *The Identity of Jesus Christ: The Hermeneutical Basis of Dogmatic Theology* (Minneapolis: Fortress Press, 1975).

Kant, Immanuel, *Religion within the Limits of Reason Alone*, translated by Theodore M. Greene and Hoyt H. Hudson (New York: Harper, 1960).

Kermode, Frank, *The Genesis of Secrecy: On the Interpretation of Narrative* (Boston: Harvard University Press, 1979).

Kümmel, Werner Georg, *Theology of the New Testament* (London: SCM, 1974).

MacDonald, Neil B., *Karl Barth and the Strange New World within the Bible: Barth, Wittgenstein, and the Metadilemmas of the Enlightenment*, rev. ed. (Carlisle: Paternoster, 2001).

Perrin, Norman, *The Kingdom of God in the Teaching of Jesus* (London: SCM, 1963).

Soulen, R. Kendall, "YHWH the Triune God," *Modern Theology* 15 (1999): 25–54; *Christian Theology and the God of Israel* (Minneapolis: Fortress Press, 1996).

Theissen, Gerd and Annette Merz, *The Historical Jesus: A Comprehensive Guide* (London: SCM, 1998).

Watson, Francis, *Text and Truth: Redefining Biblical Theology* (Edinburgh: T. & T. Clark, 1997).

Wright, N. T., *Jesus and the Victory of God* (London: SPCK, 1996); "The Servant and Jesus." In *Jesus and the Suffering Servant: Isaiah 53 and Christian Origins*, edited by William H. Bellinger Jr. and William R. Farmer (Harrisburg: Trinity Press International, 1988), 281–97.

11

Substitutionary Atonement and the Origins of Divine Triunity

To speak of the God of Israel as a judging yet desisting, forbearing self, is to say *who* God is rather than *what* God is. It is to speak of God's *identity* rather than the divine *nature*. Crucially, such an description of God is not precluded from being a designation of who God is *ad intra*. While the description "the one who released Israel from the bondage of Egypt" can be true of God only in virtue of his being the one who released Israel from the bondage of Egypt, the description "the judging yet desisting, forbearing self" can be a description of God *ad intra*. This is because we can speak of God as the judging yet desisting, forbearing self who released Israel from the bondage of Egypt. In other words, it makes sense to say that the former description can tell us *who* God was prior to his intervention on behalf of the people "Israel" when he saw their plight in Egypt. Although we can identify the divine self only on the basis of what he does in history *ad extra*, it makes sense to say that he was such a self or character even before he acted in this history. This means that the response "YHWH, the judging, desisting, forbearing self" can be an answer to the question, "Who is the God of Israel *ad intra*?"

So far, so good. If we now switch vantage points, replacing the *"ad intra"* perspective with a specific *"ad extra"* one, namely that of the gospel narrative, we get God (YHWH) the judging, desisting, forbearing self who takes his own judgement on himself – in the form of his Son, Jesus of Nazareth. If we make the assumption that this is an accurate account of what the gospel narrates as historical truth, it follows that "eternity" is, as it were, "concentrated" in this "drop" of history. Since this history is a history of substitutionary atonement, we can say that it is just this history that compels us to speak of the eternal unity of God and Jesus, one which involves a subordinate self-differentiation (self-differentiation is subordinate to unity).

The key to this conclusion is the obvious truism that God is himself eternally. God cannot be the one who takes his own judgement on himself – in the form of Jesus of Nazareth – and it not be the case that the man Jesus of Nazareth – the Jew of Galilee – be part of who this God, the God of Israel, is eternally. The reflexive pronoun has a very powerful, if not momentous, impact in this theological and historical context!

In so far as we want to attribute to God a divine identity rather than a divine nature, it is another truism to say that for God to take his own judgement on himself is to take this judgement on his divine identity, on his person. Not least of the consequences of this is that it implies the validity of the *communicatio idiomatum* or "communion of attributes." For to say that God takes his own judgement on himself in the above sense means that the man Jesus of Nazareth takes this judgement on his divine identity – the man Jesus who can be said to possess a divine identity in virtue of the fact that God takes his own judgement on himself in the form of this man Jesus of Nazareth. Though it endorses Irenaeus' description of Jesus of Nazareth as "very man and very God" it does so by saying that Jesus' human identity is identical with his divine identity.

This is something akin to the neo-Chaledonian position that Robert Jenson champions in his systematic theology. Jenson speaks of a "synthesis of hypostases" such that there is one "synthetic" hypostasis (identity or person) of divine and human character – "one and the same Lord" (one and the same soteriological identity) who is the subject of all his actions narrated in the gospel narrative (see Jenson, "Person and Work," 191–205; Jenson, *Systematic Theology*, vol. 1, 127–33).

However, if instead of saying that Jesus is a "'synthetic' hypostasis of divine and human character," we speak of Jesus' human identity being identical with his divine identity, we can more clearly see the nature of this identity. Though the identity is a metaphysical or ontological one it is not an *a priori* one; it is an *a posteriori* one – which makes it an *a posteriori* necessary identity. It is not until one locates the man Jesus of Nazareth within the narrative of God taking his own judgement on himself that one perceives the human identity to be a divine identity. This is philosophical theology of a most abstract kind but no apology must be made for it.

Conversely, the concept of "divine nature" and in particular "two-nature Christology" is intrinsic to the spirit of traditional Chalcedonian theology. To employ this conceptuality in the context of our conclusions regarding what the gospel narrative is about, is to make the following claim. When God takes his own judgement on himself – in the form of Jesus Christ – this means that Jesus Christ takes God's judgement on his human nature such that the person Jesus Christ (with both his human nature and his divine nature) is included within the divine nature. Chalcedonian language fits uncomfortably – if at all – with the fundamental theme of the gospel narrative as I understand it. The beauty of the term "divine identity" is that it is less obvious who or what kinds of things are incompatible with it or who or what are excluded from being included in it. In contrast, in the case of the term "divine nature," it appears all too clear what kinds of things are incompatible. Natures divine and human cannot be identical, one with the other.[1] But moreover, we have

---

[1] The constraints that Chalcedon imposed on our understanding of the two natures of Christ – "without division, without separation, with confusion, without change" – acknowledged the truth that one could not in principle discover that a human nature was identical with a divine nature, and vice versa. It is noteworthy that none of these classic constraints appear to be violated by a "neo-Chalcedonian" identification of a human identity with a divine identity, or the human identity of the man Jesus with the divine identity of the God of Israel. Indeed, the New Testament counterpart to the name "YHWH" in the Old Testament is "the Father, Son, and Holy Spirit" such that YHWH is now identified with "the Father." This implies an "expansion" of the divine name (now including "the Son" and "the Holy Spirit") coupled with an internal "transposition" of the name "YHWH" (now identified with "the Father," which is not in itself the locus of the divine name itself but internal to the name of "the Father, Son, and Holy Spirit"). To say that Jesus of Nazareth's human identity is identical with the divine identity is to say that he is identical with God the Father, Son, and Holy Spirit who, as God the Father, takes his own judgement on himself in the form of his Son, Jesus of Nazareth. *We perhaps speak more properly when we speak of "God the Father, Son, and Holy Spirit, the judging, desisting self."*

substantial difficulty in saying that human nature is included in the divine nature. We do not face the same degree of complication if we speak the language of "divine identity," a language that is perfectly compatible with both Nicene and neo-Chalcedonian theology.

Included within the identity of God

I claim that the gospels *in toto* are about YHWH the God of Israel taking his own judgement on himself in the form of his Son, Jesus of Nazareth. This means among other things that we identify the God of Israel – the bearer of the divine name, YHWH – as the bearer of the one divine name: "the Father, Son, and Holy Spirit." But to say that God the Father takes his own judgement on himself *in the form of his Son* seems to imply downright anomaly: in what sense can the God of Israel do something to himself and it be done to someone other than himself, namely the Son? Saying God can take his own judgement on himself is straightforward enough logically; but when one adds "in the form of his Son, Jesus of Nazareth" this seems to imply that the Father takes something on himself *in a form other than himself*. But if Jesus is included in the divine identity, this seems to circumvent the difficulty; we must understand the God of Israel taking his own judgement on himself in the form of his Son, Jesus of Nazareth, within the context of the man Jesus being included within the divine identity.

The origins of Trinitarian self-differentiation

Indeed we can go further: implicit in the statement is the notion of self-differentiation within the divine identity. God taking his own judgement on himself – in the form of his Son, Jesus of Nazareth – implies self-differentiation within the divine identity. But it is a self-differentiation subordinate to unity; God's taking of judgement on himself does not in itself imply self-differentiation, it implies unity. It is only when one adds the adverbial phrase "in the form of his Son, Jesus of Nazareth" that self-differentiation is implied. This means that the basic theme of the gospel narrative provides for the logical origins of the divine *tri-unity*. In other words, substitutionary atonement as we have it in Chapter 10 constitutes the point of departure for our thinking about the divine triunity.

This is the crucial point. This "self-differentiation within unity" takes place in history. It happened in Palestine sometime in the third or fourth decade of the first century AD that YHWH the judging yet desisting, forbearing self – "the one who released Israel from the bondage of Egypt" – took his own (eschatological) judgement on himself, in the form of his Son, Jesus of Nazareth. Now, it is obvious that *God cannot take his own judgement on himself and it be the case that the reflexive self-identity asserted here refers to a self who is not necessarily identical with this self*. That much is plain. But a necessary identity is an identity that holds in all possible worlds and is never not true; there is no time when it is not true; it is true "eternally" or "everlastingly." Therefore, if the basic theme of the gospel narrative is as Chapter 10 has it, then it follows that concentrated in this divine self in time and history – in time and history – is the eternal unity of YHWH the God of Israel and the man Jesus of Nazareth.[2] On the basis of this historical event one can make the inference endorsed by Nicaea in 325 that "there was not when he was not" (see "Neo-Chalcedonian Christology as divine identity Christology" below).

"Divine identity" Christology

In *God Crucified: Monotheism and Christology in the New Testament*, Richard Bauckham speaks of the man Jesus of Nazareth being *included within the divine identity of YHWH, the God of Israel* (Bauckham, *God Crucified*, vii). He argues that the intention of a

---

[2] Am I proposing a "Christology from below" here? Pannenberg's account of the divine unity of Jesus and God in chapters 8 and 9 of *Jesus – Man and God* is of course the classic example of a "Christology from below," which arguably achieves its objective. But where Pannenberg focuses on the proleptic nature of Jesus' resurrection in relation to divine futurity (see also his *Metaphysics and the Idea of God* esp. ch. 4), my argument takes substitutionary atonement as the primary datum, although such a datum is to be understood only in the context of the resurrection.

number of key passages in the New Testament – e.g., Philippians 2:9–11, the Prologue of John's Gospel, etc. – is to make just this claim.[3]

Divine identity, Bauckham says, can be thought of in two ways. The first is speaking of the God of Israel's identity in relation to all reality and not just Israel. The God of Israel is: the creator of all things; the unique divine sovereign presently ruling over all things; and the eschatological sovereign over all things. God therefore encompassed – just because he was *God* – protology, sovereign rule over history, and eschatology. These designations were all necessarily included in Second Temple Jewish monotheism's definition of the God of Israel (Bauckham, *God Crucified*, 10–13); such definition was the characteristic way Second Temple Jewish monotheism identified the God of Israel.

The second mode of characterisation is historically the earlier one, and one I have made much of in this essay: the God of Israel identified under the description of something like "the one who released Israel from the bondage of Egypt." God is understood as essentially "a historical identity acting in the historical life" of his people "Israel." God is the historical covenant-partner of Israel as testified pre-eminently in Old Testament narratives such as the Exodus narrative. (See Bauckham, *God Crucified*, 9).

Crucially, for Bauckham, Jesus is not understood as being *added* to the divine identity as if he were a second God. Rather, he

---

[3] Bauckham's argument at this point is in the main a *historical* one regarding what is true about earliest Christian belief about Jesus. The earliest Christians included Jesus in the divine identity of YHWH. Hence, when the New Testament witness of the earliest Christians includes Jesus in the unique divine creation, in the unique divine rule over all things, and in the eschatological sovereignty of God, it – and they – meant to include Jesus in the divine identity of YHWH. *Inter alia* their reference to Jesus as involved in the creation of the world as the Logos was a way of saying that Jesus was divine as the God of Israel was divine. If God possessed protological and eschatological sovereignty (and also ruled over all things in the present) – and Jesus was to be included in the divine identity of God – then Jesus too must be said to possess protological and eschatological sovereignty (and also ruled presently over all things). Just so: "Jesus is Lord."

is *included* within the divine identity (Bauckham, *God Crucified*, 15). The former way of thinking about the relation between God and Jesus is problematic for any account that wishes to adhere to Second Temple Jewish monotheism. The latter way, Bauckham thinks, is not contrary to a monotheistic conception of God.

Bauckham is quite clear that "divine identity" as a concept is concerned with *who* God is. It is to be contrasted with the concept of "divine essence" or "divine nature," which is concerned with *what* God or divinity is (Bauckham, *God Crucified*, 8). Patristic theology on the whole drew on the legacy of Greek *philosophy* and defined God in terms of divine nature. This meant attributing to God "a series of metaphysical attributes" or perfections defining what kind of nature he is: "ingenerateness, incorruptibility, immutability, and so on" (Bauckham, *God Crucified*, 8). In contrast, the focus of the biblical and Jewish tradition (at least in latter's earlier stages) was much more self-consciously *historical.* Though "some Jewish writers in the later Second Temple period", e.g., Josephus, "consciously adopted some of the Greek metaphysical language", even then:

> the dominant conceptual framework for their understanding of God is not a definition of divine nature – what divinity is – but a notion of the divine identity, characterized in ways other than metaphysical attributes. That God is eternal, for example – a claim essential to all Jewish thinking about God – is not so much a statement about what divine nature is, more an element in the unique divine identity, along with claims that God alone created all things and rules all things, that God is gracious and merciful and just, that God brought Israel out of Egypt and made Israel his own people and gave Israel his law at Sinai, and so on. If we wish to know in what Second Temple Judaism considered the uniqueness of the one God to consist . . . we must not look for a definition of divine nature, but for ways of characteriszing the unique divine identity (Bauckham, *God Crucified*, 8).

What this means is that, according to Bauckham, the statement that God is eternal tells us *who* God is rather than *what* God is. Hence, one should speak of the uniquely identifying description "the one who is eternal" just as one speaks of "the one who released Israel from the bondage of Egypt." Both would be an answer to the questions, Of *whom* are we talking? or *Who* are we talking about?.

In effect, Bauckham argues that speaking of the man Jesus being included in the divine identity of YHWH is a more biblical way of speaking of Jesus' relation to the God of Israel than the later efforts of the historic Councils of Nicaea and Chalcedon which, he says, did not "develop" the divine identity of Jesus "so much as transpose it into a conceptual framework constructed more in terms of the Greek philosophical categories of essence and nature" (Bauckham, *God Crucified*, viii).

Clearly, my argument that the gospel narrative is the historical truth-claiming story of YHWH the God of Israel taking his own eschatological judgement on himself in the form of his Son, Jesus of Nazareth, can be understood within the auspices of Bauckham's account. It constitutes *one* very powerful way in which Jesus could be understood as being included in the identity of the God of Israel rather than being added to it. It is therefore consistent with the monotheistic thrust of Bauckham's christological paradigm.

Divine identity contra divine nature: neo-Chalcedonian Christology

To affirm the concept of divine identity over divine nature (or for that matter, the explanatory concept of identity over the explanatory concept of nature) is conceivably to align oneself with a christological interpretation of Chalcedon that privileges the concept of person or identity (hypostasis) over the concept of nature (physis). This means a theological preference for an interpretation of Chalcedon informed by the theology of Cyril of Alexandria over the Leonine interpretation authorized by the council fathers. As Jenson puts it, the "appended 'Tome' [of Pope Leo] says that each nature is a distinct agent of the Gospel narrative; the decree speaks nowhere of an agency of the one hypostasis" (Jenson, *Systematic Theology*, vol. 1, 132). Hence famously, Leo's "Tome" declared that each nature carried out the action appropriate to it: "Each nature is agent of what is proper to it, working in fellowship with the other: the Word doing what belongs to the Word and the flesh what belongs to the flesh" (Stevenson, "Tome", 257–261). Though Chalcedon employed the confessional formula "one person (hypostasis) to be recognized in two natures (physeis)," this appeared to be understood in such a way that the real source of agency lay with the natures and not with the hypostasis. In effect, the hypostasis was construed to be reducible to, completely a function of, the two natures, even if this had not been the original intention (although there was a way of reading "one hypostasis *to be recognized in two natures*" which endorsed this).

In contrast, the interpretation of Chalcedon which would have found favor with Cyril of Alexandria (who died seven years before the council), is one which can be said to "reduce" in the other direction: it construed the two natures in terms of one unitary hypostasis. The Leonine interpretation of Chalcedon had attributed each action of Jesus Christ to one of his two natures depending on whether it was deemed to have a divine origin or a human one. The "Cyrillean" interpretation had Jesus' actions predicated on the "one and the same" hypostasis, the person or identity of "one and the same Lord" Jesus Christ. He is the active agent of his actions. Hence when Cyril spoke of "one nature, of God the *Logos*, who has been enfleshed" or "one nature after the union" he meant, as Frances Young puts it, "a theology of 'predication' which made the Logos the subject of both divine and human attributes, rather than a 'physical' theory of 'natures in union'" and only opened himself to inevitable misunderstanding with his use of the term (Young, *From Nicea to Chalcedon*, 260). For when employing the formula of "one nature" Cyril meant in fact something like a singular unitary hypostasis.

This is why he would doubtless have favored the formula "one hypostasis out of two natures" instead of the authorized "one hypostasis to be recognized in two natures" (the former was discussed at Chalcedon but failed in the end to make it into the creed). Clearly the former formula was compatible with a Jesus of Nazareth whose actions were ultimately understood in terms of the agency of hypostasis rather than the agency of the natures. In contrast, though perhaps not intrinsically impossible, it required greater effort to show how "one hypostasis to be recognized in two natures" – "without division, without separation, with confusion, without change" – could be rendered compatible with Cyril's Christology.

Notwithstanding this, Eastern Orthodoxy (for example, John of Damascus's *The Orthodox Faith*) and Reformation theology, specifically Lutheran in orientation, sought to explicate Chalcedon in ways that would bring it fully in line with Cyril's insights (see Jenson, "Person and Work," 199). This means an exposition of:

> "the notion of hypostasis as to make 'one hypostasis' denote a plausible active protagonist of the gospel's total narrative. According to this Christology, there is in Christ's case one 'synthetic' hypostasis of divine and human character, and this one hypostasis is what actually exists" (Jenson, "Person and Work," 199).

This "neo-Chalcedonian" interpretation of Chalcedon (which Jenson says was endorsed at the Second Council of Constantinople in 553, though never caught on beyond its own immediate milieu [Jenson, *Systematic Theology*, vol. 1, 133]) subsumes the natures under the singular category of "synthetic" hypostasis such that

> the phrases "Christ's divine nature" and "Christ's human nature" are then understood to be analytic. It is the one hypostasis of Christ we see acting and suffering in the gospel; and that he "has" these "two natures" means that he lacks nothing to be fully one of the Trinity and that he lacks nothing to be fully one of us (Jenson, *Systematic Theology*, vol. 1, 199).[4]

The phrase "a synthetic hypostasis of divine and human character" in effect "dispenses" with the problematic concept of "nature" by retranslating the Chalcedonian clause "one person recognized in two natures" in such a way that emphasis is put on the concept of "hypostasis" rather than "nature." One obvious reason for this is the affinity between the former and the modern

---

[4] The reason the phrases are "analytic" is because if Christ is a "synthetic hypostasis" of divine and human character then this is what it means to say that he possesses a divine and a human nature respectively. This is why Jenson does not think that Jesus Christ has a divine and a human nature according to the tenets of philosophical realism. Rather he "has" a divine nature and a human nature only in the sense that he is a "synthetic hypostasis of divine and human character."

concept of "personal identity realized in intentional action" one finds in both modern philosophy and literary theory (see Frei, *Identity of Jesus Christ*).

Neo-Chalcedonian Christology as divine-identity Christology

Can we say something more about the concept of a "synthetic" hypostasis of divine and human character such that it is more accessible to modern ears? Can we make the neo-Chalcedonian proposal more amenable to modern analytic consciousness? I think we can if the point of departure of our christological exposition is the narrative of substitutionary atonement proposed in Chapter 10 and further elucidated in the present chapter. First, if we employ this thoroughly historical account to formulate a christological position in terms of the concept of identity, we can make better analytical sense of the concept of "synthetic hypostasis" precisely because substitutionary atonement allows us to retranslate the concept of "synthetic hypostasis" in terms of "divine-identity" Christology.

To recapitulate some well-trodden themes: who is the man Jesus of Nazareth according to the gospel narrative? According to the previous chapter, he is the eschatological prophet who in his ministry declares the imminent eschatological judgement of the kingdom of God, of God's reign. He is then himself subject to, and subjects himself to, the judgement of the Jewish authorities in Jerusalem; and most tellingly, to the "judicial" judgement of Pontius Pilate, which latter leads to death by the Roman form of execution, crucifixion.

But the judgement that befalls Jesus during the passion turns out *a posteriori* to be God's judgement bearing down on him. Moreover, God makes the judgement Jesus proclaimed during his ministry the same judgement that brings Jesus from Gethsemane to Calvary. He makes it the same eschatological judgement as the one Jesus proclaimed in his ministry in Galilee. This constitutes the rationale behind the claim of substitutionary atonement in which Jesus subjects himself to the self-same eschatological judgement in the passion that he proclaimed during his ministry.

And this means crucially that the actions of Jesus of Nazareth narrated in the gospel narrative "turn out to be" included in the identity of the judging yet forbearing, desisting God who takes his own eschatological judgement on himself. The phrase "turn out to be" is indicative of an *a posteriori* metaphysical or ontological identity, not an *a priori* one. It was a seminal achievement of the philosopher Saul Kripke (Kripke, *Naming and Necessity*) to see that identities of the form "The evening star is the morning star" or "Water is H_2O" were claims whose truth could be established only by investigating the nature of the actual world we live in; in this sense the means by which we know their truth is *a posteriori* (we do not know their truth *a priori*). But once established – and this was Kripke's brilliant insight – they were necessary identities, and therefore true in all possible worlds (to use the language of possible-worlds semantics) – and therefore at all times and places. This was so even though "The morning star" did not mean "the evening star" nor "water" "H_2O." In particular, as regards the latter: had "water" meant "H_2O" then we would have been able to infer the atomic (or chemical) structure from the meanings of the word "water" alone. Patently, this could not be done! In fact, water and H_2O seemed to have different properties.

By analogy, clearly "human identity" does not mean the same as "divine identity." In fact the classical philosophical tradition without exception – from Gregory of Nyssa to Immanuel Kant – defined them or variants thereof ("divine," "human," "infinite," "finite") in such a way that they were entirely opposite, one to the other. But this did not mean that the two – in a particular case – could not turn out to be ontologically or metaphysically the same, identical. In other words, one could discover by *a posteriori* means that what diverged in the realm of meaning turned out to be identical in the realm of ontology or metaphysics. More precisely: as long as one did not interpret "the man Jesus of Nazareth" and "YHWH, the God of Israel" as excluding one another analytically (on the sometimes questionable *a priori* grounds supplied by apophasis), "revelation" might tell us that the former was to be included in the latter.

According to the gospel narrative, this is what had transpired in the particular case of Jesus of Nazareth and the God of Israel. What had transpired was an *a posteriori* "identity" or "identification of identities" such that the self-determining actions of Jesus in both his ministry and passion in the face of those who constitute the circumstances he encounters (the Sanhedrin, Pilate, etc.) "turned out *a posteriori* to be" identical with the divine identity of the God of Israel. (*Inter alia*, Pilate's judgement "turned out to be" identical with God's judgement when one looks at the same event and circumstance through the directorial lens of the evangelist.)

The upshot of all this is that where Jenson speaks of a "synthetic hypostasis of divine and human character" I prefer to translate this into something like "an *a posteriori* identification of identities" such that we speak of "God the Father, Son, and Holy Spirit, the judging, yet desisting, forbearing self" (see footnote 1 of this chapter). This is a synthetic identity and therefore not an analytic one, but this does not make it a "synthetic hypostasis" *per se* though this would be one of its implications if one wanted to employ this kind of language. Truly, God is an eternal soteriological identity. Truly, this is to speak, as Jenson does, of "Jesus in the Trinity" (Jenson, "Jesus in the Trinity").

One final point. Bauckham writes: "the inclusion of Jesus in the identity of God means the inclusion of the interpersonal relationship between Jesus and his Father. No longer can the divine identity be purely and simply portrayed by analogy with a single human subject" (Bauckham, *God Crucified*, 75). Qualified in the appropriate way, I would agree. However, he goes on to say: "Nothing in the Second Temple Jewish understanding of divine identity contradicts the possibility of interpersonal relationship within the divine identity, but there is little, if anything, that anticipates it" (Bauckham, *God Crucified*, 75). Bauckham's last point is unduly pessimistic if it makes sense to elucidate the divine self in Old Testament narrative in the way I have done: YHWH the judging, yet forbearing, desisting self.

The divine soteriological identity *ad intra*: YHWH the judging, desisting, forbearing self

Bauckham's notion that the divine nature might be understood in terms of divine identity implies that properties traditionally understood as properties of God *ad intra* can be translated into the conceptuality appropriate for the divine identity *ad intra*. We can make sense of the claim that the uniquely identifying description, "the one who is eternal" tells us *who* God is *ad intra*. We can also make sense of the claim that God *ad intra* is a soteriological identity. This means that in virtue of sub-stitutionary atonement, Jesus of Nazareth is also to be included within the identity of God *ad intra*.

As Israel's Scriptures have it, the bearer of the divine name, the God of Israel, is the creator of all things. As if to indicate this fact, Genesis 2 refers to the latter as "YHWH-Elohim." It is not unreasonable to infer from this that, immediately prior to cre-ation – prior to creation then – God is also the bearer of this divine name. This means that God *ad intra* is the bearer of the divine name, "I will be who I will be." But this "I will be who I will be" is subordinate to the divine identity characterized as this judging yet desisting, forbearing self. Unlike the identifying def-inite description "the one who released Israel from the bondage of Egypt" or its New Testament counterpart "the one who raised Jesus from the dead," this description of the divine identity as a judging, yet desisting, forbearing self is never not true of God. In this sense it is a dispositional description of God *ad intra*, though the basis of our knowledge of this – if knowledge it is – is that God acts in a way conforming to this identity.[5] I have of course

---

[5] The concept of "disposition" is central to Gilbert Ryle's classic work *The Concept of Mind* in his explanation of mental phenomena, in partic-ular personal identity. To say that this or that person "knows" this or that fact does not require that he or she is occurrently exhibiting knowl-edge of this or that fact. Indeed, were I to say of a particular person that he or she knows a particular fact, *when unbeknown to me the person in question at the time of utterance, is fast asleep*, it still follows that it is true to describe him or her thus. In general, it is not just persons but also mate-rial objects which have dispositions or propensities. These are usually expressed in the form of a subjunctive conditional. For example: of glass it can be said that it possesses the propensity to break such that if it were to be hit with a hammer it would break in actual fact. The reason it would break is of course to do with its ontological character (which makes it breakable), which it possesses prior to the blow from the hammer. For a general philosophical approach to the concept, see Armstrong, Martin and Place, *Dispositions*.

spent a large part of this book trying to argue toward just such a conclusion.

We can therefore extrapolate to the following truth. Were the human history of the exodus narrative to be present to God *ad intra* then he would be his judging yet desisting, forbearing self. We can say this without any special theological pleading. And, by extension, we can also say this: were the particular history of Israel in first-century Palestine to be present to the God of Israel in the same way, then he would be the one who takes his own eschatological judgement on himself in the form of his Son, Jesus of Nazareth.[6] The fact that both are dispositional identities respectively of the God of Israel and Jesus does not obviate the fact that God does something in the latter case that he does not do in the former case. That is, he executes a self-reflexive action in the latter, but not in the former, action. Hence, even though the eternal unity of the man Jesus and God is dispositional (though not hypothetical) in content, this must not be perceived as a problem. This is because the divine identity in terms of which the identity of Jesus of Nazareth in the gospel narrative is understood – YHWH the judging yet desisting, forbearing self *ad intra* – is also dispositional. This means the eternal soteriological identity (*ontologically* the most fundamental truth about God) is a dispositional *identity*. It can be defined outside of the soteriological acts themselves *only in terms of* a propensity or disposition to perform such acts. Hence, such divine disposition is of the very nature of a divine soteriological identity, and what we have in essence is an utterly coherent way of thinking about God's identity *ad intra*. (None of this means of course that God is not free; it only means that he is this faithful God who would act in character – as the characteristic self he is.)

---

[6] Ultimately, perhaps the best way to understand the man Jesus included in the divine identity is to apply an observation that might pass as a variation of Anselm's argument in *Cur Deus Homo*. When it is said that God takes his own judgement on himself, the judgement he takes on himself is his own judgement on "human, all too human" Israel. It is therefore a judgement on humankind. But to take this judgement on himself is to take a judgement *regarding humankind* on himself. As God, he can only do this as this one man, Jesus of Nazareth, Jesus Christ.

The identity of YHWH as the judging yet desisting, forbearing self is no less a dispositional identity than YHWH the one who takes his own judgement on himself in the form of his Son, Jesus of Nazareth.

Nicaea: "There was not when he was not"

In this "dispositional" sense then, if it is granted that it is true of the soteriological identity of the God of Israel that "there was not when he was not," then it is also true – *by inference* – that it is true of Jesus of Nazareth that "there was not when he was not." The Council of Nicaea in 325 employed this formula as a criterion of divine identity and therefore asserted of the Son as against the Arians precisely this: "there was not when he was not." *Such an inference follows as a logical deduction from the premise that concentrated in the event in history corresponding to the first two parts of the gospel narrative is the eternal unity of the God of Israel and the man Jesus, as outlined above. We "extrapolate from history back to (protological) eternity" (and indeed forward to eschatological eternity) on the grounds of this "self-differentiation within unity" in history itself.* We are entirely warranted in doing so.

To the extent that the Nicene formula "there was not when he was not" is a conceptual judgement of what Scripture says, it stands in the most intimate relation to the Prologue of John's Gospel. John's Prologue can be read in a similar such inferential manner extrapolating back from the historical unity of the man Jesus with the God of Israel to his eternal unity with the God of Israel. (Moreover, one can understand the subject-matter of John 1 to be the specific soteriological identity uniting the God of Israel and Jesus. According to this interpretation, it is this identity – and not some identity-free divine nature – about whom it is true "there was not when it was not.") In this regard, Barth's exegesis of John's Prologue in *CD II/2* is extraordinarily prescient since it presents the claim of the eternal unity of Jesus of Nazareth with the God of Israel as an inference from the historical Jesus in relation to God himself.[7]

---

[7] In *Church Dogmatics* II/2 Barth argues that the referent of John's Prologue is no other than the man Jesus of Nazareth (Barth, *CD* II/2, 95–99). That is how he reads the semantic structure of verses 1–15. The

---

[7] (*continued*) essential point of the first fifteen verses of the Prologue is that: the one of whom John the Baptist says in the present tense "was before me" – this one (the very same) – was "in the beginning with God." According to Barth, it is significant that John says "was God" rather than "is God" at 1:1c. (We may safely assume that John does not want to say that the Word "was God" but is not God *now*: clearly he does not want to say that!) The evangelist believes that, from the perspective of John the Baptist at 1:15 – speaking in the present tense – the one who "was before me" but is presently here now – "was with God" "in the beginning." To be sure. the evangelist *does* think that the one of whom John the Baptist speaks *is* God. But what is at stake is the claim that *the one of whom John the Baptist speaks is the same who, being in the beginning with God, is therefore God.* According to Barth, the Prologue is written from the perspective of John the Baptist's *present existence* coinciding with his very *present* encounter with the man Jesus. From this perspective, this present man Jesus of Nazareth is said to *have been* "in the beginning with God." This implies, that *the Prologue can be read backwards from the present perspective of 1:15 to the past, as well as forwards from 1:1 to the present.* The key moments of Barth's reading proceed as follows:

> (*i*) *1:1a: In the beginning was the Word* It is clear that the first clause is to be read with the emphasis on the phrase *en arche* ("in the beginning"); the evangelist intends to say "*In the beginning* was the Word." To be sure, the sentence does tell us *what* was in the beginning but the emphasis is on the antecedent phrase. The evangelist's intention in saying this is to make it quite clear that the Word is not merely the firstborn of all creation as in Col. 1:15 – not merely before all creation – but is there "in the beginning." The question immediately follows, where, except in or with God, can there be any being which is "in the beginning" in this sense. i.e. if the Word is in the beginning where can he be except "in or with" God? This of course implies that the statement "The Word was with God" would constitute an answer to the question, "Where was the Word if the Word was 'there' in the beginning?" In other words, it cannot be said that the Word was "there" in the beginning but not with or in God. For God *alone* – the one God – is "in the beginning."

> (*ii*) *1:1b: And the Word was with God* What of the second clause? The emphasis here is on the phrase "with God": "and the Word was *with God*." The phrase cannot mean as Augustine took it to mean (*for* God), for one does not have to be in the beginning with God if one is only for God (or in other words, one can be for God but not necessarily with God in the beginning).

> (*iii*) *1:1a and 1:1b imply 1:1c: "and the Word was God"* What does this mean? It means that *to say that Jesus was in the beginning with God (and not merely the firstborn of all creation) and was not*, in virtue of his identity, *God, is a*

⁷ *(continued)*

> contradiction. Or alternatively, to say that Jesus was in the beginning with God *is* to say that Jesus is, in virtue of his identity, God. (As Bauckham puts it, Jesus is to be *included* within the divine identity of God. But this means that he is in, within, the divine identity of God from the beginning.)

> *(iv) 1:2: "The same was in the beginning with God"* When it comes to v. 2, it is quite clear that it is not a recapitulation or a repetition of 1:1. The most important argument here is that there is no reason why it should be a consecutive verse rather than added to v. 1 itself. Verse 2 should be translated as: "the same was in the beginning with God." The fact that it has been given a whole sentence and indeed a whole verse to itself implies that it is to be given equal hermeneutical significance to the famous clauses of v. 1 – but for a functional reason not the ontic reason behind v. 1. What is this functional reason? This means that the *outos* at 1:2 points forward to the other usages of *outos* "the same" in John 1 (and as we shall see, the later usages make a backward reference to that of 1:2).

"The same" is used at both 1:3–5 and 1:10 but the most important reference is to 1:15. The Jesus *in concreto* is the one to whom John the Baptist refers as "the same." So John's argument according to Barth reads as the following inferential chain: *The Word who was in the beginning with God – in God – who was God – he is "the same" through whom all things are made; the one through whom all things are made – he is "the same" as the human Jesus to whom John the Baptist refers.* But this means that one can put the same inferential chain the other way around, which is to say, start with vv. 15ff. and work back to 1:1: *The one whom John the Baptist refers to as "Jesus" – he is "the same" as the one through whom all things are made; the one through whom all things are made – he is "the same" who is in the beginning with God, who was God.*

Crucially, if the above analysis is true it provides an explanation why it is the case that John does not say at v. 2, "the same was God in the beginning." Why? For John to have said this would have rendered one unable to make the temporally construed transitive inference that this "same" was "the same" who later on, as it were, is "the same" through whom all things are made; and this "same" is in turn "the same" of whom John the Baptist said "was before me." But to say that "the same was in the beginning with God" allows one to add "the same" who was ⁷ *(continued)* "before the creation of the world," and "the same" who was referred to by John the Baptist as "the one who was before me."

"Logos is unmistakably substituted for Jesus" (Barth, *CD II/2*, 96). This means that: "It is He, Jesus, who is in the beginning with God. it is He who by nature is God" (Barth, *CD II/2*, 96). In other words, the claim that Jesus of Nazareth possesses an eternal identity – he is the

Conclusion

I believe in God, the Father Almighty,
the Creator of heaven and earth,
and in Jesus Christ, his only Son, our Lord:
who was conceived of the Holy Spirit,
born of the Virgin Mary,
suffered under Pontius Pilate,
was crucified, died, and was buried.
He descended into hell.
The third day he arose again from the dead.
He ascended into heaven
and sits at the right hand of God the Father Almighty,
whence he shall come to judge the living and the dead.
I believe in the Holy Spirit, the holy catholic church,
the communion of saints,
the forgiveness of sins,
the resurrection of the body,
and life everlasting.

Amen.

---

[7] (*continued*) *Logos* – functions as a backwards inference in the Prologue of John's Gospel just as the eternal identity of Jesus of Nazareth is a "backwards" inference from the event of substitutionary atonement in history. To be sure, Barth's exegesis of 1:3–5 acknowledges that the term "Logos" had a previous tradition say in Philo of Alexandria (defined essentially as a metaphysical principle or explanation of the universe). But Barth argues that the term is used in a different way in John. The term is used not to honor the man Jesus but rather the term is honored by being applied to the man Jesus.

Bibliography

Anselm, *Cur Deus Homo*. In *Anselm of Canterbury: The Major Works*, edited by Brian Davies and Gillian Evans, 260–356 (Oxford: Oxford University Press, 1998).

Armstrong, D. M., C. B. Martin and U. T. Place, *Dispositions: A Debate*, edited by T. Crane (London: Routledge, 1996).

Barth, Karl, *Church Dogmatics* II/2 (Edinburgh: T. & T. Clark, 1957).

Bauckham, Richard, *God Crucified: Monotheism and Christology in the New Testament* (Carlisle: Paternoster, 1998).

Frei, Hans W., *The Identity of Jesus Christ: The Hermeneutical Basis of Dogmatic Theology* (Minneapolis: Fortress Press, 1975); *Theology and Narrative*, edited by G. Hunsinger, introduction by W. C. Placher (Oxford: Oxford University Press, 1993).

Gunton, Colin E., *Act and Being* (Grand Rapids: Eerdmans, 2003).

Jenson, Robert W., "Jesus in the Trinity." *Pro Ecclesia* 8/3 (1999): 308–18; "The Person and Work of Jesus Christ." In *Essentials of Christian Theology*, edited by William Placher (Kentucky: Westminster John Knox, 2003), 191–205; *Systematic Theology*, vol. 1 (Oxford: Oxford University Press, 1997).

Kripke, Saul, *Naming and Necessity* (Oxford: Blackwell, 1982).

Moltmann, Jürgen, *The Crucified God*, translated by R. A. Wilson and J. Bowden (London: SCM, 1974).

Pannenberg, Wolfhart, *Jesus – God and Man*, translated by L. Wilkins and D. Priebe (London: SCM, 1968); *Metaphysics and the Idea of God* (Edinburgh: T. & T. Clark, 1990).

Ryle, Gilbert, *The Concept of Mind* (London: Hutchison, 1949).

Seitz, Christopher R., "The Divine Name in Christian Scripture," *Word Without End: The Old Testament as Abiding Theological Witness* (Grand Rapids: Eerdmans. 1998), 251–62; "Handing over the Name: Christian Reflection on the Divine Name YHWH," *Figured Out: Typology and Providence in Christian Scripture* (Louisville: Westminster John Knox, 2001), 131–44.

Stevenson, J. (ed.), "The Tome of Leo the Great", *Councils, Creeds, and Controversies: Documents Illustrating the History of the Church AD 337–461*, 2nd edition, revised by W. H. C. Frend (London: SPCK, 1989), 257–261.

Taylor, Charles, *The Sources of the Self* (Cambridge MA.: Harvard University Press, 1989).

Wienandy, Thomas, *Does God Change? The Word's Becoming in the Incarnation* (Still River, MA: St. Bede's Publications, 1985); *Does God Suffer? A Christian Theology of God and Suffering* (Notre Dame: Notre Dame Press, 2000).

Wolterstorff, Nicholas, "Is It Possible or Desirable for Theologians to Recover from Kant?" *Modern Theology* 14 (1998): 1–18.

Yeago, David, "The New Testament and Nicene Dogma: A Contribution to the Recovery of Theological Exegesis." *Pro Ecclesia* 3 (1994): 152–64. Young, Frances, *From Nicaea to Chalcedon* (London: SCM, 1983).

Name Index

Alston, William, 107-110, 113, 134
Anselm, xi, xii, xiii, 11, 35, 47, 52,
    60, 69, 71, 77, 80, 98, 206,
    223, 239, 244
Aquinas, xii, xiii, xvi, 11, 14, 23,
    32, 37, 38, 39, 41, 44, 45, 51,
    52, 53, 60, 61, 62, 66, 68, 69,
    70, 71, 73, 74, 77, 78, 85, 89,
    93, 98, 118, 119, 138, 143,
    211
Arendt, Hannah, 152-156, 159
Aristotle, 11, 15, 28, 34, 70
Auerbach, Erich, xviii
Augustine, xii, xiii, 6, 10, 11, 20,
    21, 23, 29, 45, 46, 47, 52, 53,
    54, 57, 60, 61, 62, 65, 66, 69,
    70, 71, 74, 75, 77, 78, 122,
    143, 149, 157, 159, 197, 211,
    241

Barr, James, 123, 138, 147, 148,
    151, 157, 159
Barth, Karl, xii, xiii, xv, xvii, 14,
    21, 23, 32, 33, 34-36, 38, 40,
    42, 64, 65, 66, 81, 85, 86, 87,
    88, 91, 92, 93, 95, 96, 97, 98,
    101, 102, 104, 122, 138, 146,
    159, 183, 193, 195-199, 200,
    201-204, 204, 206-207,
    208-218, 220, 221-222, 223,
    224, 240-242

Bauckham, Richard, xii, xvi-xvii,
    229, 230-232, 237, 242, 244
Beethoven, Ludwig van, 20
Bernstein, Richard, 154, 159
Boethius, 14
Bonhoeffer, Dietrich, 38, 42
Bornkamm, Günther, 223
Bradwardine, Thomas, 82, 83, 84,
    85
Brunner, Emil, 62, 66
Bultmann, Rudolf, 39, 58,
    200-201, 221, 223

Calvin, John, xii, xiii, 53, 54, 57,
    60, 62, 64, 65, 66, 69, 70, 71,
    75, 77, 78, 89, 90-91, 98, 99,
    122, 143, 198, 199, 203,
    210-212, 218-219, 219-220,
    222, 223
Childs, Brevard, xvi, 32, 42, 72,
    98, 102-107, 113, 121-122,
    123-124, 126, 127-128, 134,
    138, 142, 150, 159, 160, 161,
    162, 167-168, 179, 181, 187,
    188
Craig, William Lane, 13, 23
Cross, Frank, 165, 179

Darwin, Charles, 54, 55, 56, 57,
    58, 59
Davidson, Donald, 190, 223

Dawkins, Richard, 60, 66
Democritus, 82
Dunn, James, 191, 223
Duns Scotus, xiii

Einstein, Albert, 11, 14-17, 23, 45, 77

Flannery, Kevin, 29
Frei, Hans, xviii, 25, 101, 113, 188, 223, 235, 244
Fuller, Peter, xix

Gert, Bernard, xxi, xxiv
Gödel, Kurt, xxiii
Gosse, Philip, 55-56, 58
Gregory, of Nyssa, 29, 46, 49-50, 52, 159, 236
Gunkel, Herman, 7, 21

Hegel, Georg F. W., 70
Helm, Paul, 69, 86, 98
Huizinga, Johannes, 177, 179
Hume, David, 39

Jenson, Robert, xvii, 11, 23, 31, 42, 75, 82, 90, 98, 138, 207, 226, 232, 234, 237, 244

Kant, Immanuel, 34, 68, 106, 152-153, 159, 219, 223, 236, 245
Kermode, Frank, 194, 223
Kripke, Saul, 236, 244

Lindbeck, George, 101-102, 113
Lowe, E J, 14-15, 16, 17, 23
Luther, Martin, xviii, 21, 38, 39, 60, 62, 89, 98, 99, 143, 181, 187, 197, 198

MacDonald, Neil B, 32, 35, 40, 42, 138, 224
McGrath, Alister, 26, 42, 160, 179
Mann, Thomas, xix
Migliore, Daniel, 26, 42, 160, 179
Moltmann, Jürgen, 244

Newton, Isaac, 15, 16, 45, 54, 83-84, 130
Nicholson, Ernest, 176, 179
Nietzsche, Freidrich, xviii, 156
Noth, Martin, 124, 125, 127, 138, 139, 159, 163-164, 165, 179

Ockham, William of, 37, 38, 39, 41, 42, 121

Pannenberg, Wolfhart, 11, 23, 47, 52, 229, 244
Parker, T. H. L., 69, 78, 98, 223
Pelikan, Jaroslav, 68, 98
Pickstock, Catherine, xiii
Plato, 28, 34, 37
Popper, Karl, xxii-xxiii

Rad, Gerhard von, xiii, xiv-xvi, 36, 48, 53, 63, 65, 70-72, 73-74, 75, 78, 94-95, 101, 102, 104, 106, 107, 109, 118, 123, 124, 125, 126, 130, 137, 139, 140-143, 144, 145-146, 148, 150, 151, 156, 157, 161, 163, 164-165, 166-172, 174, 175, 179
Reichenbach, Hans, 17, 23

Schleiermacher, Friedrich D. E., 59, 66, 103, 198
Schweitzer, Albert, 200-202, 205, 208, 209, 216
Seitz, Christopher R, xvii, 98, 113, 160, 244

Seters, John van, 179
Sorabji, Richard, 13, 23, 49-50, 52
Soulen, Kendall, 195, 224
Sternberg, Meir, 115, 130, 138
Swinburne, Richard, 3, 11, 12, 13,
    14, 22, 23, 80, 99

Theissen, Gerd, 221, 224
Tooley, Michael, 17, 23
Turner, Denys, 37, 43

Watson, Francis, 186, 224
Westermann, Claus, xvi, 7-10, 13,
    18, 23, 37, 43, 52, 58, 64, 65,
    66, 73, 79, 81, 99, 123, 138,
    142-144, 145, 157, 159
Wolterstorff, Nicholas, xvi, 4-6,
    18-19, 20, 22, 23, 25, 76-78,
    80, 81, 86, 99, 108, 117, 143,
    159, 190, 245
Wright, N T, 201, 205, 216, 220-
    221, 224